DOOR

UNLOCKING THE MYSTERY OF FAITH

A Journey of Prayer through the
Catechism of the Catholic Church

Doorway to Faith
Unlocking the Mystery of Faith

A Journey of Prayer through the Catechism of the Catholic Church

alive Publishing

First published in 2014 by Alive Publishing Ltd.
Graphic House, 124 City Road, Stoke on Trent ST4 2PH
Tel: +44 (0)1782 745600 Fax: +44 (0)1782 745500
www.alivepublishing.co.uk e-mail: booksales@alivepublishing.co.uk

 British Library Catalogue-in-Publication Data.
A catalogue record for this book is available from the British Library.

ISBN 978-1-906278-18-2

WELCOME TO THIS single volume edition of *Doorway to Faith* which was launched as a resource for parishioners in the Archdiocese of Birmingham during the Year of Faith declared by Pope Benedict. My hope was to provide a simple and accessible catechetical tool which would enable us to become more familiar with the teaching contained within the *Catechism of the Catholic Church* during this holy and special year.

We published four editions of *Doorway to Faith* to reflect the four parts of the catechism.

- Part One – The Profession of Faith
- Part Two – The Celebration of the Christian Mystery, in the Liturgy and the Sacraments
- Part Three – Life in Christ - The Moral Life
- Part Four – Christian Prayer

Remarkably and encouragingly *Doorway to Faith* was taken up by people far and wide, north and south, east and west, both in the UK, Ireland and overseas. There seemed to be a great hunger and thirst in many to grow in their understanding of the rich and profound teaching of the Catholic Church as contained in the Catechism.

And so, I am delighted that we now have the four editions of *Doorway to Faith* in this single volume. The beauty of this resource is that you can decide on any day of the year to begin your journey through the Catechism. The blue ribbon allows you to mark your place day by day. Each daily reflection holds out to you a rich fare of teaching from the Catechism, the Sacred Scriptures, the Fathers of the Church and the Saints, as well as references from YouCat.

The *Catechism of the Catholic Church* is one of the most important fruits of the Second Vatican Council. It is, truly a gift of the Council to the Church. For in the Catechism we see the wealth of teaching that the Church has received, safeguarded and proposed in her two thousand year history.

These four parts are all related one to another: 'the Christian mystery is the object of faith (first part); it is celebrated and communicated in liturgical actions (second part); it is present to enlighten and sustain the children of God in their actions (third part); it is the basis for our prayer, the privileged expression of which is the Our Father, and it represents the object of our supplication, our praise and our intercession (fourth part).' (Apostolic Constitution *Fidei Depositum*, Pope Saint John Paul II)

There are three different ways of understanding the Catechism. The first is to see it as a great summary of the faith of the Catholic Church. A vital key to appreciating the unity of the Catechism is to recognize the four threads that hold the Catechism together. These are: the mystery of the Trinity; the person of Jesus Christ; the mystery of Christ's death and resurrection; and finally, the immense dignity of the human person.

A second way of looking at the Catechism is to see it as divine teaching. God reveals himself in history and in the person of his Son, and by his grace enables us to respond to him in faith. Parts One and Two make present the revelation of God and his plan, while Parts Three and Four indicate the response we make in our lives and in our prayer. This teaching expresses the 'primacy of grace', because it is God who first acts and makes himself known. As we receive and

grasp God's revelation, we begin to respond in faith and are drawn into a relationship with him.

A third way to appreciate the Catechism is to see it as a great crafted work of art. On its front page is a logo which expresses the content as a symphony of truth (represented by the panpipes), by which Christ the Good Shepherd leads his sheep to rest beneath the tree of eternal life.

Throughout, the Catechism uses carefully selected pieces of art to illustrate its different parts. For example, illustrating Part Two - the section on the Liturgy and Sacraments - a picture of Jesus healing the woman with an issue of blood is chosen because it is through the sacraments of the Church that the power of Jesus goes out to heal and restore us.

But, perhaps most clearly of all, the beauty of faith is best illustrated by the lives of holy men and women who live by faith. For this reason, it is full of references to the lives and the writings of the saints, and most particularly to Mary, whose life is the embodiment of the Church, believing, celebrating, living and praying. Two pictures in the Catechism are of Mary with the Child Jesus. Mary was the first to receive the fullness of God's Word and then brought him into the world.

Key to getting the most out of the *Doorway to Faith* booklet is each of us turning to the Holy Spirit and asking for the grace to enter more deeply into the teaching and mystery of our faith; like Mary, in trust, humility and obedience. We are to be, if you like, faith detectives and, like a detective, we are to be curious, inquisitive and unwilling to settle for anything less than a deeper insight into the mystery of our faith.

As we embark on our journey to get to know the Catechism better may the Holy Spirit open our minds and our hearts to the truth, and like Mary, may we respond in faith.

+ Bernard Longley

✠ **Bernard Longley**
Archbishop of Birmingham

HOLY TRINITY

PART ONE

THE CREED

The Creed

Our journey through the Catechism begins by exploring first the desire for God which is deeply rooted in the human heart, and the Creed, the Profession of Faith.

The first part of the Catechism examines the truth that God has made himself known and very specially through the person of Jesus Christ. What has been made known and revealed came to be summarised in what we call the Creed.

The Catechism opens up the Creed, summarises our faith, and by doing so helps to put us in touch with Jesus and through him with the other persons of the Trinity but also helps us to be drawn more deeply into the communion of the Church.

The Catechism is presented to us as a great fruit of the Second Vatican Council, which was held during the first three years of the 1960's. The teaching of Vatican II is contained in a set of sixteen documents. Of these there are four principal documents or Constitutions, as they are called. They are: *Lumen Gentium* (On the Church), *Dei Verbum* (On the Word of God), *Sacrosanctum Concilium* (On the Liturgy) and *Gaudium et Spes* (On the Church in the Modern World)

As we journey together the Catechism frequently quotes from these Constitutions. In this first section, covering Part 1 of the Catechism, the main quotations are from the Pastoral Constitution on the Church in the Modern World *(Gaudium et Spes*).

A key element of *Gaudium et Spes* is a declaration to the world of the basis of the great dignity of the human person (Genesis 1:26) We will find this teaching arising again and again in different parts of the Catechism.

We shall also find references to *Dei Verbum*, especially when the Catechism deals with the great mystery of God's Revelation and also with the interpretation of Sacred Scripture. The third great Constitution is the Dogmatic Constitution on the Church or *Lumen Gentium*. We will find this document quoted in the Catechism in the sections dealing with the Church and with Our Lady. When we focus on the sacramental life of the church in the Catechism we look to *Sacrosanctum Concilium* and its rich insight into the great gift we have been given in the sacraments of the church, especially the Eucharist, the source and summit of the Christian life.

Each daily reflection begins with a question or statement inviting us to ponder and reflect on a teaching from the Catechism. These questions and statements provide us with a key to entering more deeply into the mystery of our faith. We would encourage you to read the section of the Catechism quoted at the top of each page. Also, each reflection is rich in scripture readings, insight from the Church Fathers and saints, Vatican II and, for the younger readers, cross-references to Youcat.

Our hope is that the *Doorway to Faith* booklet will help open and unlock the riches and treasures contained in the masterpiece and jewel we know as the *Catechism of the Catholic Church*.

DAY 1

THE DESIRE FOR GOD IS WRITTEN IN OUR HEARTS (CCC 27-30)

'Our dignity rests above all on the fact that we are called to communion with God.' (Gaudium et Spes 19)

YOUCAT 3

Our goal is to go through the *Catechism of the Catholic Church* and help in some way to unlock the mystery of faith – a mystery we proclaim in the Creed and celebrate in the Sacraments, and which we live and pray in our day to day lives. In striving to live like this we discover an amazing truth about ourselves – that there is in our hearts, the very centre of ourselves, a desire for God. We shall look more closely at this in the coming days, but for now let us ponder the simple but amazing reality of who we are. We are made to know God, to love God and to walk with him day by day.

What is man that you are mindful of him? You have made him little less than a god, and crowned him with glory and honour. O Lord, our God, how great is your name through all the earth. (Psalm 8)

Our Hearts are restless until they rest in God (CCC 27-30)

Day 2

Understanding the amazing dignity of us being made to know God, gives us some insight into an important part of our human experience. There is a restlessness within us. No matter what joys and pleasures we look for and experience we never quite seem to be satisfied. There is, if you like, an itch or an ache deep within. Of all the creatures that exist, we were created to find our true and ultimate happiness in God. Throughout the Catechism we shall discover many of the words and writings of saints – holy men and women, who exemplify the mystery of faith we are exploring. The first of these is St Augustine, who expressed so beautifully and powerfully our desire for God.

'The intimate and vital bond between us and God can be forgotten, overlooked or rejected by us – for many reasons.' (GS 19, CCC 29)

YOUCAT 3

You are great, O Lord, and greatly to be praised: great is your power and your wisdom is without measure … You yourself encourage him (us) to delight in your praise, for you have made us for yourself, and our heart is restless until it rests in you. (St Augustine)

Day 3

God can be known by the light of human reason (CCC 36)

'Thus in different ways, we can come to know that there exists a reality, which is the first cause and final end of all things, a reality that everyone calls God.'
(St Thomas Aquinas)

Can God really be known with certainty by human reason alone? The Catechism (CCC 31) uses a phrase from Blessed John Henry Newman: 'converging and convincing arguments'. Newman meant that there are a whole number of different evidences in the world: the existence and beauty of creation, the witness of good or holy people and so on. These things come together, like individual threads that make up a strong piece of string, and convince us of the existence of God. The signs of a spiritual soul in human beings and the order and beauty of created things all suggest something beyond ourselves and upon whom we depend – namely God!

Lord, help me to recognise both in myself and in the world around me the signs that speak to me of your existence. You are the real explanation of the beauty and order that I see, and of all the goodness, in spite of evil, that I sense in the world.

Is reason enough to know the mystery of God? (CCC 37-38)

A great dignity we possess is the capacity to come to know God by use of our reason. We cannot fully know him by reason alone. Furthermore, in reality there are many obstacles that prevent us from using our reason properly anyway. We can resist the truth in our hearts, perhaps because it makes us uncomfortable. Maybe the prevailing attitudes in our society blind us. The Catechism teaches that revolt against evil in the world, bad example on the part of believers, the power of the cares and riches of this world and finally original sin can all make us hide from God (CCC 29). Hence only with great difficulty do we find God by reason alone.

'This is why we stand in need of being enlightened by God's revelation.' (CCC 38)

YOUCAT 4

O God, although you have given me the gift of reason and have placed a desire for you in my heart, I still struggle in my search for you. I have a need for your grace. Please come to me in my need.

Day 5

Human words fall short of expressing the mystery of God (CCC 39-43)

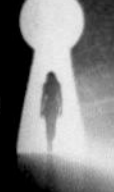

'Our human words always fall short of the mystery of God.' (CCC 42)

The Catechism speaks about our natural ability to know God and the amazing power of reason we possess. Because of this we are able to discuss and dialogue with others, believers and non-believers, about God. We are able to converse about God with everyone, even though they may know nothing about God's revelation and the gift of faith. However, it is true that our knowledge of God is limited; our language cannot really do justice to God. We open up a discussion about God by looking to the good, the true and the beautiful in our world as we see in them a reflection of the infinite perfection of God.

YOUCAT 6

Dear God, none of my words can truly grasp the fullness of your reality. And yet they can offer me a glimpse of your glory, your beauty and goodness. Only you can speak a human word that will express your divine being. Speak Lord, your servant is listening.

GOD'S PLAN OF LOVING GOODNESS (CCC 50-53)

DAY 6

We are now ready for the awesome truth that God has not left us alone in our search for him. God has himself set out in search of us, so that he could make himself known to us and make clear his call to enter into relationship with him. In Genesis (Gen 3:8-9) there is a vivid image of man and woman, because of sin, hiding from God. It is God (Genesis 3:8) who comes looking and calls out – 'where are you?' (Genesis 3:9) The word 'revelation' captures the reality of the movement of God towards us, unveiling himself, rescuing us from our wounded state and showing his plan to draw us into the very life of God.

'God... wants to communicate his own divine life to us whom he freely created, in order to adopt them as his sons and daughters...' (CCC 52)

YOUCAT 7

Heavenly Father, before we ever set out in search of you, you were already drawing us to you. You had created us to know you, but we had fallen into ignorance of you and your plan. It was your love that prompted you to rescue us from our darkness.

DAY 7

GOD REVEALED HIMSELF GRADUALLY AND IN STAGES (CCC 53-58)

'The Church, interpreting the symbolism of biblical language in an authentic way, ... teaches that our first parents were constituted ... to share in ... divine life.' (CCC 375), (LG 2)

YOUCAT 8

That God made himself known to us in stages is a testimony to his loving goodness. Blessed John Henry Newman once said that God did not reveal his full glory because that would completely overwhelm us. Instead God approached us with 'shrouded radiance and bedimmed majesty'. The first stage is captured in the biblical images of Adam and Eve and Noah. These images are intended to convey that God's plan is for all of us, and his plan to call everyone into a relationship with himself is not ended or ultimately destroyed by our turning away from him. Stories – yes; God began by speaking deep truths and realities in the simplest language.

Lord, teach me to treasure the revelation of yourself contained in the stories of our earliest ancestors. Our sinfulness does not turn you away from us. The truth I believe is that again and again, in your love, you have offered a covenant to man.

THE CALL OF ABRAHAM AND THE PEOPLE OF ISRAEL (CCC 59-64)

DAY 8

We can only think of events of history somehow revealing God if we understand that God is shaping that history and those particular events. The faith of Christians, Jews and Muslims is that God acted in history by singling out and calling a particular individual – Abraham. God's call was that Abraham be in a covenant relationship with him and his descendants to inherit the promised land that God would give him. The events are historical but also symbolic. God is revealing that Abraham is a symbol of humanity and speaks to us through the history of Abraham and his descendents, Israel, the chosen and special people of God.

'God forms Israel in the hope of salvation; in the expectation of a new and everlasting Covenant intended for all, to be written on their hearts.' (CCC 64)

YOUCAT 8

O God, you called Abraham to trust in you as you led him and his family to the promised land. You are showing yourself to me as a God who speaks and calls, a God who is love. May the events and persons of Israel's history show me ever more of yourself.

Day 9

Jesus Christ is the fullness of God's revelation (CCC 65-66)

'Christ, the Son of God made man, is the Father's one, perfect, and unsurpassable Word.' (CCC 65)

YOUCAT 9

The coming of Jesus Christ was like the announcement of the major theme in a musical performance. Often in musicals, operas and classical symphonies, different instruments of the orchestra give hints of the main theme. First the flutes, then the clarinets and the bassoon, the strings and brass instruments, all take up different variations. In its final climax, the whole orchestra sounds the theme to which everything has been moving towards. In a similar way, God acted in the events and persons of Israel's history. But it was all a preparation for the coming of Jesus. He is both the Word and Event in which God fully reveals himself.

Holy Spirit, I turn to you as the author of Sacred Scripture to open the eyes of my heart to recognise Jesus in the whole of Scripture, as Jesus opened the eyes of the disciples on the road to Emmaus.

IS THERE ANY MORE REVELATION TO COME? (CCC 67)

DAY 10

Does everything stop or come to an end with the coming of Jesus? In one sense, yes. Jesus is the definitive revelation of God. Everything about Jesus and all that he has said and done reveal completely the fullness of God. Nothing more needs to be said by God. At the same time, what God has said in Jesus is not even now fully explicit. Christian faith engages and grapples with God's revelation in order to grasp its full significance. The Catechism itself is the result of this increasing grasp of God's revelation over the centuries. Insofar as God sometimes grants private revelations to individuals, the purpose is to help people live, rather than adding to the deposit of faith.

'There have been so-called 'private' revelations, some of which have been recognised by the authority of the Church.' (CCC 67)

YOUCAT 10

Father, we have received the fullness of your revelation in the person of your Son, Jesus Christ. Help us to contemplate the glory of your Son until we become transformed into his likeness.

Day 11

Coming to Know Divine Revelation (CCC 74)

'God 'desires all men to be saved and to come to the knowledge of the truth': that is, of Christ Jesus'. (CCC 74)

God's revelation of himself in Jesus Christ remains simply an event in the past, an event of history, unless that revelation continues to be transmitted today. Now we have reached another crucial moment in the faith and life of the Church and the teaching of the Catechism. That we should come to the knowledge of the truth and by that truth be saved - this now is the great desire of God. And for those who have come to know the truth of God revealed in Jesus, there is a corresponding desire to make the truth known to others. Here we have an intimation of the great mission of the Church. To lead others to God.

I pray that the desire to hand on God's revelation to others may grow in my heart and in the heart of all believers, so that the world may come to know the good news of salvation.

We are fed from the tables of Scripture and Tradition (CCC 75-79, 83)

Day 12

There have been several centuries of dispute concerning the way that God's revelation is passed on. In other Christian traditions, the view is that 'Scripture alone' (*sola scriptura*) is the medium of transmission of God's revelation. For Catholics, the transmission of God's revelation is essentially the transmission of a person, Jesus Christ. The person of Jesus Christ, the revelation of God which he embodies, is first of all transmitted to the Apostles. Sacred Scripture comes from the Apostles and those associated with them. But the Apostles also communicated revelation in a variety of ways through their words and actions. This we call Tradition.

'The Apostles handed on ... by the spoken word of their preaching, by the example they gave, by the institutions they established, what they themselves had received ...' (CCC 76)

YOUCAT 12

Thank you, Lord, for the fidelity of the great Apostles, who gave constant witness to Christ, even to the point of death. We pray for their successors today.

DAY 13

THE RELATIONSHIP BETWEEN TRADITION AND SCRIPTURE (CCC 80-82)

'Scripture and Tradition - 'Each of them makes present and fruitful in the Church, the mystery of Christ ...' (CCC 80)

YOUCAT 12

Catholics practice their faith in a distinctive way as a result of the teaching concerning the transmission of divine revelation. We not only reverence the scriptures but we also treasure other aspects of the Church's life because they make up what we call Tradition. We are speaking here about the teachings that come to us in and through the Church (e.g. Papal teaching, the Catechism etc.) and about the liturgy and the sacraments, the witness of the lives of the Apostles and the lives of the saints. Together these two modes of transmission - Scripture and Tradition - form a great unity.

Holy Spirit, you are the life and soul of the Church, in which the Gospel of Christ is communicated and transmitted across the generations. Give me a deep love for the Church.

The Deposit of Faith belongs to the whole Church in every age (CCC 84)

Day 14

'Guarding the Deposit of Faith is the mission which the Lord entrusted to his Church, and which she fulfils in every age'. These words were written by Pope John Paul II in his introduction to the Catechism. We might find the phrase 'Deposit of Faith' a little strange. However, in ancient law the word 'deposit' referred to an agreement by which a person entrusted something to another, who was bound to both preserve and return the thing intact. God has entrusted the Apostles and their successors in the Church with his revelation. Preserving it does not imply hiding it away, but rather the opposite - interpreting it faithfully for each generation.

'I know whom I have believed, and I am sure that he is able to guard until that Day what has been entrusted to me.'
(2 Tim 1:12)

YOUCAT 13

Lord God, I thank you that I can be completely confident that the revelation of yourself and your plan for humanity, made known in Jesus and passed on to the Apostles, has been faithfully transmitted to us today in the Church.

DAY 15

THE CHURCH TEACHES THROUGH SCRIPTURE AND TRADITION WHAT HAS BEEN HANDED ON TO IT (CCC 84-85)

'Christ said to his apostles: 'He who hears you hears me'. (Luke 10:16)

'Magisterium' is the word used by the Catechism to describe what it calls 'the living, teaching office of the Church'. It comes from a Latin word meaning teacher. God spoke his Word and by his divine authority gave to the Apostles and their successors the responsibility of constantly listening to the Word he spoke, and through the help of the Holy Spirit both of preserving and expounding the truth of God's Word (which the Catechism calls the 'Deposit of Faith'). The Catechism also makes clear that the Magisterium is the true servant of the Word of God, not its master. The authority of the Church lies in its obedience to God's Word.

YOUCAT 13

Lord, I pray for the Pope and the Bishops of the Church. You have given them an awesome responsibility and yet promised the guidance of your Holy Spirit. Give them courage to expound your truth.

THROUGH ALL THE WORDS OF SCRIPTURE, GOD SPEAKS ONLY ONE SINGLE WORD - JESUS (CCC 101-104)

DAY 16

We turn now to a short but critically important section of the Catechism where the Church teaches us about Sacred Scripture - why and how it should be understood. A few days ago we saw that our human language struggles to express the reality of God. Now the Catechism states that God condescends to speak to us in human language, indeed not just in human words, but a person, his Son, Jesus Christ. The whole of Scripture (Old and New Testaments) communicate One Word - Jesus - and unveil this profound truth. There is great mystery here and we are encouraged to venerate the Scriptures as we venerate Christ in the Eucharist.

'All Sacred Scripture is but one book, and this one book is Christ 'because all divine Scripture speaks of Christ, and all divine Scripture is fulfilled in Christ'. *(Hugh of St Victor)*

YOUCAT 14

Father, I acknowledge that Sacred Scripture is not simply the work of men, but is also the living witness to your Son, Jesus Christ. Grant me the grace to treasure the Scriptures, so that I may hear your voice.

DAY 17

IN THE SCRIPTURES GOD THE FATHER SPEAKS LOVINGLY TO HIS CHILDREN (CCC 104- 108)

'God inspired the human authors of the sacred books.' (CCC 106)

An essential element of the mystery which is Sacred Scripture is that the Word of God is not primarily a written word, but a living, incarnate word. The Catechism makes the following remarkable statement: 'If the Scriptures are not to remain a dead letter, Christ, the eternal Word of the living God, must, through the Holy Spirit, 'open [our] minds to understand the Scriptures'. When Jesus opened the minds of the disciples on the road to Emmaus, he showed them that the whole Old Testament was about himself. Not seeing Christ in the Old Testament means that it remains a dead letter. Whatever Scripture is talking about, it is seeking to reveal Christ.

YOUCAT 15

Lord Jesus, I ask you to open my mind to understand the Scriptures. Like the disciples on the road to Emmaus, I am slow to believe and understand. Let your Spirit unveil the Scriptures so that I might contemplate and see your face in them.

We read and interpret Scripture in the light of the same Spirit by whom it was written (CCC 109-119)

Day 18

Scripture has a dual authorship. There are human authors and it is necessary for us to be attentive to what these authors wanted to affirm. But God is also properly called the author of Scripture. The Holy Spirit inspired the human authors to write. At the same time, there is a work of the Holy Spirit enabling the Church and all of us to both read and interpret them. There are three spiritual senses of Scripture (CCC 117) and three criteria for interpreting them (CCC 112-114). Scripture makes sense as the Word of God within the context of the Church, which receives the whole of Scripture as revealing Christ.

'The phrase 'heart of Christ' can refer to Sacred Scripture, which makes known his heart, closed before the Passion, as the Scripture was obscure.' (St Thomas Aquinas)

YOUCAT 16

In reading Sacred Scripture, Father, help me to be attentive so that I may perceive your plan, of which Christ is the centre and heart.

Day 19

The Old Testament is pregnant with Christ (CCC 120)

'Sacred Scripture comprises 46 books of the Old Testament and 27 books of the New Testament.' (CCC 120)

YOUCAT p.22

The Church has always resisted the suggestion that the Old Testament is no longer of value now that Christ has fulfilled the Old and has established a New Covenant (Testament) between God and his people. Both Old and New form a unity, both speaking of Christ, although not in the same way. The Old Testament contains all manner of God's teaching leading his people by stages to the full truth of salvation. There is much truth and wisdom, as well as a treasury of prayers, in the Old Testament. In all of these, the mystery of salvation, of Christ, is present in a hidden way and prefigures what is accomplished in the New Testament.

Lord Jesus, teach me to recognise in the Gospels the many allusions to the Old Testament, so that I might appreciate more deeply the significance of your words and actions - as the fulfilment and accomplishment of God's plan.

Sacred Scripture in the Life of the Church (CCC 131-133)

Day 20

These three paragraphs of the Catechism are a powerful incentive for us to love and read the Scriptures. They speak of the force and power of the Word of God that can serve the Church - giving support and vigour. For the members of the Church (the Church's children) the Word is 'strength for their faith, food for the soul, and a pure and lasting font of spiritual life'. Theologians are reminded that 'study of the sacred page' is the very soul of theology. Preachers, catechists and teachers will be nourished in their ministry through the Word of Scripture, *Dei Verbum,* the Constitution on the word of God says: 'access to Sacred Scripture ought to be open wide to the Christian faithful'.

'Ignorance of the Scriptures is ignorance of Christ.' (St Jerome)

YOUCAT 17-19

Father, your desire is that I should learn 'the surpassing knowledge of Jesus Christ'. This is my desire also. May I discover more and more in the scriptures this knowledge of your Son.

DAY 21

FAITH IS BEING SURE OF WHAT WE HOPE FOR AND CERTAIN OF WHAT WE CANNOT SEE (CCC 176, 142-3)

'Faith is a supernatural gift of God, by which we believe without doubting whatever God has revealed.' (Penny Catechism)

YOUCAT 20

One of the principle teachings of the Catechism has been described as the 'primacy of grace'. This means that God is always the first to act and take the initiative in his dealings with us. The very structure of the Catechism bears witness to this. Part One and Two speak of God's action in revealing himself, especially in Jesus, and also of the way in which God's action continues to be made present in the liturgy and the sacraments. The response we make in our day-to-day living and prayer are the subject of Part Three and Part Four. In paragraphs (CCC 142-3) we see the same principle. Our first response to God's revelation is faith.

Lord God, help me to see and understand that my faith is first and foremost a decision to respond in love to you, and that I can respond as I begin to receive your revelation - handed on to me in the Church.

WE ARE CALLED TO LIVE BY 'THE OBEDIENCE OF FAITH' (CCC 144-149)

DAY 22

A feature of the Catechism is the witness of real people. The three paragraphs to read today speak of many witnesses of faith to be found in the Old Testament. Hebrews 11 gives a list of some of these. Two persons are of particular importance – Abraham and the Virgin Mary. Abraham is called 'the father of all who believe' because he is the beginning of Israel's history and illustrates that God's people were gathered on the basis of faith. When we first read of Mary in the New Testament we see her responding in faith to the message of the angel Gabriel and then being hailed by Elizabeth – 'blessed is she who believed'.

'The Church venerates in Mary the purest realization of faith.' (CCC 149)

YOUCAT 20

I thank you, Father, for the life of Mary and of Abraham. They are wonderful models of faith. I thank you also for those who have been models of faith in my own life and experience.

DAY 23

THE CHURCH PROCLAIMS THAT GOD IS FATHER, SON AND HOLY SPIRIT (CCC 150-152)

'It is right and just to entrust oneself wholly to God and to believe absolutely in what he says.' (CCC 150)

YOUCAT 21

Although it has been implicit in many of the Catechism paragraphs that we have already looked at, CCC 150-152 now leads us explicitly into the revealed truth that there is only one God: Father, Son and Holy Spirit, the Holy and Blessed Trinity. For the Catechism, believing in God is unpacked as belief in Jesus Christ, who is revealed as the Father's beloved Son, and who is the only one who can reveal the Father. Belief in God the Father and the Son cannot take place without sharing in the Spirit, for it is the Spirit who reveals who Jesus is. We cannot say or profess that 'Jesus is Lord except by the Holy Spirit' (1 Corinthians 12:3) and it is the Spirit who helps us comprehend God.

With the whole Church, I proclaim my faith in the one God, who is Father, Son and Spirit. With the grace of the Holy Spirit I can enter more deeply into the mystery of three persons in one God.

FAITH IS A GIFT OF GOD AND YET A TRULY HUMAN ACT (CCC 153 - 165)

DAY 24

It is not a contradiction to hold that faith is truly an act of our will and our understanding and simultaneously understand that faith is a grace or a gift from God. We choose to believe and entrust ourselves to God and his truth. In order to make the free choice of mind and will to believe, we need the interior help of the Holy Spirit, who moves the heart and converts it to God. Faith then is a gift of God, a supernatural virtue infused by him. There are exterior proofs of God's revelation also – the miracles of Christ, the witness of the saints, prophecies, and, in spite of the many sins, the sheer endurance and growth of the Church and the witness of holy lives.

'The assent of faith is 'by no means a blind impulse of the mind'.' (CCC 156)

YOUCAT 21

O Lord, you teach me that it is entirely reasonable to believe in you. For you are the very source of truth, you are truth itself. I thank you that my dignity as a human being is enhanced not lessened by my faith in you.

DAY 25

FAITH IS MORE CERTAIN THAN ALL HUMAN KNOWLEDGE (CCC 158-9)

'Ten thousand difficulties do not make one doubt.' (Blessed John Henry Newman)

YOUCAT 23

There is a mutual relationship between faith and understanding. Because it is in our nature to question and seek understanding, it should not be surprising that we would want to understand our faith more deeply. Understanding does not lead to a loss of faith, but rather leads to and calls for a deeper faith. The Catechism suggests that knowing God better and understanding better what he has revealed will lead to a faith increasingly set aflame by love. Faith is in no way in conflict with, or opposed, to the things of reason or science. How can it be so - when the same God is the source of both?

Help me not to be afraid of questioning and seeking to understand my faith more deeply. Lord, to understand you is to love you. The more I see, the more I am overwhelmed with the beauty of your mystery.

The Profession of the Christian Faith – the Creeds (CCC 185-197)

Day 26

The 'Symbol of Faith' is a phrase sometimes used to describe what we usually know as the Creed. It is the essential summary of the principal truths of the faith. From the beginning the Church was in the habit of developing formulae or summaries so that members of the Christian community would always know and be able to call to mind the very heart of the faith they believed. The word 'symbol' came from the Greek use of tokens as a sign of identity. It is a kind of badge, both identifying and gathering believers into unity and communion. The Creed shows the Church being responsible for both preserving and handing on the 'deposit of faith'.

'This Creed is the spiritual seal, our heart's meditation and an ever-present guardian; it is unquestionably, the treasure of our soul.' (St Ambrose, CCC 197)

YOUCAT 24-27

O God, the Creed was handed over to me on the day of my baptism. Since that day I have learned to proclaim this summary of Christian faith every Sunday. May I grow in treasuring the truth that you are a trinity of persons, Father, Son and Holy Spirit.

DAY 27

I BELIEVE IN ONE GOD (CCC 198-202)

'The Creed tells the story of salvation in three stages: the Father, origin of everything, created the world; the Son redeems it by his death; the Spirit makes the Gospel known.' (CCC 190)

We have now completed the first section of Part One, having looked at our capacity to know God, at God's self-revelation, and our response of faith. The remainder of Part One deals with the content of God's revelation as summarised in the Creed. The opening affirmation of the Creed 'I believe in one God' is described as the most fundamental. Why is this? The oneness of God was a central element of the faith of Israel and Jesus also affirmed that God is the 'one Lord'. The Father is the most important reality, because he is also the source of all reality. To know the full meaning of everything must begin with knowing God.

Along with Jews, Muslims and all Christians, I acknowledge you, Father, as the one God, source of all that is. May our common faith in you draw us into greater unity rather than division.

God revealed himself to Israel progressively and under different names (CCC 203-213)

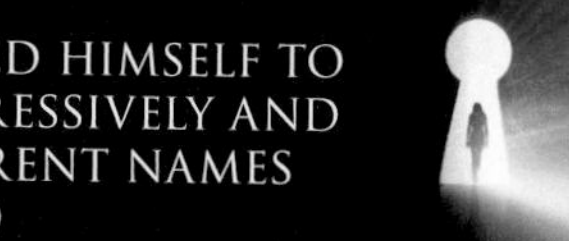

DAY 28

The name under which God revealed himself to Moses is at once mysterious and fascinating. The name in Hebrew is YHWH and can be translated 'I am He who is' or 'I am who (I) am'. There is a double effect here. On the one hand, the name seems to refuse the giving of a name and thus expresses a truth about God – that he is a reality beyond what can be expressed. At the same time, God's desire to express himself to Moses reveals God's will to come close to humanity. Moses later received further unveiling of the name – God is goodness, faithfulness and mercy.

'Jesus reveals that he himself bears the divine name – 'then you will realise that 'I am'.' (John 8:28)

YOUCAT 30

Like Moses before the burning bush and at the pronouncing of your name, I stand in awe. Like Isaiah and Peter before your holy presence, I confess that I am a sinner in need of your mercy.

DAY 29

GOD IS EVERLASTING LOVE (CCC 214-221)

'Out of respect for the holiness of God, the people of Israel do not pronounce the divine name. Instead they use the divine title 'Lord'.' (CCC 209)

YOUCAT 32-33

We might consider that the whole history of the Old and New Testament is a gradual unveiling of the meaning of the divine name, the unveiling of God's identity. There are many words used in the Catechism and taken from Scripture which express the characteristics of God as they became known to Israel, and that were understood through Israel's experience of being in a relationship with God. We should meditate on such words as graciousness, constancy, trustworthiness, faithfulness and truth. Jesus Christ is also the embodiment of these qualities. The history of Israel and the life of Jesus reveal one single motive for God revealing himself: his sheer gratuitous and everlasting love.

My Lord and my God, I desire to live in the light of your revelation, trusting each day in the faithfulness and love you have revealed, most of all, in the sending of your Son, Jesus Christ.

The Trinity is the central mystery of our faith (CCC 261, 232-237)

Day 30

Although we speak of the mystery of the Trinity, the word mystery does not imply that nothing can be said. CCC 234 says that the Trinity is 'the source of all the other mysteries of faith, the light that enlightens them. It is the most fundamental and essential teaching in "the hierarchy of the truths of faith"'. It is however a truth that cannot be accessed by reason alone. It is hidden in God and could not be known unless revealed by God. Although hinted at in creation and Israel's history, the mystery of the Trinity only becomes explicit with the incarnation of God's Son and the sending of the Holy Spirit.

'A golden key to the Catechism is to see every teaching in the light and context of the Trinity.' (CCC 234,261)

YOUCAT 35-36

In your great love, O God, you have revealed the mystery of your Trinitarian life. You have called me to share in that life. Keep this mystery always before my mind and heart.

THE REVELATION OF THE TRINITY TOOK PLACE GRADUALLY IN TIME (CCC 238-248)

'With the Father and the Son, he (the Holy Spirit) is worshipped and glorified.' (Nicene Creed)

The revelation of God as Trinity took place gradually in Israel over a long period of time. The concept of God's fatherhood came from God's authorship of all things as their creator and from the image of his paternal love towards Israel. Only with the coming of Jesus is God revealed as Father in an unheard of sense. 'He is eternally Father in relation to his only Son, who is eternally Son only in relation to his Father' (CCC 240). The eternal origin of the Spirit is revealed by the actual coming of the Spirit in time as promised by Jesus. The Gospel of John relates that Jesus was to ask the Father to send the Spirit to the Apostles.

Glory be to the Father, and to the Son and to the Holy Spirit. As it was in the beginning, is now and ever shall be, world without end. Amen.

Creation and Salvation is the Work of the Three Divine Persons (CCC 249-260)

Day 32

When we make the Sign of the Cross we proclaim our faith in God as Trinity. 'In the name of the Father, and of the Son and of the Holy Spirit. Amen.' It was necessary in the early centuries of the Church to articulate the doctrine of the Trinity using language and concepts from the philosophy and culture of the day. For sure the Trinity is a mystery, and words like 'person', 'substance' and 'hypostasis' were adopted to express the revelation that God is three persons in One divine nature. In this way the Church was guarding the deposit of faith against errors that were undermining this teaching which is at the heart of Christian revelation.

'In every action of God, the three persons are wholly involved, but each according to his unique divine property.' (CCC 267)

YOUCAT 37-39

Father, you are the one source of all that is; and you Jesus Christ, the one through whom all things came to be and through whom humanity is restored; and you, Holy Spirit, make known the Father and the Son.

DAY 33

OF ALL THE DIVINE ATTRIBUTES, ONLY GOD'S OMNIPOTENCE IS NAMED IN THE CREED (CCC 268-289)

'Only faith can embrace the mysterious ways of God's almighty power.' (CCC 273)

The universal power of God is constantly affirmed in the Sacred Scriptures. But as God is also revealed as Father, we must understand his omnipotence in a way which is fatherly. In fact, God's almighty power is revealed in all the actions of God – in creation, in the plan of salvation brought to completion in Christ, and in the gift of the Spirit raising us to the dignity of children of God. God can sometimes appear as either absent or weak in the face of the evil in the world. However, the voluntary weakness and humiliation of Jesus on the cross was precisely the means of revealing the great power of God overthrowing evil and transforming humanity.

YOUCAT 40

Almighty God, in confessing the greatness of your power, I acknowledge that all things are possible for you. And yet, the greatest manifestation of your power is in your mercy and forgiveness.

GOD WHO IS THE CREATOR IS A FOUNDATIONAL TEACHING OF THE CATECHESISM (CCC 282, 290-301)

DAY 34

After confessing the one God to be Father, almighty, the Creed acknowledges God as Creator of heaven and earth. Creation is described as the beginning of the history of salvation. This implies that from the beginning God envisaged the glory of the new creation in Christ. Creation is the first purposeful step towards the Covenant between the One God and his people, and as such is the first indication of God's universal love. The teaching about the Creator and creation is crucial regarding our questions about our origins and our destiny. Please read these key paragraphs in the Catechism. Creation sets the stage and the scene for all of God's actions in history.

'God gave a beginning to all that exists outside of himself.' (CCC 290)

YOUCAT 41-42

I praise you, Father, for you created all things in the beginning as a reflection of your infinite majesty and power, and established the stage for accomplishing your plan of sharing your life with humanity.

DAY 35

GOD CARRIES OUT HIS PLAN, DIVINE PROVIDENCE (CCC 302-308)

'Many are the plans in the mind, but it is the purpose of the Lord which will be established.' (Proverbs 19:21)

The Catechism spells out several different aspects of God's providence. On the one hand, providence is an element of the omnipotence of God and his absolute mastery over the whole of creation. As the Psalmist prayed: 'Our God is in the heavens; he does whatever he pleases'. The same is true of Christ, 'who opens and no one shall shut, who shuts and no one opens.' (Revelation 3:7) And yet, it also speaks of the concern of God, who cares for all, from the least things to the great events of the world and its history. God's loving care for creation and human history is such that he knows when a sparrow falls to the ground and has counted every hair on our head (Matthew 10:29).

Father, we thank you that we are not subjects of faceless fate or mere pawns in a purposeless universe. We live under the loving care of your providence. Help me to trust you like a child in every aspect of my life.

THE PROBLEM OF EVIL (CCC 309-314)

The question of evil has no simple answer. One element of the answer, however, lies in God's free decision to create the universe, as we have seen, in a state of journeying. In this state the less perfect exists alongside the more perfect; good is accompanied by evil as long as creation has not reached the goal of its journey – perfection. Intelligent and free creatures, angels and men, make their journey towards perfection through their free choices. God has permitted the free choice of moral evil, thus respecting the freedom of his creatures, yet he knows he can bring good from evil. The greatest evil - the rejection of God's Son - has led to the greatest good.

'Only at the end... will we fully know the ways by which God has guided his creation to that definitive Sabbath rest.' (CCC 314)

YOUCAT 51

In the Lord's Prayer we ask the Father to deliver us from evil. Father, we know that at times you do permit evil in our lives. We pray that, when the times of trial come, we may remain steadfast in trusting your loving care for us.

Day 37

God created heaven and earth (CCC 325-327)

'The totality of what exists (expressed by the formula 'the heavens and the earth') depends on the One who gives it being.' (CCC 290)

YOUCAT 41-48

The two words 'heaven' and 'earth' represent two different and distinct realities, but the fact that they appear in the same phrase indicates a unity between them. 'Earth' stands for all of the visible creation, including the stars and planets, sun and moon, the earth and everything on the earth. 'Heaven' refers to what is invisible in the sense of spiritual beings, the angels; it can also indicate that God's presence is not limited to the created universe, but transcends the world. Also there is the suggestion of eschatological time (beyond human time) where the saints live in glory. We are unique in being made up of a combination of material and spiritual.

Holy, holy, holy, Lord God of power and might. Heaven and earth are full of your glory. Hosanna in the highest.

Angels in the Life of the Church (CCC 328-336)

Day 38

Relying on the witness of Scripture and on a unanimous Tradition, the Church has always understood that the existence of angels is a truth of our faith. The word angel describes the role rather than the nature of angels. Their nature is spirit. Their role is as servants and messengers of God. Scripture testifies to this role in many places, but the culmination is with Christ. The angels are described as Christ's – having been created through him and for him (Col 1:16). They were present all through Jesus' life, death and resurrection. They are also present in the life and liturgy of the Church. Each believer is accompanied by an angel in the role of protector and shepherd.

'In her liturgy, the Church joins with the angels to adore the thrice-holy God.' (CCC 334)

YOUCAT 54-55

O Angel of God, my guardian dear, to whom God's love commits me here, ever this day be at my side, to light and guard, to rule and guide.

DAY 39

GOD CREATED EVERYTHING THAT EXISTS (CCC 337-344)

'The immense beauty of creation reflects the infinite beauty of the Creator and ought to inspire the respect and submission of man's intellect and will.' (CCC 341)

YOUCAT 46

The Catechism summarises the Church's interpretation of Sacred Scripture. Today we explore the Church's interpretation of Genesis 1. Scripture presents the divine work of the Creator symbolically as a succession of six days concluded by a day of rest. The truth being revealed in Genesis 1 is the truth necessary for our salvation, namely, that creation's inner nature and value and its ordering is directed towards the praise and worship of God. Every part of creation has its own goodness and perfection, but each part is interdependent, completing and serving the others. There is a hierarchy of creatures from the less to the more perfect, and humankind is at the summit.

O God, you have made all things out of nothing. All things depend upon you for their existence. Help me to be in awe of your splendour through the things that I see.

THE RELATIONSHIP BETWEEN CREATION AND THE WORK OF REDEMPTION (CCC 345-349)

DAY 40

In Israel the Sabbath was a day for setting work aside and for giving God worship and adoration. By stating that God completed the work of creation on the seventh day, the Scriptures indicate that the whole of creation was ordered towards worship. It is as though creation is the stage setting for the worship of God. The Catechism goes on to speak of an eighth day – the day of Christ's Resurrection. This day is the beginning of a new creation in Christ. The work of creation, therefore, culminates in the greater work of redemption. The two – creation and redemption – are linked together. The purpose of both is to draw us into the worship of God.

'Worship is inscribed in the order of creation.' (CCC 347)

YOUCAT 46-48

Lord God, St Benedict has taught us that our greatest work is the act of worship and adoration. Help me to give time to prayer and to worship you each day.

DAY 41

WE ARE CREATED IN THE IMAGE AND LIKENESS OF GOD (CCC 355-359)

'God attached so much importance to his salvation that he did not spare his own Son for the sake of man.' (St John Chrysostom)

YOUCAT 58-60

We have already seen the uniqueness of humanity in God's creation. We share in the reality of both heaven and earth. We are composed of both the material (body) and spiritual (soul). It is this unique combination of material and spiritual that places us in a unique relationship to God. We are able to know and love God. Our great dignity is that we have the capacity and the consequent destiny of sharing in the very life of God. We are in the image of God: called by God to a covenant with him and to bring all of creation as a returned offering to him. Our eternal destiny however is only made clear in the mystery of the Word made flesh.

Lord God, what great dignity you have bestowed upon us to discover that only we are able to know and love you our good Creator; and that we alone are called to share, by knowledge and love, in God's own life.

We are created in the image of God and are composed of body and soul (CCC 362-368)

Day 42

The human person is most especially described as being in the 'image of God' because he possesses a soul. The soul is the spiritual principle in a human being, and is directly created by God. The soul does not perish. At death, the soul separates from the body, but will be reunited with the body at the final resurrection. We are the apple of God's eye and the pinnacle of his creation. As the Psalmist so beautiful prays: 'You created me in my inmost self, knit me together in my mother's womb... your eyes could see my embryo.' (Psalm 139:13, 17) Our bodies possess a wonderful dignity and is not to be despised.

'It is the whole human person that is intended to become, in the body of Christ, a temple of the Spirit.' (CCC 364)

YOUCAT 62-63

I bless you Father, that you have made me a unity of soul and body. Through my body I share in the creatureliness of all created things and acknowledge my dependence upon you. Through my soul I am called into loving communion with you.

DAY 43

God created man and woman together and willed each for the other (CCC 369-373)

'The woman... elicits on the man's part a cry of wonder, an exclamation of love and communion.' (CCC 371)

YOUCAT 64

In various ways the first two chapters of the book of Genesis reveal a great deal about the relationship between men and women. Over the centuries the Church has read these chapters symbolically in order to penetrate the great mystery that men and women were created to be a communion of persons. 'Man discovers woman as another 'I' sharing the same humanity' (CCC 371). Men and women also discover in themselves a complementarity. As they come together in marriage, God forms a unity between them, which is life-giving. They can transmit human life and in so doing become cooperators in the Creator's work. They also participate in God's providential care over all of his creation.

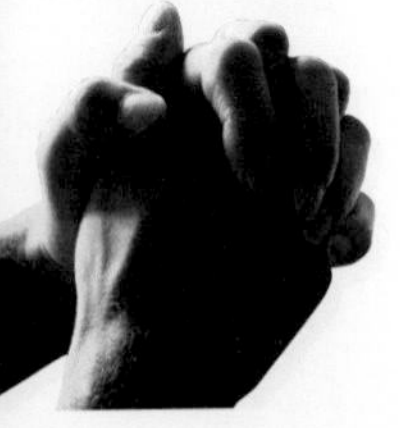

Blessed are you, Lord, God of all creation. You have wonderfully created men and women in your own image, and have called them to a communion of life-giving love.

OUR STATE OF ORIGINAL JUSTICE IN PARADISE BEFORE THE FALL AND SIN (CCC 374-9)

DAY 44

The opening chapters of Genesis reveal another profound mystery about human life, namely, that we were constituted in an original state of holiness and justice. Contemplating and interpreting the scriptures, the Church came to the understanding that the original justice of human beings consisted of an inner harmony within the human person; a harmony between men and women; and a harmony between them and the rest of creation. This harmony was the goodness of God's creation and persisted as long as they remained in communion with God. Before the Fall we lived in a state of profound friendship and intimacy with our good Creator.

'In paradise work is not yet a burden, but collaboration with God in perfecting the visible creation.' (CCC 378)

YOUCAT 66

Only by your revelation, O God, can we glimpse the great glory and dignity of your plan for us. Only by our restoration in a new covenant with you can we find our true destiny.

DAY 45

THE TRAGEDY OF THE FALL (CCC 379, 385-389)

'We cannot tamper with the revelation of original sin without undermining the mystery of Christ.' (CCC 389)

YOUCAT 66-67

We have wrestled for centuries for a solution to the question of the origin of evil in the world. St Augustine realised that an answer was to be found only in his conversion to the living God. The mystery of evil is unmasked in the same moment as one recognizes the call to be in a relationship with God. The true reality of sin is the rejection of God and our continued rebellion and resistance to him. Attempts to explain evil in any other terms fall short of helping us to understand the problem of evil. Only the full revelation of Christ as the source of grace can make possible a full understanding of Adam as the source of sin. Sin is a fact of life to be faced.

Lord God, help me to understand that the only way for me to understand the depth of the Fall is to grasp the depth of your love for us in sending your Son, God made man, Jesus of Nazareth.

THE FALL OF THE ANGELS (CCC 391-395)

DAY 46

The Catechism confirms what revelation has made known a primal event – a Fall - and that the whole of human history is marked by the original fault of our first parents. However, it is also affirmed that, behind the choice of Adam and Eve, there lurks a seductive voice, opposed to God, which tempts us into turning away from God. This seductive voice has been given the name of Satan, the devil, the father of lies. Some angels, though created naturally good, turned from the goodness and the plan of God. From the beginning the evil one has sought to turn humanity away from God. Jesus came to break the mastery and works of Satan.

'The power of Satan is, none the less, not infinite. He is only a creature, powerful from the fact that he is pure spirit, but still a creature.' (CCC 395)

YOUCAT 67

Lord Jesus, you entered into conflict with the devil in order to rescue us from the hold that the devil exercised. We praise you for your death and resurrection that has led us from captivity into the kingdom of God.

DAY 47

THE SIN OF ADAM (CCC 396-403)

'When we look into our own hearts we find that we are drawn to what is wrong and sunk in many evils which cannot come from our good creator... often refusing to acknowledge God at his source.' (Gaudium et spes)

YOUCAT 68

The Catechism helps us to interpret the meaning of Adam's sin. 'Man, tempted by the devil, let his trust in his Creator die in his heart and, abusing his freedom, disobeyed God's command. All subsequent sin would be disobedience toward God and lack of trust in his goodness.' (CCC 397) God, in friendship with us, set out the conditions and limits of our freedom, including respect for our dependence upon God as well as respect for the laws of all creation and the moral teachings that govern the use of freedom. We opted for a false freedom without God. We opted to rebel against the good Creator. We chose to be independent and separated from God.

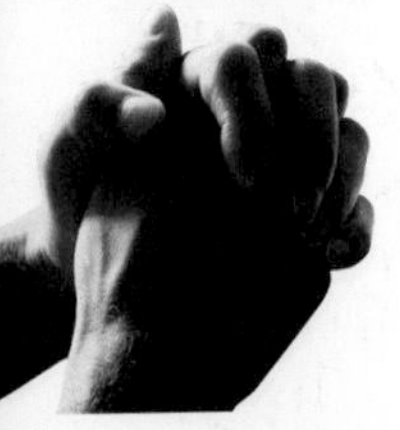

Lord, through the disobedience of Adam we were separated, but through the obedience of Christ we are reconciled. We who were far away from God have been brought close and made friends of God once again.

We share in the sin of Adam (CCC 404)

DAY 48

The fuller understanding of the mystery of sin is only reached when we grasp our redemption in Christ. There is a certain parallel between Adam and Christ. Christ is the head of a new creation, and through Baptism Christ's life of grace is imparted to us. This grace of Christ has the effect of erasing original sin, which had been transmitted through Adam. The nature that is passed on to us all through this unity, is a fallen nature – damaged by the effects of sin. Even though it was not our personal sin, we all experience its effects – an inclination to sin, which is called 'concupiscence'.

'...original sin is called 'sin' only in an analogical sense. It is a sin 'contracted' and not 'committed' – a state and not an act.' (CCC 404)

YOUCAT 68

O Lord Jesus Christ, the first Adam was made a living soul, but you have become a life-giving spirit. Only through immersion into your death and resurrection can I be liberated from the power of the fallen nature inherited from Adam.

IGNEM VENI MITTERE
TERRA

DAY 49

THE DRAMATIC SITUATION OF THE WHOLE WORLD... MAKES MAN'S LIFE A BATTLE (CCC 405-409)

'Finding himself in the midst of a battlefield man has to struggle to do what is right.' (Gaudium et Spes 37)

YOUCAT 68-69

The Church's teaching on the transmission of original sin was articulated both in the 5th century and then again in the 16th century. Firstly, against the monk Pelagius, who reduced Adam's sin simply to bad example and nothing more. And then, later against the idea, that original sin has radically perverted and even depraved humanity, destroying his freedom in an insurmountable way. The Church, however, taught that our nature is not depraved but rather deeply wounded, inclined to evil, and in need of healing. The mystery of evil and sin means that we are born into a sinful condition and have to battle daily with our own sin and the sin of the world. (John 1:29)

Holy Michael, Archangel, defend us in the day of battle, be our safeguard against the wickedness and snares of the devil. May God rebuke him, we humbly pray, and do thou, prince of the heavenly hosts, cast down to hell, Satan and all wicked spirits who wander the world for the ruin of souls.

GOD DID NOT ABANDON US TO THE POWER OF DEATH (CCC 410-412)

DAY 50

Genesis 3:15 has always held an important place in the tradition of the Church. The Church interpreted this verse, which speaks of an enmity between the serpent (devil) and the woman and a conflict in which the final victory will go to the woman's descendant. This verse is understood as the first announcement of the gospel, the Good News. The full revelation of this gospel is revealed in the obedience of Jesus. Through his obedience to the Father, and through his death on the cross, Jesus became the new Adam, thereby overcoming the effects of the sin of the first Adam. God permitted the sin of Adam to reveal his Son as our redeemer.

'I will put enmity between you and the woman, and between your offspring and hers; he will crush your head, and you will strike his heel.' (Gen 3:15)

'O happy fault that earned so great, so glorious a Redeemer!' (The Easter Proclamation – Exsultet)

YOUCAT 70

O Father, the dreadful tragedy of the sin of Adam is far surpassed by the infinite grace of your mercy towards us. For your Son not only erased the effects of original sin, but also raised us to a share in his divine Sonship.

DAY 51

THE GOOD NEWS IS A PERSON: JESUS OF NAZARETH (CCC 426)

'From this loving knowledge of Christ springs the desire to proclaim, to 'evangelize', and to lead others to the 'yes' of faith in Jesus Christ.' (CCC 429)

YOUCAT 71

On the road to Emmaus the disciples said that their hearts burned within them as the Lord talked with them and opened up the scriptures (Luke 24:32). This burning love and desire to tell others about Jesus was the hallmark of the first believers. As Ss Peter and John testified so eloquently, 'We cannot but speak of what we have seen and heard.' (Acts 4:20). The Good News isn't a set of teachings or an ideology or even a way life. No, the Good News is first and foremost a Person, Jesus of Nazareth. The whole of God's eternal plan finds fulfilment through him, with him and in him.

Lord God, may the Holy Spirit burn within me a deep desire to share with others my own experience of Jesus of Nazareth, the Lord of my life.

The Hebrew word Messiah translates into Greek as Christ, which means 'anointed.' In Israel, priests, prophets and kings were chosen for a special mission and were anointed with oil (Exodus 29:7, Leviticus 8:12). Jesus was chosen by God to be the Saviour of the world and was anointed by the Spirit as priest, prophet and king. From the very beginning Jesus was recognized as the Christ. 'To you is born this day in the city of David a Saviour, who is Christ the Lord.' (Luke 2:11). Jesus' glory as the Servant King, who came down from heaven and became the Suffering Servant, is fully revealed only when he is raised high on the cross.

'It was necessary that the Messiah be anointed by the Spirit of the Lord at once as king and priest, and also as prophet.' (CCC 436)

YOUCAT 72-73

'Let all the house of Israel therefore know assuredly that God has made him both Lord and Christ, this Jesus whom you crucified.' (Acts 2:36)

DAY 53

JESUS IS GOD'S ONE AND ONLY SON (CCC 441-445)

'The Church .... believes that the key, the centre and the purpose of the whole of man's history is to be found in its Lord and Master.' (Gaudium et Spes 10)

YOUCAT 74

Jesus' titles shed light on who he is and why he came. The title 'son of God' was used in Israel for angels, kings and the Chosen people of God. When St Peter acknowledged Jesus as 'the Christ, the Son of the Living God', Jesus responded that this grace of revelation could not have come 'by flesh and blood' but only from the heavenly Father. (Matthew 16:16-17). Jesus is God's only Son, God from God, light from light, true God, true man, begotten not made, con-substantial with the Father. YHWH is the name by which God revealed himself to Moses. YHWH is translated into the Greek as Lord. Jesus is God, therefore Jesus is Lord.

Lord, I confess with my heart and proclaim with my lips, in the power of the Holy Spirit, that Jesus is Lord.

THE INCARNATION SHEDS LIGHT ON THE MYSTERY OF HUMANKIND (CCC 456 - 463)

DAY 54

C.S. Lewis said: 'The central miracle asserted by Christians is the incarnation. They say that God became man.' Belief in the incarnation, that God became man, is the distinctive truth of our faith. This truth is holy and sacred and the Church from the very beginning has defended attempts to challenge it. Jesus' divinity did not overwhelm his humanity; nor did his humanity undermine his divinity. The Council of Nicea in 325 confessed in its Creed that the Son of God is 'begotten not made' and is of the same substance as the Father *(homoousious)*. Whenever we celebrate the Eucharist we profess and proclaim this same Creed today. This is our faith.

'The only-begotten Son of God, wanting to make us sharers in his divinity, assumed our nature, so that he, made man, might make men gods.' (CCC 460)

YOUCAT 76

'Though he was in the form of God, Jesus did not count equality with God a thing to be grasped, but emptied himself, taking the form of a servant, being born in the likeness of men.' (Philippians 2:5-6)

Day 55

The Church confesses that Jesus is true God and true man (CCC 469)

'Sing with joyous conviction the hymn of faith: 'He was manifested in the flesh.' (1 Timothy 3:16)

To enter the mystery of the incarnation we need to let grace take us by the hand and lead us to an ever deeper revelation so that we might grasp this profound and central truth of our faith. Jesus was not part God, part man, nor was he some kind of mix of human and divine. Jesus assumed our human nature; he did not absorb it. The Scriptures themselves bear eloquent and beautiful testimony to the truth that God became man. 'In the beginning was the Word: the Word was with God and the Word was God. Through him all things came into being' (John 1:1-3). And, 'Who, being in the form of God, did not consider equality with God something to be grasped' (Philippians 2:6).

YOUCAT 77

'The Son of God... worked with human hands; he thought with a human mind. He acted with a human will, and with a human heart he loved. Born of the Virgin Mary, he has truly been made one of us, like to us in all things except sin.' (Gaudium et Spes 22)

Jesus is Lord of Glory and One of the Holy Trinity (CCC 468)

Day 56

In the early centuries of the Church's growth, a number of theological battles were fought between those who questioned Christ's humanity or indeed his divinity. Paul of Samosata argued that Jesus was Son of God by adoption not by nature. Arius claimed that Jesus came from another substance than that of the Father. The Nestorian heresy held that Jesus was a human person joined to the Son. The Monophysites suggested that Jesus' humanity was subsumed by his divinity. We owe a great debt to saints such as St Cyril of Alexandria and St Athanasius and the Fathers of the early Church Councils, who preserved and defended the doctrine of the incarnation.

'The Church has always acknowledged that in the body of Jesus 'we see our God made visible and so are caught up in love of the God we cannot see'.' (CCC 477)

YOUCAT 77

We confess that Jesus is inseparably true God and true man. He is truly the Son of God who, without ceasing to be God and Lord, became a man and our brother.

DAY 57

THE FATHER BLESSED MARY MORE THAN ANY OTHER CREATED PERSON (CCC 492)

'By the grace of God Mary remained free of every personal sin her whole life long.' (CCC 493)

YOUCAT 83

God chose a young Jewish woman from Nazareth in Galilee to be the Mother of his Son. Through the holy women of old Mary's mission was prepared. Firstly, Eve who despite her disobedience received a promise that evil would be conquered (Genesis 3:15). Then Sarah, who conceived in old age. God chose the weak, the poor and humble: Hannah, Deborah, Ruth, Judith and Esther. But in the fullness of time God sent his Son born of a woman and that woman was Mary. Mary was filled with grace and her 'Yes' to God was a defining moment in the history of the world and in our salvation. We are indebted to Mary for her willingness to humbly co-operate in God's plan of salvation.

Lord, we thank you for Mary, the Mother of God, our Mother in faith. For she was blessed in Christ with every spiritual blessing and was chosen by Christ to be holy and blameless before the foundation of the world.

THE LITURGY OF THE CHURCH CELEBRATES MARY AS THE 'EVER VIRGIN' (CCC 499)

DAY 58

Mary was pledged to marry Joseph. The scriptures tell us that, on discovering she was pregnant, he had in mind to divorce her quietly. He was a good man and did not want to expose her to public disgrace (Matthew 1:18). It is not difficult to imagine his distress, anguish and indeed his suffering as he grappled with this devastating news. In a dream he was told that Mary had conceived by the Holy Spirit (Matthew 1:20). Truly a virgin birth is beyond human understanding; physically impossible. But what is impossible for us is possible for God. The Church has always confessed that Mary is for ever virgin.

'Against this doctrine the objection is sometimes raised that the Bible mentions brothers and sisters of Jesus. The Church has always understood these passages as not referring to other children of the Virgin Mary.' (CCC 500)

YOUCAT 80

'Mary remained a virgin in conceiving her Son, a virgin in giving birth to him, a virgin in carrying him, a virgin in nursing him at her breast, always a virgin.' (St Augustine)

Day 59

Christ's whole earthly life is both mystery and revelation (CCC 561)

'No one – whether shepherd or wise man, can approach God here below except by kneeling before the manger at Bethlehem and adoring him hidden in the weakness of a new born child.' (CCC 563)

YOUCAT 86

Jesus is the mystery of God revealed, and unveiled. Jesus reveals God. Jesus, the Son of God, says, 'Whoever has seen me has seen the Father' (John 14:9) and the Father says, 'This is my Son, my Chosen; listen to him.' (Luke 9:35). At Christmas we enter into this mystery with joy and a sense of expectancy of the Lord coming into our own lives. The events surrounding Jesus' birth touch on the deeper mystery of 'God's love among us.'(1 John 4:8). In the humble stable, a poor family and simple shepherds were led into the mystery that 'the Word became flesh and dwelt among us.' (John 1:14). Before this mystery we bow low in humble adoration.

Lord Jesus Christ, in you are all the treasures and riches of God. Through you we have received every spiritual blessing. Lead me by the grace of revelation ever deeply into the mystery of Christ.

At his baptism Jesus accepted his mission as God's suffering servant (CCC 536)

Day 60

St John the Baptist was surprised by Jesus' request for baptism for his baptism was for repentance. Had he not declared Jesus to be 'the Lamb of God who takes away the sin of the world' (John 1:29)? Why did the Saviour of the world need to be baptized? Why did he who had no sin identify himself with those on the very margins of society: tax collectors, prostitutes? Through his cross and resurrection he who had no sin, the perfect and sinless One, took upon himself the sin of the world. On account of sin God 'made him to be sin who knew no sin, so that in him we might become the righteousness of God.' (2 Corinthians 5:21).

'The baptism of Jesus is on his part the acceptance and inauguration of his mission as God's Suffering Servant.' (CCC 535)

YOUCAT 87

'Let us be buried with Christ by baptism to rise with him; let us go down with him to be raised with him; and let us rise with him to be glorified with him.' (St Gregory of Nazianzus)

DAY 61

THE TEMPTATIONS OF CHRIST (CCC 538)

'Jesus' victory over the tempter in the desert anticipates victory at the Passion, the supreme act of obedience of his filial love for the Father.' (CCC 539)

YOUCAT 88

Oscar Wilde famously said, 'I can resist everything except temptation.' We are all tempted in many different and varied ways. Some succumb to pride and arrogance, others to more sensual things like food and sex. We are weak and fallen and find temptation hard to resist. Jesus was tempted in every way that we are but he did not sin (Hebrews 4:15). Jesus suffered when he was tempted and, because of this, is able to help us when we are being sorely tempted. Jesus is the perfect man, the New Adam, the One who did not sin; nor was he seduced to turn away from God. We resist temptation by God's grace: 'Lead us not into temptation but deliver us from evil'.

Lord Jesus Christ, you are the Victor and the Conqueror. You bind the strong man and take back his plunder. (Mark 3:27)

Everyone is called to enter the kingdom (CCC 541)

Day 62

Jesus' invitation to enter the kingdom is uniquely found in the parables. The key that unlocks all of the parables is the Parable of the Sower (Mark 4:1-9). Jesus encourages us to strive to understand this parable in particular because it allows us entry into the mystery of all the others (Mark 4:13). The seed of God's word is sown in our hearts. We receive God's seed in baptism but we also receive it whenever we read or hear God's word in Scripture, prayer or when celebrating the Eucharist. To mature in faith and understand the secrets of the kingdom requires a radical and daily choice on our part to follow the Lord. Ask yourself today: will you be good soil for the Lord?

'The kingdom of God will be definitively established through Christ's cross. 'God reigned from the wood.' (CCC 550)

YOUCAT 89

Lord Jesus, teach me to sit at your feet and learn from you for you are humble and gentle of heart, and your Spirit pours out the wisdom that I may grasp ever more deeply the secrets of the kingdom of heaven.

Day 63

The Transfiguration of Jesus (CCC 554)

'He also reveals that he will have to go by the way of the cross at Jerusalem to 'enter into his glory'.' (CCC 555)

YOUCAT 93

Just before Jesus began his public ministry he was baptized. Just before Jesus entered his Passover he was transfigured. At both events the Father, the Son and the Spirit were revealed. St Thomas Aquinas said of the Transfiguration: '..the Father in the voice, the Son in the man Jesus, the Spirit in the shining cloud.' Through baptism we are immersed into the death and resurrection of Jesus and become partakers in the very life of God. Our destiny and dignity rests on the hope that at the coming of Jesus and the resurrection of the dead we will be raised up body and soul, just as Jesus was raised body and soul. The Transfiguration gave us, if you like, a glimpse of the eternal life to come.

Lord, in your Transfiguration we had a foretaste of the life to come when you will change our lowly body to be like your glorious body. But before this blessing comes trial and persecution.

The Paschal Mystery is the Good News (CCC 571)

In St John's Gospel Jesus spoke of his hour of glory. 'The hour has come for the Son of Man to be glorified.' (John 12:23). He was referring to the glory of the cross. We understand the following events in Jesus' life as the Paschal Mystery: his suffering, death on the cross, resurrection from the dead and ascension into heaven. These events are the very heart, essence and core of the Good News. We cannot separate them – they are linked together in a mystical union of faith. In this journey through the Catechism we can dedicate ourselves to becoming more familiar with the Gospels and their account of Jesus' death, resurrection and ascension.

'God's saving plan was accomplished 'once and for all' by the redemptive death of his Son Jesus Christ.' (CCC 571)

YOUCAT 95

Lord, teach me to glory in nothing but the cross of Christ and to rejoice in the Paschal Mystery by which we are saved and redeemed.

DAY 65

JESUS IS THE FULFILMENT OF THE LAW (CCC 577-591)

'The perfect fulfilment of the Law could be the work of none but the divine legislator, born subject to the Law in the person of the Son.' (CCC 580)

YOUCAT 96

Jesus was perceived as a serious threat by the religious leaders of his day. They accused him of not abiding by the Law of Moses, although he taught that he had not come to abolish the law but to fulfil it (Matthew 5:17). They also accused him of being hostile to God's Temple, although for him the Temple was the dwelling place of the Father and, in order not to cause offence, he paid the Temple-tax. They were threatened by him and saw him as undermining the very stability of Israel's faith because he claimed to forgive sin – and who could forgive sin but God alone (Mark 2:7)? Their hearts were hard and resistant through ignorance and unbelief.

Lord, protect me from being hardened by the deceitfulness of sin. I hold firmly to the faith with the confidence and joy which comes by grace. Today, Lord, help me not to harden my heart.

From the very beginning the cross has been at the heart of God's plan of salvation (CCC 599-611)

Day 66

From the moment we fell away from God his plan of redemption began. We see this in Genesis 3:15. This scripture verse is called the *Protoevangelium,* which means 'first gospel' because it announces the coming of a Saviour. It also speaks of a battle between the serpent and the woman. Tradition has seen in this verse the promise of the 'new Adam' who 'became obedient unto death, even death on a cross.' (Philippians 2:8). We fell away from God's grace through the wood of the tree; we are reconciled to God by the wood of the cross. Jesus identified himself from the very beginning with the Suffering Servant of Isaiah (Isaiah 53:7-8).

'The desire to embrace his Father's plan of redeeming love inspired Jesus' whole life.' (CCC 607)

'And I will put enmity between you and the woman, and between your offspring and hers; he will crush your head, and you will strike his heel.' (Gen 3:15)

YOUCAT 98

Lord God, your death on the cross was not the result of blind chance or simply the violence of human beings but was part of your mysterious and divine plan of salvation.

DAY
67

IN GETHSEMANE JESUS ACCEPTED THE CUP OF SALVATION (CCC 612)

'My Father, if it be possible, let this cup pass from me.' (Matthew 26:39)

In the Garden of Gethsemane Jesus underwent a dreadful anguish. It was so intense that he sweated blood (Luke 22:44). Can you imagine how stressed and overwhelmed you have to be to perspire blood? What was happening in this moment? How can we understand this suffering? One way is by looking at gardens in the Bible. In the Garden of Eden we rebelled against God. In the Garden of Gethsemane Jesus, unlike Adam, was obedient even unto death on a cross. Jesus' agony in the Garden of Gethsemane showed the utter horror and desolation of human death. By drinking his cup of suffering Jesus conquered sin and death.

YOUCAT 100

Lord, I know the wages of sin is death. Only in Jesus, the sinless and perfect One, the Author of Life and the Living One, could death be conquered. Jesus destroyed death once and for all.

What is the result of Christ's sacrifice for us? (CCC 613-618)

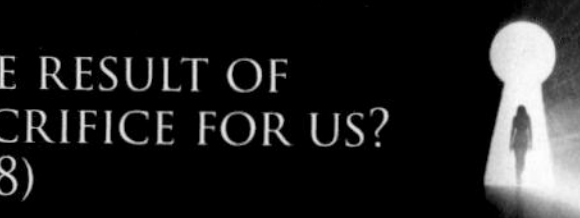

Through the cross of Jesus we are blessed with every spiritual blessing and gift. Through it we are restored to communion with God. We are reconciled with the Father through the blood of the covenant which was poured out for many for the forgiveness of sins. Through the cross Jesus bore our sins and iniquities. Jesus atoned for, paid the price, if you like, for our sins. No mere human being, regardless of how holy they were, could take upon themselves the sins of us all. Jesus' death on the cross was unique and special, the most important death in human history and the source of our salvation.

'Apart from the cross there is no other ladder by which we may get to heaven.' (St Rose of Lima)

YOUCAT 101

Lord, today I take up my cross and follow you. You suffered for us and left an example for us to follow in your steps. Hail, O Cross, our only hope.

DAY 69

JESUS DESCENDED INTO HELL TO SET CAPTIVES FREE (CCC 632-637)

'Christ, that Morning Star who came back from the dead, and shed his peaceful light on all mankind, your Son who lives and reigns forever. Amen.' (CCC 631)

Today we reflect on a profound mystery of faith: Jesus' descent into hell to proclaim the Good News to those imprisoned there. What happened to Jesus after he died, when his soul left his body? The Church has taught since the beginning that like all humankind Jesus experienced death and in his soul he joined the realm of the dead. The Hebrews referred to this realm as '*Sheol*', also known as '*Hades*' in Greek, or hell as we know it today. The Church has taught that the souls here were deprived of the vision of God; this did not mean that they were all damned. Jesus descended into hell to liberate them, the just and righteous souls who awaited their Saviour.

I am your God, who for your sake have become your son... I order you, O sleeper, to awake. I did not create you to be a prisoner in hell. Rise from the dead, for I am the life of the dead. (Ancient homily for Holy Saturday)

Many signs give witness to the resurrection of Jesus (CCC 639-644)

Day 70

The resurrection of Jesus is understood as the climax of the incarnation. Many signs witness to Jesus' resurrection. The living tradition of the resurrection is rooted in the historical witness firstly of the empty tomb (John 20:23). Secondly, in the witness of Mary Magdalene and the holy women who were the first to witness the resurrection. Thirdly, the Lord appeared to Peter and after this the Twelve. However St Paul records that the Risen Lord also appeared to more than five hundred people on a single occasion (1 Corinthians 15:5-6).

'Thus the women were the first messengers of Christ's resurrection for the apostles themselves.' (CCC 641)

YOUCAT 106

I want to know Christ and the power of his resurrection and the fellowship of sharing in his suffering, becoming like him in his death, and by God's grace to attain to the resurrection from the dead.

DAY 71

THROUGH THE RESURRECTION WE ARE FORGIVEN, JUSTIFIED AND RECEIVE NEW LIFE (CCC 651-655)

'Christ's resurrection is closely linked to the Incarnation of God's Son, and is its fulfilment in accordance with God's eternal plan.' (CCC 653)

YOUCAT 104,108

Through Jesus' death on the cross we are liberated from sin and by the resurrection a new way of life is opened to us. St Paul said: '...as Christ was raised from the dead by the glory of the Father, we too might walk in newness of life.' (Romans 6:4). Through baptism we are adopted children of God and become partakers in God's divine nature. The Catechism refers to this process as justification – in other words, we are reinstated into God's grace and friendship. Jesus' resurrection is the source of our own future resurrection. In our prayer, reading of scripture and supremely in the Eucharist we taste something of the eternal and divine life to come.

Lord God, teach me that by your grace I no longer live for myself but for Jesus the Lord, who for my sake died on the cross and was raised to new life.

WHAT DOES THE ASCENSION OF JESUS INTO HEAVEN MEAN? (CCC 659-667)

DAY 72

St Mary Magdalene was the first to witness the resurrection and the first to hear the Lord's mysterious words about his ascension in to heaven: 'I have not yet ascended to the Father; but go to my bretheren and say to them, I am ascending to my Father, and your Father, to my God and your God' (John 20:17). The glory of the Risen Lord was different from the exaltation of the Ascended Lord. The glory of the Risen Lord was veiled compared to the complete divine glory of the Ascended Lord. Jesus is our great High Priest, he is seated at the right hand of the Father and always lives to make intercession for us. He who ascended in glory will return in glory. 'Come, Lord Jesus, Come.'

'By the 'Father's right hand' we understand the glory and honour of divinity, where he who exists as Son of God before all ages, indeed as God, of one being with the Father, is seated bodily after he became Incarnate and his flesh was glorified.' (St John Damascene)

YOUCAT 109

'To him was given dominion and glory and kingdom, that all peoples, nations and languages should serve him; his dominion is an everlasting dominion which shall not pass away, and his kingdom one that shall not be destroyed.' (Daniel 7:14)

DAY 73

WE CELEBRATE CHRIST'S FIRST COMING AND LOOK FORWARD TO HIS SECOND (CCC 668-674)

'Since the Ascension Christ's coming has been imminent even though 'it is not for you to know times or seasons which the Father has fixed by his own authority'.' (CCC 673)

YOUCAT 110

St Bernard of Clairvaux taught there are three comings of Christ. The first is the birth of the Saviour in a manger in Bethlehem. The second, his coming into our lives, takes place at baptism, but also as adults as we re-dedicate and give our lives more fully to him. The third and final coming is the Second Coming, the return of Christ in glory. Since Jesus ascended into heaven his return has been imminent. Jesus is the Lord of the cosmos and Lord of human history. All of creation now groans and longs for the return of the King. The whole of creation is waiting, longing and groaning for the Lord to come again.

Lord, we are living in the age of the Church, the time of the Spirit and of witness. Today, when we celebrate the Eucharist, pour out your Spirit into my heart as I pray, 'Maran atha! Our Lord, come'.

THE CHURCH'S FINAL AND ULTIMATE TRIAL (CCC 675-677)

DAY 74

Since the ascension of Jesus into heaven we have been living in the last times or the 'last hour' (1 Peter 4:7). Since the beginning this has been a time of trial and suffering. The martyrdom of St Stephen highlights the persecution unleashed upon the first believers (Acts 7:54-59). The Church teaches that before Jesus' return in glory the Church will pass through a final trial in which 'the mystery of iniquity' in the form of a religious deception called the Antichrist will lead many astray. We do not know dates or times of the Antichrist nor do we know when the Lord will return. We are simply invited to watch, pray and be faithful to the Lord.

'Before Christ's Second Coming the Church must pass through a final trial that will shake the faith of many believers.' (CCC 675)

YOUCAT 111

Lord, teach me to be self-controlled and alert. Our enemy the devil prowls around like a roaring lion looking for someone to devour. We resist him standing firm in faith in the power of the name, the blood and the Cross of Jesus.

'Full right to pass definitive judgement on the works and hearts of men belongs to him as redeemer of the world. He 'acquired' this right by his cross.' (CCC 679)

YOUCAT 112

The idea of judgement is a difficult one and, if we are honest, rather frightening. There is no escaping the fact that Jesus spoke a lot about it. He taught that the Father had given 'all judgement to the Son' (John 5:22). Jesus, the Son of God, did not come to judge, but to save and to give his life that we may know the life he has in himself (John 3:17). How will we be judged? Our behaviour, our conduct and the secrets of our hearts will be laid bare and brought to light before the Living God (Romans 2:16). All unbelief and rejection of God's grace will be condemned. We must be careful not to reject God's grace in this life because in doing this we judge ourselves.

Lord, teach me to love and serve my neighbour by grace and by the power of your love. Teach me also the wisdom of your teaching: 'Truly I say to you, as you did it to one of the least of these bretheren you did it to me.' (Matthew 25:40)

We confess our faith in God the Holy Spirit (CCC 683-690)

Day 76

The Holy Spirit is the third person of the Blessed Trinity. With God the Father and God the Son, God the Holy Spirit is worshipped and glorified. The Holy Spirit is the Lord and the giver of the new life of grace. To be in touch with Christ we need to be in touch with the Holy Spirit. Faith is kindled or awakened in us through the grace and fire of the Holy Spirit. We cannot proclaim that Jesus is Lord without the Holy Spirit (1 Corinthians 12:3), and because God the Father sent the Spirit into our hearts we proclaim God as 'Abba' Father!' (Galatians 4:6) The Holy Spirit is our Counsellor, Advocate, Intercessor and Friend. We turn to the Spirit today.

'Baptism gives us the grace of new birth in God the Father, through his Son, in the Holy Spirit.' (St Irenaeus)

YOUCAT 113-114

O Lord, at the beginning of the Second Vatican Council, Pope John XXIII prayed, 'Send forth your Spirit and renew the face of the earth.' We make this our prayer today.

Day 77

The Holy Spirit spoke through the Old Testament prophets (CCC 702-706)

'The Spirit of the Lord is upon me, because the Lord has anointed me to bring good tidings to the afflicted; he has sent me to bind up the broken hearted, to proclaim liberty to the captives, and the opening of prison to those who are bound; to proclaim the year of the Lord's favour.' (Isaiah 61:1-2)

YOUCAT 116

God's Holy Spirit helps us to read the Old Testament in a way that helps us to understand God's plan of salvation. The Spirit leads us to recognize that, when reading the Old Testament, God's Spirit from the very beginning was preparing for the time of the Messiah. We are invited by the Holy Spirit to search the Old Testament to discover there what the Spirit has spoken through the prophets. Ask the Spirit to open up the Scriptures to you during this journey. Search for Christ in the Pentateuch (the first five books of the Bible), the Prophets and Writings (the Psalms and the books of Wisdom).

Lord, you proclaimed through the prophet Isaiah, 'Behold, I am doing a new thing! (Isaiah 43:19). That new thing was the birth of the Saviour, our salvation and the revelation of God as Holy Trinity.

THE HOLY SPIRIT PREPARED MARY BY HIS GRACE (CCC 721-726)

DAY 78

The Catechism describes Mary as 'the masterwork of the mission of the Son and the Spirit in the fullness of time' (CCC 721). In Mary, God the Father found the perfect dwelling place where the Son and the Spirit could dwell. Mary's consent and co-operation was a pivotal moment in human and salvation history because, through the work of the Spirit in her, God's plan of redemption got underway. Mary was full of grace by the power of the Holy Spirit. Mary was full of wisdom by the power of the Holy Spirit. The liturgy proclaims and recognizes Mary as the 'Seat of Wisdom' and we in turn proclaim and recognize her as our Mother in faith.

'It was fitting that the mother of him in whom 'the fullness of deity dwells bodily' should herself be 'full of grace'.' *(CCC 722)*

YOUCAT 117

Lord, Mary is the 'mother of the living', the mother of the 'whole Christ', and we give thanks and praise to the Father for pouring out upon her every grace and blessing in the spiritual realm.

DAY 79

GOD SENT THE HOLY SPIRIT AT PENTECOST (CCC 727-732)

'Through the Holy Spirit we are restored to paradise, led back to the kingdom of heaven and adopted as children, given confidence to call God 'Father' and to share in Christ's grace, called children of light and given a share in eternal glory.' (St Basil the Great)

YOUCAT 118

The birth of a new year is marked with joy all over the world. The birth of the Church at Pentecost was celebrated with joy and the fire of the Holy Spirit. The coming of the Holy Spirit, fifty days after the resurrection, fully revealed God as Holy Trinity. His coming transformed those gathered in the upper room. God's love was poured into their hearts through the Holy Spirit (Romans 5:5). With the Spirit we can bear much fruit for God; we can produce the fruits of the Holy Spirit: love, joy, peace, patience, kindness, goodness, faithfulness, gentleness and self-control (Galatians 5:22).

We have seen the true Light, we have received the heavenly Spirit, we have found the true faith; we adore the indivisible Trinity, who has saved us. (Byzantine Liturgy, Pentecost Vespers)

THE CHURCH'S MISSION IS TO PROCLAIM CHRIST AND ESTABLISH THE KINGDOM (CCC 751-769)

DAY 80

Mary's mission was to give birth to Christ. This is our mission and the mission of the Church too. The Church is called to proclaim and establish God's kingdom on earth. The first Christians had a saying, 'The world was created for the Church.' From age to age God has gathered a people to himself, first in his people Israel and now in the People of God, the Church. The Church journey is to the Father's house, where at Christ's glorious return she will be reunited with Christ her spouse. We dedicate ourselves to the mission of the Church to win souls for Christ and to live life in the power of the Spirit.

'St Paul calls the nuptial union of Christ and the Church 'a great mystery'.' (Ephesians 5:32)

YOUCAT 121-122

The Spirit and the Bride, the Church, pray with heartfelt conviction: 'Come, Lord Jesus, Come.'

Day 81

We are the Church – the People of God (CCC 781-801)

'Once you were not a people, but now you are the people of God; once you had not received mercy, but now you have received mercy.' (1 Peter 2:10)

When we think of the word Church, we tend to think of a building. But the church is much more than a work of architecture or construction. It is first and foremost made up of people. The bishops at Vatican II referred to the Church as the People of God. We are the People of God; we are the Church. We belong to a body different from any other religious, ethnic, political or cultural group found in history. To quote St Peter, we are a 'chosen race, a royal priesthood, a holy nation.' (1 Peter 2:9). We are children of God, as St John says, 'children born not of natural descent, nor of human decision or a husband's will, but born of God' (John 1:13).

YOUCAT 122-123

Lord, through the grace of baptism and as members of the church we participate and share in your three-fold ministry of priest, prophet and king.

THE CHURCH IS HOLY (CCC 813-829)

DAY 82

The Church is holy because Christ was holy. Christ gave himself up for his Bride, the Church, and joined her to himself. The Church then is made holy and sanctified by the Lord, through him, in him and with him. However, although the church itself is holy we are constantly in need of conversion, reform and renewal. The Catechism expresses this beautifully when it says: 'The Church however clasping sinners to her bosom, at once holy and always in need of purification, follows constantly the path of penance and renewal' (CCC 827). We look to the saints of the Church as our brothers and sisters in holiness, for encouragement and strength to live good and holy lives.

'Love, in fact, is the vocation which includes all others; it's a universe of its own, comprising all time and space – it's eternal.' (St Therese of Lisieux)

YOUCAT 129,132

Just as he who called you is holy, so be holy in all you do, for it is written, 'Be holy, because I am holy.' (1 Peter 1:15)

DAY 83

WE BELONG TO THE COMMUNION OF SAINTS. PRAISE GOD! (CCC 946-953)

'Do not weep, for I shall be more useful to you after my death and I shall help you more effectively than during my life.' (St Dominic's last words)

YOUCAT 146

We belong not only to a worldwide communion of believers but also to the souls in purgatory and to the blessed in heaven. We have friends both in heaven and on earth. Through this communion of saints we share in a common fund of every spiritual grace and blessing *(sancta)*. These blessings are many and include: the sacraments of the Church, especially the Eucharist, the charisms and every spiritual gift. We belong to each other in faith, and at the heart of our communion or fellowship is love and charity. Our communion with each other is rooted in the vision of the Acts of the Apostles, when the early believers 'had everything in common' (Acts 4:32).

Heavenly Father, I give thanks and praise to you, for the communion of saints, the family of believers, both living and dead, to which I belong.

Mary, United with Her Son Helps and Aids the Church in So Many Ways (CCC 963-972)

Day 84

Mary is our Mother, Advocate, Helper, Benefactress and Mediatrix (CCC 963-972). Mary is the perfect and model disciple. She is the Church's most pre-eminent and wholly unique member, the 'exemplary realization' *(typus)* of the Church *(Lumen Gentium 53)*. She helps us today in so many ways. From the beginning she has taught us how to pray (Luke 1:46-55). Since the Ascension she has prayed for the Church. Through her Assumption into heaven we have hope that, just as she was redeemed body and soul, God will raise us up on the Last Day. Mary is our sign of hope and she lives now in heaven to intercede and pray for us.

'We believe that the Holy Mother of God, the New Eve, Mother of the Church, continues in heaven to exercise her maternal role on behalf of the members of Christ.' (Pope Paul VI)

YOUCAT 147-149

Lord, we lift up our hearts in praise and worship to you for the gift of Mary, our Mother in faith. For by her co-operation, obedience, faith, hope and burning charity she is a mother of grace to us all.

Day 85

By the Sacraments of Baptism and Penance our sins are forgiven (CCC 976-980)

'Penance has rightly been called by the holy fathers 'a laborious kind of baptism'.' (St Gregory of Nazianzus)

YOUCAT 151

In baptism our sins are completely wiped out, totally forgiven and we are reconciled to God. This forgiveness is so full and complete that, as the Catechism itself teaches, 'there remained in us absolutely nothing left to efface, neither original sin nor offences committed by our own will.' (CCC 978). The Church received power to forgive sins from the Lord Jesus himself: 'Receive the Holy Spirit. If you forgive the sins of any, they are forgiven; if you retain the sins of any they are retained.' (John 20:22-23). But we are sinners and sinners sin. However, in the Sacrament of Reconciliation the Church offers us again the wonderful and healing gift of forgiveness.

Lord God, even if I should sin until the last moment of my life the grace of forgiveness is always available to me.

WE WILL BE RAISED FROM THE DEAD – BODY AND SOUL (CCC 990)

DAY 86

When St Paul preached about the resurrection of the body he was ridiculed and mocked. 'When they heard of the resurrection of the dead, some scoffed' (Acts 17:32). James Joyce, the Irish novelist, many centuries later mocked it also: 'Once you are dead you are dead. The last day idea. This knocking them all up out of their graves.' In sharp contrast, St John the Evangelist, himself a witness of the resurrection, in what must surely be one of the most exciting promises of the New Testament, wrote: 'We will be like him, for we will see him as he is' (1 John 3:2). Our faith teaches us that, on the Last Day, we will be raised body and soul to live with God for ever.

'The body that is sown is perishable, it is raised imperishable, it is sown in dishonour, it is raised in glory, it is sown in weakness, it is raised in power, it is sown a natural body, it is raised a spiritual body.' (1 Corinthians 15:42-44)

YOUCAT 152

'For the perishable must clothe itself with the imperishable, and the mortal with immortality. Then the saying that is written will come true: 'Death has been swallowed up in victory'. (1 Corinthians 15:54)

DAY 87

ON THE LAST DAY WE WILL RISE AGAIN FROM THE DEAD (CCC 992-1004)

'Just as bread that comes from the earth, after God's blessing has been invoked upon it, is no longer ordinary bread, but Eucharist, formed of two things, the one earthly and the other heavenly; so too our bodies, which partake of the Eucharist, are no longer corruptible, but possess the hope of resurrection.' (St Irenaeus)

YOUCAT 154

The Church teaches us that, when we die, our soul separates from our body. The body corrupts in the ground but the soul, which is immortal, goes to meet God. The Church also teaches us that the soul will reunite with the body on the 'last day' when Christ returns. This is a mystery and, for sure, exceeds both our understanding and our imagination. We can only penetrate this mystery through prayer and ask the Spirit to help us grasp it more fully. However, what we do know is that when we participate in the Eucharist we are given a foretaste of the life to come and of our transfiguration and resurrection, body and soul.

For the Lord himself will descend from heaven, with a cry of command, with the archangel's call, and with the sound of the trumpet of God. And the dead in Christ will rise first. (1 Thessalonians 4:16)

GOD HAS GIVEN US EVERLASTING LIFE (CCC 1020-1022)

We know many things about the world we live in. We have made amazing advances in science and technology. However, despite this progress, death defeats us and no one is exempt. We rebel against death and sense deep within that death is not the end as the sage taught 'God has set eternity in our hearts' (Ecclesiastes 3:11). Through baptism we carry within us an eternal seed which death cannot extinguish. What is everlasting life? 'Now this is eternal life: that they may know you {the Father} and Jesus Christ, whom you have sent' (John 17:3). Through baptism we are united with Christ to Christ's death and on dying we enter into everlasting life.

'Although the mystery of death utterly beggars the imagination, the Church has been taught by divine revelation and firmly teaches that man has been created by God for a blissful purpose beyond the reach of earthly misery.' (Gaudium et Spes 18)

YOUCAT 156-157

Go forth, Christian soul, from this world, in the name of God the almighty Father, who created you, in the name of Jesus Christ, the Son of the Living God, who suffered for you, in the name of the Holy Spirit, who was poured out upon you. Go forth faithful Christian. (Prayer of Commendation)

DAY 89

TO LIVE IN HEAVEN IS TO BE WITH CHRIST (CCC 1023-1029)

'For life is to be with Christ; where Christ is, there is life, there is the kingdom.' (St Ambrose)

YOUCAT 158

We don't tend to think a lot about heaven. Why is this? Perhaps we don't want to be presumptuous or assume we will one day get there. C S Lewis, that great apologist for the Christian faith, gently challenged this: 'A continual looking forward to the eternal world is not a form of escapism or wishful thinking, but one of the things a Christian is meant to do.' Heaven is the goal, the purpose and the blissful destiny we hope for in Christ. True, what heaven is like is beyond our understanding and description. However, the Bible helps us by using images which shed some light: the Father's house, life, light, peace and paradise.

Lord, by your cross and resurrection you have opened heaven to us, by the grace of revelation open up heaven in a way that I may contemplate the divine mystery of heaven, the beatific vision, to see God face to face.

After Death We Undergo a Purification (CCC 1030-1031)

Day 90

The Church teaches the need for purification or a cleansing after death so as to enter the holiness and joy of heaven. Both scripture and the tradition testify to this. In the book of Maccabees it says: 'Therefore [Judas Maccabeus] made atonement for the dead, that they might be delivered from their sin' (2 Maccabees 12:46). The Church has always honoured the memory of the dead and celebrated the Eucharist for their intention so that once purified they may finally enter their eternal reward. St Catherine of Genoa said of the souls in Purgatory: 'I believe no happiness can be found worthy to be compared with that of a soul in Purgatory except that of the saints in Paradise'.

'...[the] fire which both burns and saves is Christ himself. The encounter with him is the decisive act of judgement. Before his gaze all falsehood melts away. This encounter with him, as it burns us, transforms and frees us, allowing us to become truly ourselves.' (Spe Salvi 47)

YOUCAT 159

If Job's sons were purified by their father's sacrifice, why should we doubt that our offerings for the dead bring them some consolation? Let us not hesitate to help those who have died and to offer our prayers for them. (St John Chrysostom)

WE CAN REJECT GOD OF OUR OWN FREE CHOICE (CCC 1033-1041)

DAY 91

One of God's greatest gifts is free choice. We were created to freely choose to love God but we also have the capacity to finally and ultimately reject this love. The Church's teaching on hell can only be understood in the light of free will, because God predestines no one to hell but rather, through a persistent refusal to turn to God and a wilful turning away, we cut ourselves off finally and ultimately from God's love and mercy and risk being eternally separated from his love. God does not want anyone to perish but for all to come to repentance and the joy of eternal life (2 Peter 3:9). The invitation to repentance and conversion is held out to us throughout our lives.

'...graciously accept this oblation of our service, that of your whole family; order our days in your peace, and command that we be delivered from eternal damnation and counted among the flock of those you have chosen.' (EP 1, New Roman Missal)

YOUCAT 161-163

Lord, you call us to conversion and so to enter by the narrow gate. The gate that leads to eternal separation from you is wide and easy. Help me, by your grace, to choose the narrow gate of repentance and holiness of life and so enter the joy of the blessed.

DAY 92

WHAT IS THE MEANING OF AMEN? (CCC 1061-1065)

'The faithful must believe the articles of the Creed so that believing they may obey God, by obeying may live well, by living well may purify their hearts, and with pure hearts may understand what they believe.' (St Augustine)

YOUCAT 165

The last word of the Creed is 'Amen'. The last word of the Bible is 'Amen' (Revelation 22:21). The root of the meaning of 'Amen' is 'believe.' When we say 'Amen' we are saying, 'Yes I believe.' Our vocation, to walk with the Lord and live the life in the power of the Spirit, is to be a daily 'Amen, yes I believe.' We have journeyed together through the Creed, our Profession of Faith. We have proclaimed together, 'We believe, I believe.' The Holy Spirit is the One who unlocks the mystery of faith and gives us fresh insights, so that our hearts burn within us with a new desire to witness to Christ and spread his word.

Through him, and with him, and in him, O God, almighty Father, in the unity of the Holy Spirit, all glory and honour is yours, for ever and ever. Amen.

PART TWO

The Celebration of the Christian Mystery

The Celebration of the Christian Mystery

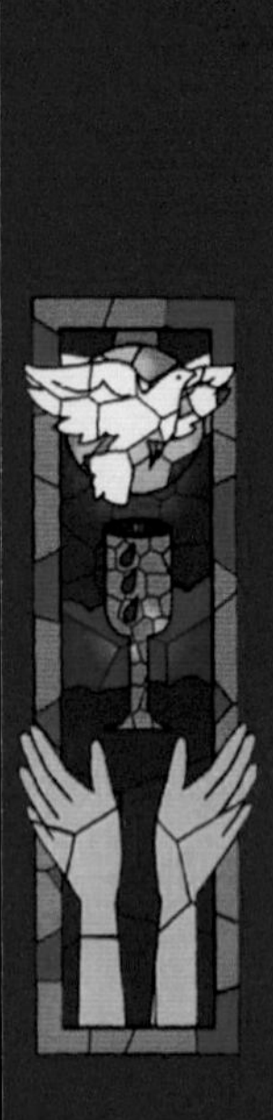

THE CATECHISM OF THE CATHOLIC CHURCH is one of the most important fruits of the Second Vatican Council. It is, if you like, a gift of the Council to the Church. For in the Catechism we see the wealth of teaching that the Church has received, safeguarded and proposed in her two thousand year history.

In *Doorway to Faith* (Part Two) we journey together to discover the riches and treasures contained in the Church's teaching on the celebration of the Christian Mystery in the liturgy and the sacraments.

This part of the Catechism outlines the Church's understanding of her doctrinal teaching and her practice of the Liturgy and the Seven Sacraments.

Each of the seven sacraments is an example of liturgy, as is also what is called the Liturgy of the Hours or the Divine Office – which is a system of times of prayer during the day and

every day, practised by priests, deacons and religious and, increasingly, by many lay people.

In presenting the Church's understanding of the great beauty and profound nature of liturgy and sacraments, this part of the Catechism has two main sections. The first deals with the nature of the liturgy and sacraments generally; while the second section focuses on each of the sacraments in particular.

In the liturgy we are being brought into the very centre of our faith, the very heart of God's plan to reveal himself and draw us back from our fallen condition to a new and intimate relationship with the living God. In and through the liturgy God the Father, who accomplished the plan of salvation by sending his Son and the Holy Spirit, gradually draws all of humanity to himself.

This is, in summary, what is happening in each and every liturgy and sacrament. This is what will continue to happen

until the end of time, when our union and communion with God and with one another will be complete.

An essential element of our relationship with God is the use of material things as signs and symbols. We are created in God's image and likeness. And yet, God is pure spirit – God is not in our image and likeness. In order to reveal himself God first created the material world and then uses it as a means of communication.

This is what is meant when the Catechism speaks of created things as God's blessings. These same blessings become for us the means by which we love and worship God.

We see this very clearly in the Offertory Prayers in the Mass: 'Blessed are you, Lord God of all creation, for through your goodness we have received the bread/wine we offer you ...'.

In the history of Israel God involved himself in the very

events of their history. He is their God; they are his people. God established with them a covenant, so that the Chosen People of God would became a sign of his plan to restore us to a right relationship with God.

Both creation and the history of Israel were a preparation and, ultimately, a shadow of a new reality that was to take place, namely, the Incarnation of God's own Son and the Paschal Mystery of Jesus' death and resurrection.

As an eternal act, the Paschal Mystery of Christ's redeeming sacrifice can now enter into time in any place and at any moment. This is what occurs in the Church's liturgy, wherever and whenever it is celebrated.

This was Christ's will and purpose in establishing the Church and its sacraments. Christ willed also that certain created signs – bread, wine, water, oil and even marital love – should become signs of the eternal Paschal Mystery entering into our time.

When we begin to have some insight into this awesome reality of the liturgy, our minds and our hearts begin to be opened to the amazing thing that is taking place when we enter our churches on a Sunday and celebrate the Eucharist.

At the Baptism of Christ in the river Jordan, 'the heavens were torn apart' (Mark 1:10). This metaphorical phrase

refers to a deep reality. The heavens were closed because of our rebellion and original sin. We were no longer capable of truly knowing God or of worshipping him in a way that truly united us with God. With the coming of Jesus, everything was changed, heaven has been opened again! Jesus' Baptism was an anticipation of what was to occur when Jesus died on the Cross – the veil of the Temple was torn open (Matthew 27:51).

The Temple veil is another image of the closed heaven, of the barrier that separated humanity from God because of sin. In Jesus' death this barrier between God and us is destroyed, true worship can take place and we can receive the full blessing of God (Ephesians 1:3).

This blessing is, first and foremost, the gift of the Holy Spirit, who draws us all into the very life of the Trinitarian God through the Paschal Mystery made present for us and fills us with God's love.

Whenever we celebrate the Church's liturgy this 'open heaven' becomes a reality for us. Our full participation occurs through our awareness of and interiorising in our hearts this most amazing celebration of the Christian Mystery.

DAY 93

WHY THE LITURGY? (CCC 1066)

'The Father accomplishes 'the mystery of his will' by giving his beloved Son and his Holy Spirit for the salvation of the world and for the glory of his name'. (CCC 1066)

YOUCAT 166; p.102

We begin now to explore the second part of the Catechism, which is devoted to the liturgy, the Celebration of the Christian Mystery. The liturgy is principally the Church coming together to worship God and celebrate the Sacraments. The first ten paragraphs of this second part of the Catechism form a sort of preamble to what follows. Today's paragraph reminds us of Part One, which explored our faith as the work of God as Trinity bringing salvation to humankind. Today we read that the accomplishment of the Father's will is 'for the glory of his name'. This is where liturgy begins – it is the act of glorifying the Father.

Heavenly Father, I rejoice to be among the number of your children and to be called to share in worship of you in the Church. Please give me the grace during the following weeks to understand more deeply the great treasure of the liturgy.

The Liturgy celebrates the Paschal Mystery (CCC 1067)

Day 94

There are many wonderful things God did for his people in the Old Testament. They were all a shadow or an anticipation of the greatest work that Christ himself was to accomplish, and by which he would give perfect glory to God, namely, his Passion, Death, Resurrection and glorious Ascension. We saw in Part One of the Catechism that this Paschal Mystery of Christ was a sacrificial act of love and obedience whereby the whole of humanity is restored and reconciled to the Father. The Church is the first fruit of Christ's work. It is fitting that the Church would want to celebrate the work that gave rise to its existence.

'... the Church celebrates in the liturgy above all the Paschal Mystery by which Christ accomplished the work of our salvation'. (CCC 1067)

YOUCAT 166; p.102

Father, I am privileged to be able to share in the act of worship by which your Son obediently glorifies your name. Help me to participate in the weekly liturgy and to give glory to you more and more consciously.

'...the Liturgy is the summit toward which the activity of the Church is directed; it is also the fount from which all her power derives.' (Constitution on the Sacred Liturgy, 10)

YOUCAT 166; p.102

Later on in *Doorway to Faith* we shall explore the way in which the Church's liturgy makes present the saving work that Jesus accomplished. We shall be seeing also why it is that Christ's work is the most perfect act of worship. Today we focus on how it is from the liturgy that we live because in the liturgy the mystery of Christ is proclaimed and celebrated. This is something for us to reflect on: to what extent do we really draw life from the mystery of Christ contained in the liturgy? When we participate in the liturgy, especially the Eucharist we receive the grace to express something of the mystery of Christ and the nature of the Church.

Lord Jesus, please grant me the grace to draw nourishment from the celebration of the Eucharist so that my whole day and week will be infused by your saving presence.

WHAT DOES THE WORD LITURGY MEAN? (CCC 1069-70)

DAY 96

In the ancient Greek world 'liturgy' was a public work or service, an act carried out on behalf of others. The word was taken up in the Christian world to refer to the act that Christ performed on behalf of the whole human race, namely, that of offering a perfect sacrifice of love to his Father. As a very public act, the Paschal Mystery of Christ is also a proclamation that something wonderfully new has occurred – humanity rescued and reconciled to God, and is an act of love towards the human race. No action surpasses the liturgy, for the Church acts along with Christ in making his sacrifice present and in proclaiming it to the world as a service to the world.

'In a liturgical celebration the Church is servant in the image of her Lord' – as Priest (worshipping); Prophet (proclaiming the Gospel) and King (serving in love). (CCC 1070)

YOUCAT 166; p.102

Open my eyes and heart, Lord God, to see in every liturgy a 'sacred action surpassing all others' so that my desire to participate may grow ever more strong.

DAY 97

THE LITURGY AS SOURCE OF LIFE (CCC 1071-2)

'... liturgy is the summit toward which the activity of the church is directed... it is the fount from which all her power flows.' (Sacrasanctum Concilium 10)

YOUCAT 166; p.102

Liturgy has a profound implication for the Church. It is where the Church is most truly the Church. Celebrating the liturgy, the Church is seen as a visible sign of the union in Christ between God and humanity. The celebrating Church is a sign that we have been brought into an intimate relationship with God. A key aspect of that visible sign is that we are participating in the worship, the celebration of the mystery, in a conscious active and fruitful way. Here the Catechism has drawn on the Second Vatican Council Constitution on the Sacred Liturgy. We shall gradually see more clearly what conscious, active and fruitful participation means.

Lead me, Holy Spirit, into deeper conversion to Jesus and to fuller understanding of my faith, so that I may be ever more effectively prepared to celebrate the sacred liturgy.

Christian prayer is essentially a participation in Christ's own prayer to the Father. It is a sharing in the very relationship of sonship that Jesus enjoys with the Father. What is true of all Christian prayer generally is especially true of the liturgy. In fact, the Catechism here tells us that the liturgy is both the source upon which all prayer really draws and the goal to which all prayer tends. Source, because personal prayer is an echoing of the prayer of Christ to the Father in the liturgy. Goal, because the Spirit, teaching and moving us to pray in Christ, is ultimately leading us to the liturgy.

'Prayer can progress ... to the point of rendering the person wholly possessed by the Divine Beloved, vibrating at the Spirit's touch, resting filially within the Father's heart' (Novo Millennio Ineunte, 32)

YOUCAT 166; p. 102

In my private prayer and in the liturgy, my goal is to share in Jesus' love and worship of the Father, and so today with Jesus I pray 'Our Father, who art in heaven …'

'But we with unveiled faces contemplate the glory of Christ and are being transformed into his likeness from one degree of glory to another.' (2 Corinthians 3:18)

YOUCAT 168

Yesterday we saw how the liturgy is both the source and the goal of prayer. The phrase 'source and goal' or 'fount and summit' is also taken from the Constitution on the Sacred Liturgy. It describes the centrality of the liturgy in the life of the Church and indicates why it is so vital for each of us as individual members of the Church. The liturgy is also a privileged place for catechising or teaching the People of God. Liturgical catechising is a very particular kind of teaching called 'mystagogy'. This refers to the unveiling of hidden things – visible realities reveal the invisible, signs lead us to the things signified – ultimately we are taken into the divine mysteries.

O Holy Spirit, lead me from the visible signs I see in the liturgy to the deeper realities and divine mysteries veiled by these signs. As you unveil the signs for me, help me to assist in unveiling the mysteries for others.

The Sacramental Economy (CCC 1076)

Day 100

On the day of Pentecost, the Holy Spirit was poured out and the Church appeared before the world. The coming of the Holy Spirit ushered in a new era which we call 'the dispensation of the mystery' or 'the age of the Church'. We are living in the age of the Church and Christ himself lives and acts in and through the sacraments until he comes again. As St Paul says, 'Whenever you eat this bread, then and drink this cup, you are proclaiming the Lord's death until he comes' (1 Corinthians 11:26). We call Christ living and acting through the sacraments 'the sacramental economy'. In the days ahead we shall explain and unpack what is meant by sacramental economy.

'To accomplish so great a work, Christ is always present in his Church, especially in her liturgical celebrations.' (Sacrosanctum Concilium 7)

YOUCAT 169

Holy Trinity, my heart is filled with wonder to be living in the Age of the Church, when I am surrounded by life-giving signs in the liturgy that draw me into the mystery of your life and love.

DAY
101

THE FATHER, THE SOURCE AND GOAL OF THE LITURGY (CCC 1077)

'Blessed be the God and Father of our Lord Jesus Christ, who has blessed us in Christ with every spiritual blessing' (Ephesians 1:3)

YOUCAT 170

Today's Catechism paragraph is simply a quotation from Scripture – Ephesians 1:3-6. It begins the Article in the Catechism that will consider the liturgy as the work of the Holy Trinity. Every part of the Catechism is rooted in the Trinity – our Faith, the Creed is Trinitarian; Prayer is Trinitarian – sharing, in the Spirit, in Christ's own prayer to the Father. Now we will see that the liturgy is also essentially Trinitarian. The Ephesians passage makes clear that the action of liturgy, namely, that of blessing or worshipping, is directed towards the Father as its goal. But the Father is also the origin, because it has always been his plan to draw us in Christ to himself.

Father, you have greatly blessed me with the gift of your Son and the presence of the Holy Spirit. In the power of the Spirit and in the name of your Son, I bless you.

Blessing is a Divine and Life-Giving Activity (CCC 1078-83)

Day 102

Blessing means everything that God has done in the creation and salvation of humanity – indeed, one vast blessing. The Catechism here summarises some of the blessings of salvation history, showing that in spite of our sin, God was always seeking to redirect us to its source. The Old Testament Scriptures, which also became part of the worship or liturgy of Israel, recalls God's many blessings and at the same time respond to them 'with blessings of praise and thanksgiving'. Now, in the Church's liturgy, the gift of Jesus and the Holy Spirit is both made known and communicated and returned to the Father as a perfect gift of worship.

'The dual dimension of the Christian liturgy as a response of faith and love to the spiritual blessings the Father bestows on us is thus evident.' (CCC 1083)

YOUCAT 170; p.104

'I bless you, Father, Lord of heaven and of earth, for hiding these things from the learned and the clever, and for revealing them to mere children; yes, Father, for such was your gracious will' (Luke 10:21).

DAY 103

CHRIST'S WORK IN THE LITURGY (CCC 1084-9)

'Christ, indeed, always associates the Church with himself in this great work in which God is perfectly glorified and men are sanctified.' (CCC 1089)

YOUCAT 171

The very essence of liturgy is rooted in the Paschal Mystery of Christ's death and resurrection which happened at a specific time and place. The Paschal Mystery now belongs in eternity. Time is not destroyed, but it is transcended. This means that the sacrificial mystery can be made present in any place or time. Christ willed that this should happen through the ministry of his apostles and their successors – through their preaching of the gospel and especially through their ordering and structuring of the liturgy – the Eucharistic sacrifice and the sacraments – the heart of liturgical life. Through this liturgical life, Christ himself continues to communicate and dispense his work of salvation.

Lord Jesus, open my eyes to see that you are truly present acting in the sacraments, speaking in the Scriptures, offering yourself through the ministry of priests, and praying and singing with and in the Church as she worships the Father.

Participating in the Liturgy of Heaven (CCC 1090)

Day 104

This paragraph, a direct quotation from the Constitution on the Sacred Liturgy, shows the link between the age of the Church and the final age of heavenly life. The Fathers of the Church described these ages as, first, the time of 'image', when the full reality of salvation is present in signs. Second, the eternity of 'likeness' where the full reality of salvation is eternally complete. The Church's liturgy today, and in all times, shares already in the heavenly liturgy, where Christ worships his Father along with the saints and angels. Today's liturgy is both a sharing in and a foretaste of the liturgy of heaven. This makes our liturgy a help in our journeying towards the final goal.

'Our union with the Church in heaven is put into effect in its noblest manner especially in the Sacred Liturgy...' (Lumen Gentium 50)

YOUCAT 170

Hail Mary, full of grace, the Lord is with thee. Blessed art thou among women and blessed in the fruit of thy womb, Jesus. Holy Mary, mother of God, pray for us sinners, now and at the hour of our death. Amen.

Day 105

The Holy Spirit and the Church in the Liturgy (CCC 1091-1103)

'In the celebration of the liturgy, sacred Scripture is extremely important.' (Sacrosanctum Concilium 24)

YOUCAT 170

The Holy Spirit's desire is that each of us draw life and strength from the life of the risen Christ. The Spirit not only desires this, but enables it through inspiring us to faith. The Spirit's work is described as threefold: preparing the Church for the encounter with the Lord in the liturgy; making the mystery of Christ present here and now; uniting the Church to the life and mission of Christ. It is the work of preparation that is described in the paragraphs we are considering today. Today we focus especially on the Spirit's role of unveiling the Old Testament, wherein the mystery of Christ lies hidden, and also of preparing us to share fruitfully in the liturgy.

Come Holy Spirit, prepare my mind and heart for the Sunday liturgy and Holy Eucharist. May I encounter Christ in the readings from Scripture and welcome him as a gift in Holy Communion.

THE HOLY SPIRIT MAKES PRESENT THE MYSTERY OF CHRIST (CCC 1104-09)

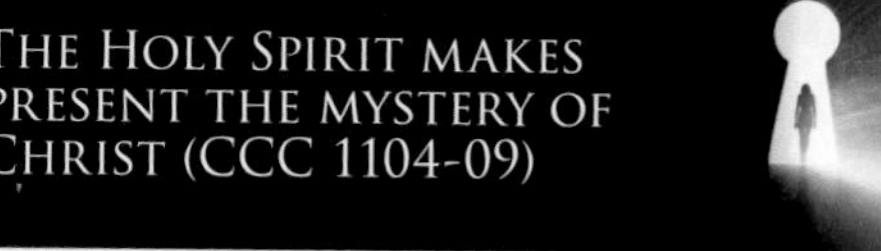

DAY 106

The Holy Spirit not only enables the Church to recall the great works of God, and in particular, the Paschal Mystery of Christ, the Spirit also makes the mystery actually present. The one unique event of our redemption is continually made present in each and every celebration. It is the celebration, not the event, that is repeated. This work of the Spirit is highlighted in the liturgical celebration by the '*epiclesis*' – the prayer to the Father to send the Holy Spirit. The '*anamnesis*' or remembering the saving action, and the '*epiclesis*' or calling on the Holy Spirit, are at the heart of every sacramental celebration, most especially the Eucharist.

'In every liturgical action the Holy Spirit is sent in order to bring us into communion with Christ and so to form his Body.' (CCC 1108)

YOUCAT 171

Glory be to the Father, and to the Son and to the Holy Spirit. As it was in the beginning, is now and ever shall be, world without end. Amen.

Day 107

The Church's Sacraments (CCC 1113)

'The whole liturgical life of the Church revolves around the Eucharistic sacrifice and the sacraments' (CCC 1113)

Many years ago young people were tested on how familiar they were (or not) with the contents of the Catechism. For example they were asked: how many sacraments are there? The answer to this is that there are seven sacraments. Baptism, Confirmation, Eucharist, are sacraments of Christian initiation. The sacraments of healing are: Penance and Anointing of the Sick. The sacraments of service are: Holy Orders and Marriage. Over the coming days we will unpack and explore what is common to each them in terms of their teaching (doctrine) and celebration but also what is distinctive about each of them.

YOUCAT 172 p.105

Lord God, as I spend time in prayer prepare me to explore the treasure of the sacraments of the Church and to see their unity in the sacrament of the Eucharist.

Today we explore the theological understanding of the words and actions of Jesus' hidden life and public ministry. They were anticipations of the power of the Paschal Mystery, and they were also the preparation and the announcement of what Jesus was going to give to the Church after the Paschal Mystery was accomplished, especially the sacraments. The Catechism offers an illustration of this between pages 236-7 – a fresco of the woman with an issue of blood touching the hem of Jesus' garment. This is also an example of the literal sense of Scripture, in this case, the gospel account of the miracle, being transformed into the spiritual sense.

'What was visible in our Saviour has passed over into his mysteries.' (Pope St Leo the Great)

YOUCAT 173

Lord Jesus, as I read the accounts in the Gospels of your actions (acts of forgiveness, healing and deliverance), help me to see that these very actions continue today in the sacraments of the Church.

Day 109

The Sacraments of the Church (CCC 1117-21)

'The Sacraments are 'by the Church' – because the Church is itself the sacrament of Christ's action in her; and 'for the Church' – because 'the sacraments make the Church'. (St Augustine, CCC 1118)

YOUCAT 175

Over time, the Church has recognised gradually, under the Spirit's guidance, that there are seven sacraments. These seven are related to one another, but we first focus on Baptism, Confirmation and Holy Orders. Through Baptism and Confirmation we are enabled to truly participate in and celebrate the liturgy. Through the sacrament of Holy Orders, the ministerial priesthood guarantees that it is really Christ who acts in the sacraments. The priest is the link to the apostles, who are in turn the link to Christ. Each of these three sacraments confers a seal or character conforming the individual to Christ and to a particular state and function in the Church.

Holy Spirit, open my mind and heart to a renewed appreciation of the seal I received in Baptism and Confirmation. I have been forever claimed for God and have received the responsibility to worship him and to serve the Church and her mission.

THE SACRAMENTS OF FAITH (CCC 1122-26)

DAY 110

The sacraments presuppose faith but also nourish, strengthen and express it. The mission of evangelisation, preaching the word of God, leads to Baptism and to the sacramental life. But this preaching also awakens the response of faith, which is our assent to the Word of God. Once faith has been awakened, the sacraments will nourish and strengthen faith even further. Participation in the sacraments is, in fact, the principal way of expressing faith. But it is always the faith of the Church that is expressed and thereby nourished. Hence, the Catechism strongly affirms that the sacramental rites may not be modified by the minister or the community.

'Lex orandi, lex credendi means: The law of prayer is the law of faith: the Church believes as she prays.' (Prosper of Aquitaine CCC 1124)

YOUCAT 177

By faith, Lord Jesus, I humbly receive from you the gift of the liturgy and of the sacraments. Forgive me for any impatience with the liturgy and any desire to change it to suit my perceived needs.

DAY 111

THE SACRAMENTS OF SALVATION (CCC 1127-28)

'Celebrated worthily in faith, the sacraments confer the grace that they signify.' (CCC 1127)

Since the Council of Trent the Church has taught that the sacraments act '*ex opere operato*'. This means that they are efficacious – they bring about the grace, the work of salvation, that they signify, simply by virtue of the fact that they are performed. They do not depend upon the disposition of the minister or the recipient. This is because it is Christ who is acting and communicating the grace of his Paschal Mystery. The Church calls for the Holy Spirit to touch the sacramental signs, and the Father always hears this prayer, so that, as fire consumes what it touches, the Holy Spirit divinises whatever is brought under the Spirit's power.

YOUCAT 178

Lord God, I perceive, with amazement and love, the mystery that is hidden from view – the Holy Spirit transforming bread and wine, so that they may become for us the Body and Blood of our Lord, Jesus Christ.

Sacramental Grace (CCC 1129)

The Catechism affirms that for believers the sacraments are necessary for salvation. This is a salutary doctrine of our faith, especially as we consider, for example, our motivation for and our own practice of celebrating the Sunday Eucharist or of the Sacrament of Reconciliation. The grace of the sacraments is the Holy Spirit, the third person of the Trinity, who heals and transforms those who receive the sacraments. The Spirit, through the sacraments, unites us to God's only Son, the Saviour, makes us adopted sons and conforms us to the likeness of Christ. Without the sacraments, how is all this to take place?

'Grace is first and foremost the gift of the Spirit who justifies and sanctifies us.' (CCC 2003)

Grant me the grace, Lord God, to treasure the sacraments and draw upon the grace that they confer. Help me to seek regularly grace from the Sacrament of Reconciliation, so as to be more tuned to celebrate the sacred mysteries of the Eucharist.

DAY 113

THE SACRAMENTS OF ETERNAL LIFE (CCC 1130)

'A sacrament is a sign that commemorates what precedes it – Christ's Passion; demonstrates what is accomplished in us through Christ's Passion – grace; and prefigures what that Passion pledges to us – future glory.' (St Thomas Aquinas, CCC 1130)

The sacraments have a certain momentum. They are straining towards the future, towards the final state of everlasting life in heaven. The very nature of signs is that they have something hidden about them, something not yet fully and completely manifest. While in the form of signs the sacraments make present and communicate to us the reality of what Christ accomplished through his Paschal Mystery, at the same time, the sacraments also, as signs, point to the future, to the end of time, when the whole Body of Christ is complete and totally conformed to its Head, Jesus Christ. The sacraments, therefore, reveal the pilgrim nature of the Church.

Keep us free from sin, as we await the blessed hope and the coming of our Saviour, Jesus Christ. (Prayer before Holy Communion)

Celebrants of the Heavenly Liturgy (CCC 1136-1139)

Day 114

The liturgy is a celebration of the whole Church on earth as it is in heaven (*Christus totus*). The heavenly liturgy no longer requires the sacramental signs; it is a banquet of total communion and eternal feast. Powerful imagery from the book of Revelation helps us grasp something of this mystery. 'A throne stood in heaven, with one seated on the throne, the Lord God.' (Revelation 4:2,8). The Lamb is there, Christ crucified, the high priest of the sanctuary. He is the one 'who offers and is offered, who gives and is given' (Revelation 5:6). Finally, we have the image of 'the rivers of the water of life' (Revelation 22:1) flowing from the throne; truly a beautiful symbol of the Holy Spirit.

'A great multitude which no one could number, from every nation, from all tribes and peoples and tongues.' (Revelation 7:9)

YOUCAT 179

Lord, unworthy as I am, I rejoice with the Spirit and the Bride as they enable me to participate in the heavenly banquet whenever we celebrate the liturgy and the sacraments of the Church.

Day 115

Celebrants of the Sacramental Liturgy (CCC 1140-44)

'Liturgical services are not private functions but are celebrations of the Church, ... the holy people united and organised under the authority of the bishops.' (CCC 1140)

YOUCAT 179

The Church assembled is the community of the baptised, who are consecrated to be 'a spiritual house, and a holy priesthood'. As such 'they may offer spiritual sacrifices' as a 'common priesthood', which is that of Christ, the sole priest, in which all his members participate. The Church desires that all of us 'be led to full, conscious and active participation in liturgical celebrations' – in other words, participation that fully engages our minds, hearts and even our bodies. While participation refers primarily to the action of worship, certain individuals do have particular functions – those ordained and those with particular ministries, who act in special service to the whole Body.

I pray for all in the Church who perform particular acts of service or ministry in the liturgy. May their hearts and minds be in union with the reality that their actions signify.

SIGNS AND SYMBOLS (CCC 1145-50)

DAY 116

The sacramental liturgies are full of signs and symbols. Two kinds of sign and symbol find their place in the Church's sacramental life. There are symbols whose meaning is rooted in creation and in human culture. Other signs and symbols are specifically taken from Israel and the Old Covenant (for example, anointing, laying on of hands). Signs and symbols belong to the created world and are an essential part of human communication. They can express spiritual realities. They can, in principle, also become a means of expressing and communicating the action of God and also our response in the worship of God.

'As a being at once body and spirit, man expresses and perceives spiritual realities through physical signs and symbols. As a social being, man needs signs and symbols to communicate with others ... the same holds true for his relationship with God.' (CCC 1146)

YOUCAT 181

Help me, Lord, not to take for granted the holy signs that are so familiar to me – from the blessed water in which I dip my fingers on the way into the Church to the lighted sanctuary lamp revealing the presence of Christ in the tabernacle.

Day 117

Signs taken up by Christ (CCC 1151-52)

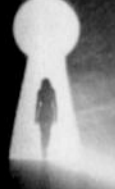

'And beginning with Moses and all the Prophets, he explained to them what was said in all the Scriptures concerning himself.' (Luke 24:27)

YOUCAT 181

Jesus in his public ministry frequently uses signs and symbols to make known the realities of the kingdom of God. His more radical action was to take the deeds and signs of the Old Covenant to himself and give them new meaning. Jesus showed that he himself is their truest meaning. We see this unpacked by the Lord as he joined the disciples on the road to Emmaus (Luke 24) and explained in the whole of Scripture (the Old Testament) those things that were about himself. After Pentecost, many of these two groups of signs and symbols have been taken up into the sacramental liturgies.

Jesus teach me not to be embarrassed to surround myself with spiritual signs and images. You took many signs from human culture and the faith of Israel and made them vehicles for mediating your presence and your salvation.

WORDS AND ACTIONS (CCC 1153-55)

DAY 118

Although sacramental actions are already a language, in the dialogue between God and man words also have a place – both the word of God in Scripture and the words that are the response of faith. All of these words accompany the symbolic actions and give life and meaning to them. The Liturgy of the Word is an integral part of sacramental celebrations. Special emphasis in celebrations should be given to the signs and actions that are part of the Liturgy of the Word – the book of the Gospels, its veneration, the place of its proclamation, its audible and intelligible reading, the homily and the responses of the people.

'The liturgical actions signify what the Word of God expresses: both his free initiative and his people's response of faith.'
(CCC 1153)

YOUCAT 182

As the book of the Word is venerated in the sacred liturgy, so may I give the Scriptures a place of veneration in my home.

'How I wept, deeply moved by your hymns, songs and the voices that echoed through your Church! A feeling of devotion surged within me, and tears streamed down my face - tears that did me good.'
(St Augustine of Hippo)

YOUCAT 183

Singing and music in the liturgy can be traced back to the liturgical celebrations of Israel in the Old Testament. The first account of singing is the spontaneous response of Moses and the freed slaves of Egypt to their deliverance by God through the Red Sea. The Church has continued to develop a vast treasury of music. When music and song are closely connected to the liturgical action, they fulfil their function as signs, especially when they are chosen according to three key criteria: beauty expressive of prayer; the unanimous participation of the assembly at the designated moments; and the solemn character of the celebration.

Father, I treasure those moments when the beauty of the liturgy touched my emotions – a melody, a poetic phrase from a psalm, the scenes of Christmas or the emptiness of the Church on Holy Saturday.

In the earlier Christian centuries, great controversies raged over images. The first commandment of the Decalogue forbids graven images of any likeness of things in heaven or on earth. The controversies centred on the true meaning of the Incarnation. In Christ, God has become not only accessible, but visible. Images now express faith in the Incarnation of God's Son. Icons in particular seek to unveil the inner reality of the Risen Christ rather than any outward appearance. The same is true of the images of Mary and the saints. They are presented to the eyes of faith as those who have become conformed to the likeness of Christ.

'Through the contemplation of sacred icons, united with meditation on the Word of God and the singing of liturgical hymns, the mystery celebrated is imprinted in the heart's memory and is then expressed in the new life of the faithful.' (CCC 1162)

I thank you, Father, for the simple power of statues, crucifixes, rosaries and other religious objects. They remind me that the incarnation of your Son was real, not imaginary.

DAY 121

LITURGICAL SEASONS (CCC 1163-65)

'In the course of the year ... she (the Church) unfolds the whole mystery of Christ ...she opens up to the faithful the riches of her Lord's power and merits, so that these are in some way made present in every age.' (CCC 1163)

YOUCAT 185

Over the next few days we shall be looking at when and where the liturgy is celebrated. We have already seen that, although Christ's work of redemption was carried out at a particular moment in history, the Paschal Mystery is now part of God's eternity. In the liturgy, the Catechism teaches us, we make contact with 'This "today" of the living God' (CCC 1165). God's "today" is the hour of Jesus' Passover. The Church believes that she should celebrate Christ's saving work on certain days throughout the year. Easter is the most solemn of all feasts, along with the celebration of the Passion on Good Friday. Each Sunday, the Lord's Day, recalls the memory of the resurrection.

Help me, Lord, to view my time in the same way as the Church – as filled with your presence and consecrated by the memorials and celebrations of the mysteries of your life, death and resurrection.

Today we look at the importance of the Lord's Day, which from apostolic times took its origin from the day of Christ's Resurrection. The Paschal Mystery is celebrated every Sunday, which is seen, in our weekly cycle, as both the first day of the week, recalling the first day of creation, and also the eighth day. The Catechism describes this 'eighth day' as 'the day that the Lord has made'. Quoting from a liturgical text of the Syriac Office of Antioch, the Catechism tells us: 'Blessed is Sunday, for on it were opened the gates of paradise so that Adam and all the exiles might enter it without fear.'

'Even if our word Sunday has a pagan origin – 'the day of the sun', we recognise that the risen Jesus is the light of the world who was raised; 'the sun of justice with healing in his rays.' (CCC 1166)

YOUCAT 187

Father, I praise you for the great power you displayed in raising your Son from the dead. May that same power raise me from my sinful ways and lead me back to you.

'In the liturgical year the various aspects of the one Paschal mystery unfold.' (CCC 1171)

YOUCAT 186

Through the liturgy the Paschal Mystery of Christ has a transforming effect on time itself. Because of the liturgy, celebrated day by day throughout the Church, time is drawn into the redemption accomplished by Christ. Time for us is no longer a simple passing of the hours and days or the cyclic return of the seasons. Time is now the occasion for encountering the mysteries of Christ. In particular, the mystery of the resurrection permeates time with its powerful energy until, the Catechism says, 'all is subjected to him' (CCC 1169). The liturgical year also anticipates, as a foretaste, the final accomplishment of salvation at the end of time.

We thank thee that thy Church unsleeping, while earth rolls onward into light, through all the world her watch is keeping, and rests not now by day or night. (From 'The day thou gavest Lord is ended', a designated hymn for Night Prayer)

DAY 124

THE SANCTORAL IN THE LITURGICAL YEAR (CCC 1172-3)

'When the Church keeps the memorials of martyrs and other saints during the annual cycle, she proclaims the Paschal Mystery in those 'who have suffered and have been glorified with Christ'.' (CCC 1173)

YOUCAT 186

As well as celebrating the mysteries of Christ throughout the year, the Church also honours the Blessed Mary, Mother of God and the martyrs and other saints. Mary is 'inseparably linked' with the saving work of Christ – through her *fiat* (let it be done), she cooperates with God in his plan of salvation through Christ. She accompanies Christ to the Cross and suffers with him. The Church honours her with a special love and sees her as the most perfect fruit of Christ's redemption, an image of what the Church desires and hopes to be. In a similar way, the saints are also honoured. They too are models for us and to them we pray and ask for their intercession.

Mary, Mother of Christ and Queen of all the saints, pray for us.

The Church's year is filled with a rich array of celebrating Solemnities and Feasts as we remember the great events of salvation history. We also have memorials of the saints and the Liturgy of the Hours through which the hours of each day are also sanctified. The Divine Office ensures that the course of the day and night is made holy by the praise of God. Through the Liturgy of the Hours the Church 'prays constantly', for as one group finishes a particular Office (eg. Morning Prayer), another group takes it up. The Liturgy of the Hours is truly the voice of the Bride herself (the Church) to her Bridegroom (Christ).

'The laity, too, are encouraged to recite the divine office, either with the priests, or among themselves, or even individually' (CCC 1175, SC100)

YOUCAT 188

'O Lord open my lips and my mouth shall declare your praise' (From the beginning of the Divine Office each day)

DAY 126

WHERE IS THE LITURGY CELEBRATED (CCC 1179-86)

'The Catechism also lists and explains the various elements to be found in our churches (altar, tabernacle, lectern etc.). Each of these shows Christ to be present and active in this place.' (CCC 1182-86)

YOUCAT 189

The Church is not primarily a building. The Church is the assembly of the people of God, wherever that might be. The members of the Church are described in the First Letter of St Peter as 'living stones' that are being 'built into a spiritual house' (1 Peter 2:4-5). There is something very dynamic about this concept of the Church. It is the Holy Spirit dwelling within us who incorporates us all into Christ. The assembled Church is a visible sign of God's dwelling among us, who are reconciled to him through Christ. The church buildings themselves are also visible signs – of God among us, and also of the Father's house to which we journey.

Lord Jesus, I pray today for my parish, my priest and deacon and for the whole neighbourhood of people, to whom you have called us to be a witnesses. May our church building and our gatherings for the liturgy speak of you to the world.

Whenever the liturgy is celebrated it is always the Paschal Mystery that is made present. However, the forms by which this mystery is celebrated are diverse. This is similar to the diversity of the four Gospels. The mystery of Jesus is so rich that it is not exhausted either by one Gospel or by one liturgical tradition. As the Gospels were written because the Good News was proclaimed in different places and different milieux, so the diverse liturgical traditions arose through celebrating the mystery of Christ in diverse geographical and cultural areas. All the authentic riches of the cultures can be integrated into the Church's liturgies.

'In the liturgy the Church... respects and fosters the genius and talents of the various races and peoples... so long as they harmonize with its true and authentic spirit.' (Sacrosanctum Concilium 37)

YOUCAT 192

I thank you, Lord God, for the whole Church spread throughout the world. Wherever it gathers to celebrate the liturgy, the same mystery of your death and resurrection is present.

DAY 128

THE SACRAMENTS OF INITIATION (CCC 1212)

'The Sacraments of Initiation – Baptism, Confirmation, and the Eucharist - lay the foundations of every Christian life.' (CCC 1212)

YOUCAT 193

We now turn to the seven sacraments of the Church, These sacraments touch different stages of our Christian life – our birth and initiation, our healing and our mission in the life of the Church. There is a certain organic unity to the sacraments and the Eucharist stands at their centre as the sacrament to which all the others are ordered and in which they find their goal. The three sacraments of Initiation are Baptism, Confirmation and the Eucharist, and they lay the foundations of the Christian life. They provide in increasing measure the treasures of the divine life and the impulse to a life of holiness.

I pray for all those who have received the sacraments of initiation this Easter, that their Christian lives will now continue to be nourished and that they may grow in the likeness of Christ.

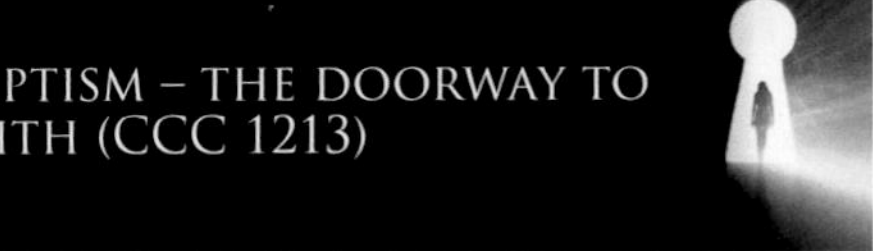

Baptism – The Doorway to Faith (CCC 1213)

Day 129

The Sacrament of Baptism is the first point of contact between ourselves and the Risen Christ. Unlike other initiation ceremonies, which focus on the acceptance by the community of the initiated individual, a Baptism brings about a deep change in the individual. It is described as a regeneration or a being re-born as children of God. In the Scripture, Jesus said that the Holy Spirit gives birth to our spirit (John 3:6). With this regenerated spirit and the indwelling of the Holy Spirit, the fruit of the Paschal Mystery, we are set free from original and actual sin and become adopted sons of God.

'If anyone is in Christ, he is a new creation; the old has passed away, behold, the new has come.' (2 Corinthians 5:17)

YOUCAT 194

Holy Spirit, please fill me with gratitude for the grace of my Baptism. Help me to call to mind each day that, through you, I have become a new creation in Christ.

DAY 130

WHAT IS BAPTISM (CCC 1214-16)

Jesus said: 'Truly, I say to you, unless one is born of water and the Spirit, he cannot enter the kingdom of God. That which is born of the flesh is flesh, and that which is born of the Spirit is spirit.' (John 3:5-6)

YOUCAT 194

The first sacrament of initiation is called Baptism because the word, from the Greek, means to plunge or immerse into water. We are immersed into Christ's death and through resurrection with Christ become a new creation. The sacrament has other names too. It is called 'the washing of regeneration and renewal by the Holy Spirit' and also enlightenment. Enlightenment indicates the communication of the Word, Christ himself, who is the true light that enlightens every person. Through our union with Jesus in Baptism, we also become light in the world.

Lord Jesus, enlighten my mind and heart today. Keep me conscious that through my Baptism I am immersed into you. In your death, I am dead to sin; in your resurrection, I am alive to God.

Creation, Noah's Ark, the Crossing of the Red Sea, the Crossing of the Jordan are 'The great events of salvation history that already prefigured the mystery of Baptism' (CCC 1217). We see here an example of spiritual interpretation of the Old Testament. While the events of the Old Testament refer primarily to the actions of God in history, their truest meaning is that they were shadows or prefigurations of Christ himself - The New Testament hidden in the Old. Those Old Testament events enable us to understand the full reality of Christ, This reality has now passed into the Sacrament, in this case of Baptism.

'And beginning with Moses and all the prophets, he interpreted to them in all the Scriptures the things concerning himself.' (Luke 24:27)

YOUCAT p.116-117

Lord God, you have taught us the true meaning of the mystery of Christ through the Old Covenant. The events of salvation history prefigured Christ and the sacraments. Teach me always to treasure the Old Testament.

DAY 132

CHRIST'S BAPTISM (CCC 1223-25)

'At his Baptism, Jesus is revealed as the suffering servant (Isaiah 53). He identified himself with sinful humanity. 'I have appointed you as covenant of the people.' (Isaiah 42:6)

Christ's commission to the apostles to baptise all nations in the name of the Father and of the Son and of the Holy Spirit reminds us once again of the centrality of the Trinity in every aspect of our faith. Baptism immerses us into the reality and communion of the life of the Trinity. This occurs through our union with Christ; with his own Baptism and with his death on the cross. In his own Baptism, Jesus, the Beloved Son, is also revealed as the suffering servant who identifies himself with us and takes upon himself the iniquity of us all. His death on the cross has opened for us all new life in the Spirit: the life now available to us through the sacraments.

Lord Jesus, at your Baptism the heavens were torn open and the Father's voice was heard declaring his delight in you. Lead us all into the Father's presence.

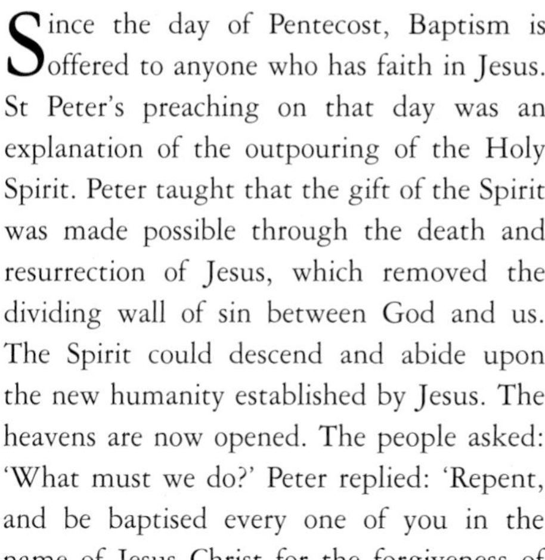

Since the day of Pentecost, Baptism is offered to anyone who has faith in Jesus. St Peter's preaching on that day was an explanation of the outpouring of the Holy Spirit. Peter taught that the gift of the Spirit was made possible through the death and resurrection of Jesus, which removed the dividing wall of sin between God and us. The Spirit could descend and abide upon the new humanity established by Jesus. The heavens are now opened. The people asked: 'What must we do?' Peter replied: 'Repent, and be baptised every one of you in the name of Jesus Christ for the forgiveness of your sins, and you shall receive the gift of the Holy Spirit' (Acts 2:38).

'Always Baptism is seen as connected with faith.' (CCC 1226)

YOUCAT 197

Come Holy Spirit, renew my faith and fill my heart with the fire of your love.

'Baptism is a bath of water in which the 'imperishable seed' of the Word of God produces its life-giving effect' (CCC 1228)

Anyone who is baptised is baptised into Christ's death, and is also raised, in the likeness of Christ's resurrection, to 'walk in newness of life' (Romans 6:4). How is it that a material element such as water can produce such an effect? St Augustine said: 'The word is brought to the material element, and it becomes a sacrament' (CCC 1228). It is the Word, who is Christ, and the word spoken by Christ, through the Church, that transforms the water into a means of grace and into a place of union with Jesus' death and resurrection. Paul describes this Baptismal union as 'having put on Christ'. His death and resurrection has become a reality in us.

Heavenly Father, the sacraments are the crowning of your work of creation, for now certain created things (water and oil) not only remind us that you are the Creator, but they have become a vehicle of your grace.

Becoming a Christian (CCC 1229-33)

Most of us are baptised as babies. We then receive the Sacrament of Reconciliation and First Holy Communion around the age of seven years and finally the Sacrament of Confirmation two or more years later. Catechesis has an essential role in uniting the three sacraments of initiation and ensuring the taking hold of and growing in Baptismal grace. Initiation for adults follows a different process. It begins with a period of catechesis, then a series of liturgical actions take place, and also celebrations of the Liturgy of the Word (usually during Lent). This reaches a culmination in the celebration of all three sacraments together in a single liturgy.

'By its very nature infant Baptism requires a post-Baptismal catechumenate ... (there is) a need for instruction after Baptism, but also for the necessary flowering of Baptismal grace in personal growth.' (CCC 1231)

YOUCAT 195

Give us both strength and wisdom, Lord God, to ensure that our baptised children are not deprived of the catechesis they need in order to take hold fully of the Baptismal grace.

DAY 136

THE SIGN OF THE CROSS (CCC 1234-5)

'The Christian community welcomes you with great joy. In its name I claim you for Christ our Saviour by the sign of his cross. I now trace the cross on your forehead and invite your parents and godparents to do the same.' (From the Rite of Infant Baptism)

The Catechism takes us through the gestures and words of the celebration of Baptism. By understanding these words and gestures we shall see clearly both the meaning of this sacrament and the action of God (grace) that is taking place. The signs in a sacrament point to the very reality that is conferred upon the one receiving the grace. The very first sign is that the person to be baptised is marked with the sign of the Cross. This signifies that the person is set apart to belong to Christ and to receive from him the effects of the redemption, won by Christ through his cross.

Lord Jesus, I begin each day with the sign of the Cross. Help me to live my day in union with you. In the name of the Father and of the Son and of the Holy Spirit, Amen.

THE PROCLAMATION OF THE WORD OF GOD (CCC 1236)

DAY 137

An essential element of any sacrament is the proclamation of the Word of God. This usually takes place in a Liturgy of the Word, in which passages of Scripture and the Gospel are read. These are followed by a homily, so that the hearers are enabled to appreciate that God's living word is addressed to them here and now. The purpose of this is to elicit a response of faith, not least from the person receiving the sacrament. Infants receive the gift of faith, but the response of faith is made by parents and godparents. Faith is always and foremost a gift we receive from God. Through nurturing, the hope is that the baptised infant will make a personal response of faith in later years.

'Baptism is 'the sacrament of faith' in a particular way, since it is the sacramental entry into the life of faith.' (CCC 1236)

I believe in one God, the Father almighty, maker of heaven and earth. I believe in his Son, our Lord Jesus Christ, who for us men and for our salvation came down from heaven; I believe in the Holy Spirit, the Lord, the giver of life.

'Make these into a sacred anointing oil, a fragrant blend, the work of a perfumer. It will be the sacred anointing oil.' (Exodus 30:25)

YOUCAT 195

Each year on Holy Thursday, the Bishop blesses two great containers of oil – Oil of Catechumens and Oil of the Sick. He also consecrates sacred chrism – perfumed oil. In Baptism, anointing with the Oil of Catechumens along with prayers of exorcism signifies the liberation from sin and from its instigator, the devil. The Christian life will be a battle against sin and evil and a daily living and professing of the faith entrusted by Baptism. Immediately after Baptism, the child or adult is anointed with Sacred Chrism. This oil is a sacramental sign of the Holy Spirit, who joins us to Christ and makes us part of his saving mission.

Since I have been anointed with the oil of catechumens and of sacred Chrism, grant, O Holy Spirit, that their effects may remain with me today. May I be strong in confessing the Church's faith and live in union with Christ.

Just as Sacred Chrism is consecrated on Holy Thursday, so Baptismal water is consecrated on Holy Saturday. The Holy Week ceremonies are the central celebrations of our Catholic Faith – the Paschal Mystery of Jesus' death and resurrection. The consecration of oil and water during these liturgies and their later use in the sacrament of Baptism vividly demonstrate how Baptism immerses us into the mystery of Christ's redemption. The Church asks the Father to send the Holy Spirit upon the water so that those baptised in it will be united with Jesus' death and resurrection and so die to sin and be raised in a new birth to life with God.

'You have called your children to this cleansing water and new birth, that they may share in the faith of your Church and have eternal life. By the mystery of this consecrated water lead them to a new and spiritual birth.' (Rite of Baptism)

YOUCAT 195

Father, I confess and believe that in Christ I am dead to sin and have been raised up to a new life as your child. And so, I say, 'Our Father ...'.

'I baptise you in the name of the Father, and of the Son, and of the Holy Spirit.' (Rite of Baptism)

The heart of the sacrament of Baptism is the triple pouring or immersion into the water of Baptism. Immersion into the consecrated water is in reality an immersion into the very life of the Trinity. This is accomplished through immersion into the death and resurrection of Christ. By his Paschal Mystery, Christ has freed us from the sin (original and personal) that separated us from God, and has now reconciled us to the Father. We can now know the same relationship with the Father that the risen Son enjoys. The Spirit draws the baptised into this mystery and commits to dwell from now on in the baptised person.

YOUCAT 195

Holy Trinity, help me to meditate upon the unfathomable privilege and mystery of sharing in your life. Glory and praise be to the Father and to the Son and to the Holy Spirit.

THE WHITE GARMENT AND CANDLE (CCC 1243)

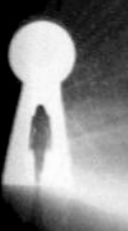

The white Baptismal garment recalls a parable of Jesus in which a king held a wedding feast and provided the guests with garments. One man refused to put on the garment and was excluded from the feast. Just as the second person of the Trinity has clothed himself in our humanity, so we, who are baptised, have become clothed in Christ. We have 'put on Christ' and can share in the Eucharistic banquet. United with Christ, we are part of his Body, the Church. The Baptismal garment is a visible sign of this. We have been enlightened by Christ, and this is signified by receiving a candle lit from the Paschal Candle, symbolising the risen Lord. We share his light and shine to others with it.

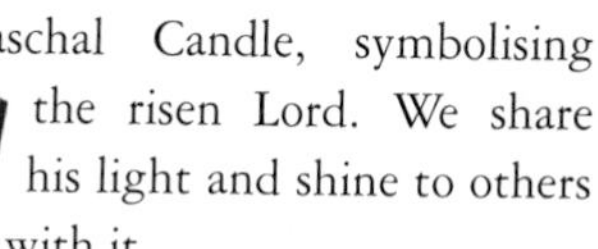

'You have become a new creation and have clothed yourself in Christ. See in this white garment the outward sign of your Christian dignity ... bring that dignity unstained into the everlasting life of heaven.' (Rite of Baptism)

YOUCAT 195

In Baptism I was outwardly clothed in a white garment signifying Christ. Lord, help me to be unashamed to be clothed with you today, so that my life may bear witness to you.

'The Church and the parents would deny a child the priceless grace of becoming a child of God were they not to confer Baptism shortly after birth.' (CCC 1250)

YOUCAT 196

The Code of Canon Law (864) states starkly that 'every person not yet baptised and only such a person is able to be baptised'. In the beginning, and in countries where the preaching of the Gospel is new, adult Baptism is the common practice. Where the faith is long established, infant Baptism is the usual mode of Christian initiation. What is essential is the catechumenate, which aims at bringing conversion and faith to maturity. Adults being prepared for Baptism and baptised children need to be properly initiated into the mystery of salvation, the practice of the virtues and the Church's liturgical life. Parents and godparents create the environment in which children can grow in faith.

Lord God, I pray for the work of catechesis in the Church and especially for those who have special responsibility – parents, bishops, priests and deacons, catechists and teachers. Fill them with the grace of the Holy Spirit.

The necessity of Baptism (CCC 1256-61)

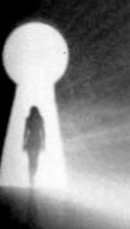

Day 143

Jesus told Nicodemus that in order to see the kingdom of God a person must be born of water and the Holy Spirit (John 3:5). He also told his disciples to proclaim the Gospel to all nations and to baptise them (Matthew 28:19). Baptism is necessary for salvation. At the same time, God is not himself bound by his sacraments. There are those who are saved without the sacrament. The Catechism mentions martyrs, catechumens who die before being baptised, and those who are ignorant of the Gospel yet live according to their best lights. They receive Baptism of blood or Baptism by explicit or implicit desire.

'The great mercy of God ... and Jesus' tenderness towards children ... allow us to hope that there is a way of salvation for children who have died without Baptism' (CCC 1261)

YOUCAT 197-198

Heavenly Father, we commend to your loving mercy all those infants who have died without Baptism. We pray especially for the many conceived babies who have been aborted.

DAY 144

THE GRACE OF BAPTISM FOR THE FORGIVENESS OF SINS (CCC 1262-64)

'Immersion in water symbolises not only death and purification, but also regeneration and renewal.' (CCC 1262; Acts 2:38)

On the one hand water is a symbol of death and purification; on the other, it is a sign of new life and renewal. This permits us to consider two principal effects of Baptism: forgiveness and purification of sins, and new birth in the Holy Spirit. By Baptism all sin is removed, and nothing remains that would impede entry into the kingdom of God. Notwithstanding this amazing grace, certain 'temporal consequences of sin' do remain in the baptised – suffering, sickness, death, human frailty and what is called concupiscence or the inclination to sin. These remain for us to wrestle with and, in various ways, overcome by the grace of Christ.

YOUCAT 200

Lord Jesus, I rejoice in my Baptism, but I know that I must still struggle with sin and other weaknesses each day. Help me with your grace to do battle and experience victory in you.

Baptism and a new creation (CCC 1265-6)

Day 145

The second principal effect of Baptism is transformation into a 'new creation'. This remarkable change identifies the individual as one who partakes in the divine nature, is a member of Christ and co-heir with him, and a temple of the Holy Spirit. This new identity also brings new abilities through what is called sanctifying grace or the grace of justification. The Catechism mentions three: being enabled to believe and hope in God and to love him; power to live and act under the prompting of the Holy Spirit, especially through the gifts the Spirit makes present in us; and ability to grow in goodness through the moral virtues.

'The Most Holy Trinity gives the baptised sanctifying grace, the grace of justification.' (CCC 1266)

YOUCAT 200

Grant, Lord, that I may devote at least as much time and attention to taking care of my moral and spiritual health and growth as I give to my physical health and well-being.

Day 146

Baptised into the Church (CCC 1267-70)

'As baptised persons we are called to serve one another in the Church, respect and obey its leaders and to receive the spiritual helps of the Church.' (CCC 1269)

In Baptism we are joined to Christ and share in the life of the Trinity, we also become members of the Body of Christ. We become 'incorporated into the Church'. These words describe something much more than simple membership. Incorporation implies something organic – a union that transcends nations, cultures, races and sexes – deeper even than biological family ties or the union of husband and wife. Indeed, Scripture teaches that the marriage union is itself a sacramental sign of the union between Christ and his Body. We share in Christ's priestly worship of the Father; his proclamation of salvation and his establishment of God's kingdom on earth.

Lord, teach me to love the Church. It is your body on earth. All of its leaders and members are united by the deepest bonds.

THE SACRAMENTAL BOND OF THE UNITY OF CHRISTIANS (CCC 1271)

DAY 147

Baptism establishes the basis for unity among all Christians, even though that unity may as yet be imperfect. There is a real sacramental bond of unity among baptised Christians of all denominations. Division among Christians is a contradiction of the will of Christ and a scandal, and it impedes the proclamation of the Gospel to the world. The Second Vatican Council declares that God has, in recent times, 'begun to bestow more generously upon divided Christians remorse over their divisions and longing for unity' (*Unitatis Redintegratio* 1). This longing has its basis in the grace of Baptism. We pray that all believers may be one as Jesus and the Father are one.

'Christ prayed to his Father for those who believe – 'that all may be one, as you, Father, are in me, and I in you; I pray that they may be one in us, that the world may believe that you sent me.' (John 17:21)

YOUCAT 200

Father, I grieve for the disunity among Christians. I repent and ask your forgiveness for any ways I may contribute to division. In the Paschal Mystery of Christ make us all one.

'The Holy Spirit has marked us with the seal of the Lord ... 'for the day of redemption.' (CCC 1274)

Baptism confers on us an indelible spiritual mark or character of belonging to Christ. This character remains even when a person is no longer living in accordance with it. It offers therefore the possibility of return. This spiritual mark also consecrates us for religious worship – and therefore for vital participation in the holy liturgy of the Church; for the witness of holy lives and practical charity. Finally, the spiritual mark is the guarantee that the person who has remained faithful to the demands of Baptism will depart this life 'marked with the sign of faith'. That person can look forward with expectation to the 'blessed vision of God' and 'the hope of resurrection'.

YOUCAT 200

Holy Spirit, keep me daily aware that you have marked me with the seal of the Lord. Increase in me the sense of belonging to Christ and my consecration to worship of the Father.

THE SACRAMENT OF CONFIRMATION (CCC 1285)

The sacrament of Confirmation brings the completion of Baptismal grace. From the earliest times in the Church Baptism was administered by the apostles and those who were their successors, the bishops. As the Church grew into more and more areas, Baptisms were carried out by priests. It was the presence of the bishop that brought about the complete grace of Baptism because the baptised person was then brought into full and visible union with the Church, of which the bishop is the clearest sign. The separation of the sacrament of Baptism and the presence of the bishop ultimately led to the practice of a sacrament which completes and confirms Baptism – it is called Confirmation.

'By the sacrament of Confirmation, [the baptised] are more perfectly bound to the Church ...' (CCC 1285)

YOUCAT 203

O Holy Spirit, through the grace of my Confirmation help me to appreciate the special unity you have created between me and my bishop and that through him I am one with the whole Church, even back to the apostles.

DAY 150

CONFIRMATION IN THE ECONOMY OF SALVATION (CCC 1286-92)

'The imposition of hands is rightly recognised by the Catholic tradition as the origin of the sacrament of Confirmation, which in a certain way perpetuates the grace of Pentecost in the Church.' (CCC 1288)

YOUCAT 203; p.120

From the beginning of the life of the Church the sacrament of Baptism was completed by the apostolic 'laying on of hands'. This gesture signified the handing on of the gift of the Holy Spirit, received by the apostles at Pentecost. A little later on oil of Chrism (perfumed oil) began to be used as an additional sign of the Holy Spirit, who through the Apostles' action, was given to strengthen a person for sharing in the mission of the apostles and of the whole Church. The gift of the Spirit leads us into the unique relationship between Jesus and the Spirit, prophesied in the Old Testament; revealed in his birth; and in the anointing he received to carry out his mission of obedience.

Lord Jesus, as you promised, I have been anointed with the Holy Spirit even as you received the Spirit without reserve from the Father so that you could complete your mission.

The Signs and Rite of Confirmation (CCC 1293-96)

Day 151

In the Gospel of John, Jesus is speaking of himself and his mission; he then declares: 'For on him has God the Father set his seal' (John 6:27). What is meant by the seal? It surely expresses something of Jesus' relationship with the Father. He is the Son and he belongs to the Father. Not in the narrow sense of property ownership, but rather in the sense that the Son has his origin in the Father; he is begotten of the Father. The Father has a loving claim upon him and the Son gives himself to the Father and, in so doing, to the mission he has given him. Through the Holy Spirit, in Confirmation we received a similar mark or seal of belonging to Christ and his mission.

'It is fitting to consider the sign of anointing and what it signifies and imprints: a spiritual seal.' (CCC 1293)

YOUCAT 203

Lord Jesus, sealed with your Spirit, I acknowledge that I belong to you. In love you have redeemed me and have set me apart to serve you in the particular path of my life. Keep me faithful to the end.

Day 152

The celebration of Confirmation (CCC 1297-1301)

'Be sealed with the gift of the Holy Spirit' (The Rite of Confirmation, CCC 1300)

There are various elements of the rite of the Sacrament of Confirmation. They are all signs that Confirmation completes the grace of Baptism and establishes a special relationship with the bishop, and through him, a full and visible union with the Church. The key elements of the rite are; the renewal of Baptismal promises; the very presence of the bishop conferring the sacrament through the laying on of hands and anointing with Chrism; the prayer of Confirmation, the sign of peace signifying and bringing about ecclesial communion with the bishop and with all the faithful. This union is also signified on Holy Thursday when the same bishop consecrates the Chrism for use in the whole diocese.

YOUCAT 203

Lord God, I pray for the bishop of my diocese and for the ministry that you have given him. Please bless him with your grace and give him wisdom, strength and courage.

The effects of Confirmation (CCC 1302-5)

Day 153

When we read the summary of the effects of Confirmation in the three paragraphs (CCC 1303-5), it is clear that an important element of completion of Baptismal grace is a deeper insertion into the life of the Trinity – a deeper, firmer relationship with each of the persons of the Trinity. Once again, we see how our Catechism is saturated in the Trinity. It surely helps us to raise our own consciousness of living within the Trinitarian life. The Trinity is not a mere abstract truth, but a dynamic life in which we participate. Our bond with the Trinity necessarily involves a bond or union with the whole Church. Jesus clothes us with his Spirit, 'with power from on high' so that we may be his witnesses.

'It is evident ... that the effect of the sacrament of Confirmation is the special outpouring of the Holy Spirit as once granted to the Apostles on the day of Pentecost' (CCC 1302)

YOUCAT 203

Through the grace of my Confirmation, may I become wholly possessed by the Divine Beloved and tremble at the Spirit's touch, and rest filially in the Father's heart.

WHO CAN RECEIVE THIS SACRAMENT? (CCC 1306-11)

DAY 154

What is the right age to be confirmed? The Church has referred to the long tradition of taking the 'age of discretion' as a reference point. The Sacrament of Confirmation is sometimes called the 'sacrament of Christian maturity'. Adult faith is not the same as adult in age; it is possible for children to have a spiritual maturity. It is vital however that it is accompanied by good catechesis, fostering closer union with Christ and familiarity with the Holy Spirit - his actions, gifts and biddings. Growth in these renders us more capable of taking on the apostolic responsibilities of the Christian life.

'To receive Confirmation one must be in a state of grace. More intense prayer should prepare one to receive the strength and graces of the Holy Spirit with docility and readiness to act.' (CCC 1310)

YOUCAT 203

Father, I pray today for all Confirmation sponsors and also for godparents. Renew the grace of the Spirit in us all.

DAY 155

THE MINISTER OF CONFIRMATION (CCC 1312-14)

'The minister and administration of the sacrament demonstrates that its effect is to unite those who receive it more closely to the (apostolic) Church,... and to her mission of bearing witness to Christ.' (CCC 1313)

YOUCAT 203

The ordinary and appropriate minister of Confirmation is the bishop. We have seen the central role of the bishop and also that the bishop's absence was the impetus for Baptism and Confirmation becoming separated. The visible link with the bishop in the sacrament is the effective sign that those receiving Confirmation are being more closely united with the Church, to her apostolic origins, and to her mission of bearing witness to Christ. The oil, consecrated by the bishop, is the visible and effective sign of the inner presence of the Holy Spirit who strengthens this union with the apostolic Church and empowers the confirmed person for witness.

Most Holy Trinity, I pray for all who have been confirmed and for all preparing for this sacrament. Grant that the grace of the Holy Spirit may draw us all into closer union with you and inspire greater love and unity with the Church and her mission.

Eucharist: The Source and the Summit (CCC 1322-1327)

Day 156

The bishops at the Second Vatican Council coined the phrase that the Eucharist is the 'source and summit of the Christian life.' (*Lumen Gentium* 11). It is an awesome truth that all the sacraments, all ministry, all mission, all apostolates, whatever they are, are bound up with and orientated towards the Eucharist. In other words, the Eucharist is the very core, the very essence of our Catholic life. The Eucharist is Christ himself, the author of grace. The other sacraments are actions of Christ but the Eucharist is Christ himself under the appearance of bread and wine. In the Eucharist the sacrifice of Christ on the cross is made present for us.

'Our way of thinking is attuned to the Eucharist, and the Eucharist in turn confirms our way of thinking.' (St Irenaneus)

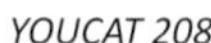

YOUCAT 208

Lord, teach me to grow in love for the Eucharist and deepen within me a sense of awe and wonder before this sacrament of love and unity.

Day 157

The Name of the Eucharist (CCC 1328-1332)

'The Church's whole liturgy finds its centre and most intense expression in the celebration of the Sacred Mysteries.' (CCC 1330)

YOUCAT 208; p.123

The word Eucharist comes from the Greek *eucharistein* meaning literally 'to give thanks' and recalls the Jewish blessing in which God's works of creation, redemption and sanctification are invoked and praised. The Eucharist has many names highlighting its different aspects: the Lord's Supper, the Wedding Feast of the Lamb, the Breaking of Bread, the Eucharistic Assembly, the Memorial of the Lord's Passion and Resurrection. We also speak of the Holy Sacrifice of the Mass, Sacrifice of Praise, Spiritual Sacrifice, Pure and Holy Sacrifice. We speak also of 'receiving the Eucharist' or 'receiving Holy Communion.'

Lord, we give you thanks and praise for the gift of the Eucharist. We rejoice in the inexhaustible riches of this sacrament expressed in the many different names we give it.

THE SIGNS OF BREAD AND WINE (CCC 1333-1336)

DAY 158

From the very beginning the Eucharist and the Cross have been stumbling blocks. When the Lord spoke of his cross, St Peter declared, 'Never, Lord! This shall never happen to you.' (Matthew 16:22). When the Lord first announced the Eucharist, the disciples reacted negatively: 'This is a hard saying; who can listen to it?' (John 6:60). The Cross and the Eucharist are the same mystery. The Lord asks of us the same question he asked of the disciples: 'Will you go away?' (John 6:67). The question is a loving invitation for us to discover anew that only Jesus Christ, our Lord and Saviour, has 'the words of eternal life' (John 6:68).

'At the heart of the Eucharistic celebration are the bread and wine that, by the words of Christ and the invocation of the Holy Spirit, become Christ's Body and Blood.'. (CCC 1333)

YOUCAT p.126

Thank you, Lord, that in the Eucharist the bread and wine are changed by your word and the invocation of the Holy Spirit into your Body and Blood.

Day 159

The Last Supper (CCC 1337-1340)

'When it comes to the consecration of the venerable sacrament, the priest no longer uses his own language, but he uses the language of Christ. Therefore the word of Christ consecrates this sacrament.' (St Ambrose)

YOUCAT p.126

The Jewish festival of Passover was celebrated to commemorate Israel's deliverance from captivity in Egypt and when God 'passed over' them and protected them from his judgement (Exodus 12:13). Jesus celebrated his Last Supper with his disciples and so gave the Jewish Passover its definitive and fullest meaning. By his death and resurrection Jesus passed over to his Father and instituted the new Passover, the Eucharist. The Eucharist is the memorial of his death and resurrection, and the Lord commanded that it be celebrated until he comes again in glory. Every time we celebrate it we share in Christ's death and resurrection, perfected in receiving his Body and Blood.

'This is my body which is given for you. This cup which is poured out for you is the New Covenant in my blood. Do this in memory of me.'

The Institution of the Eucharist (CCC 1341-1344)

Day 160

We know that from the very beginning the Church has been faithful to the celebration of the Eucharist. 'They devoted themselves to the apostles' teaching and fellowship, to the breaking of bread and the prayers. Day by day, attending the temple together and breaking bread in their homes, they partook of food with glad and generous hearts.' (Acts 2:42, 46). The Eucharist is the source, summit and centre of the Church's life. The Eucharistic is a remarkable and wonderful institution which we are so blessed and privileged to receive. Day after day all over the world the Eucharist is celebrated and will be until the end of time when the Lord returns in glory.

'It was above all on 'the first day of the week,' Sunday, the day of Jesus' Resurrection, that the Christians met 'to break bread'.' (CCC 1343)

YOUCAT p.126-127

Lord God, we are the Pilgrim People of God and we proclaim with joy and enthusiasm the Paschal Mystery. For the joy set before us we follow the narrow way of the cross toward the heavenly banquet.

'On the day we call the day of the sun, all who dwell in the city or country gather in the same place.' (St Justin Martyr)

Since the Last Supper the Eucharist has been celebrated. As early as the second century St Justin outlined the basic order of the Eucharist which has remained unchanged since then. The basic structure of the Eucharistic liturgy has been preserved by the Church right down through the centuries. The two fundamental parts of this liturgy are: first, the Liturgy of the Word (Scripture readings, homily and general intercessions); And secondly, the Liturgy of the Eucharist (presentation of the bread and wine, the consecratory thanksgiving and the distribution of holy communion). Together these two form one single act of worship in praise and adoration of God.

Lord, you are the Word of God and the Bread of Life. We feed our spirits and are refreshed in body and soul when we read your Word and receive your Body and drink your Blood.

There is a beautiful symphony and order to the celebration of the Eucharist. Christ himself is the principal agent of the Eucharist. The bishop or priest acts in the person of Christ the head (*in persona Christi capitis*). We all participate in the celebration and reflect this in our 'Amen.' The heart and summit of the Eucharist are the *anaphora* (the Eucharistic prayer), which includes the *epiclesis* (the prayer asking for the Father's blessing on the bread and wine so that they become the Body and Blood of Christ), the *anamnesis* (the calling to mind of the Passion, Resurrection and glorious return of Christ), and the intercessions.

'We call this food Eucharist and no one may take part in it unless he believes that what we teach is true, has received Baptism for the forgiveness of sins and new birth, and lives in keeping with what Christ taught.'
(St Justin Martyr)

YOUCAT 214

Lord, I give thanksgiving and praise for the gift of the Body and Blood of Christ who offered himself for the life of the world.

Day 163

The Mass as Thanksgiving (CCC 1356-1361)

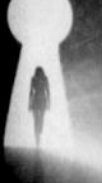

'Eucharist means first of all thanksgiving.' (CCC 1360)

Why do you go to Mass? Perhaps we don't think about this too much and go because it has become our custom and practice. However, the reason we go to Mass is to thank God for all the blessings and grace we have received in our lives. Praise of God is the highest form of prayer. When we praise God the focus shifts from ourselves and our own needs and wants to worship, praise and thanksgiving to God. The holy sacrifice of the Mass is quite simply a sacrifice of praise and thanksgiving to God the Father. We thank the Father for the gift of creation. We thank the Father for sending the Son. We thank the Father for sending the Spirit.

YOUCAT p.123

Through Christ, with Christ and in Christ we offer up to the Father a sacrifice of praise and thanksgiving to the Father. We thank God for all the blessings in our lives.

THE SACRIFICE OF CHRIST (CCC 1362-1372)

DAY 164

The great mystery of the Eucharist is that Jesus' sacrifice on the cross is in a certain way made real and present. The Holy Spirit is the One who moves in us to instil a sense of Eucharistic awe and wonder at what takes place on the altar. The Eucharist re-presents (makes present) the sacrifice of the cross. Jesus' cross remains a once and for all event but his priesthood did not end with his death. At the Last Supper 'on the night he was betrayed' he left us the gift of the Eucharist. The Holy Mass, then, is a visible sacrifice which is re-presented and remembered until the end of time so that we can receive the forgiveness for our sins that we commit daily.

'Put this body anywhere! Don't trouble yourselves about it! I simply ask you to remember me at the Lord's altar wherever you are.' (St Monica)

YOUCAT 216

Lord God, deepen within me a real sense of awe, adoration and worship before the Lord who is real and present in the Mass. I bow before the Eucharist - 'Sweet Sacrament most holy, sweet Sacrament divine.'

DAY 165

THE REAL PRESENCE (CCC 1373-1381)

'Could not Christ's words, which can make from nothing what did not exist, change existing things into what they were not before? It is no less a feat to give their original nature than to change their nature.' (St Ambrose)

Christ is present in many ways to us: in the Scriptures, in prayer, in the poor, the sick and those in prison. He is present in the sacraments, in the priest celebrating Mass but most of all Christ is present in a unique and special way in the Eucharist. St Thomas Aquinas said of the Eucharist that it was, 'the perfection of the spiritual life and the end to which all the sacraments tend.' At the consecration of the bread and wine a change takes place of the whole substance of the bread and wine into the whole substance of the body and blood of Christ. This change is called transubstantiation, and before Christ made real and present we bow down and worship.

YOUCAT 217; p.129-130

Godhead here in hiding, whom I do adore masked by these bare shadows, shape and nothing more, see, Lord, at thy service low lies here a heart lost, all lost in wonder at the God who art.' (St Thomas Aquinas)

The Eucharistic Banquet (CCC 1382-1390)

Day 166

The altar is the most important place in every Church. The altar represents the altar of the sacrifice where the Paschal Mystery is made real and present to us. It also represents the table of the Lord, the Eucharistic Banquet, from which we are fed and nourished. St Ambrose said: 'For what is the altar of Christ if not the image of the Body of Christ? The altar represents the Body of Christ and the Body of Christ is on the altar.' We approach the altar of the Lord in silence, prayer and reverence. In receiving the Eucharist we echo the humble prayer of the Centurion: 'Lord, I am not worthy that you should enter under my roof, but only say the word and my soul will be healed.'

'Bodily demeanour (gestures, clothing) ought to convey the respect, solemnity and joy of this moment when Christ becomes our guest.' (CCC 1387)

Lord, I cherish your words about the Eucharist: 'Truly, I say to you, unless you eat the flesh of the Son of man and drink his blood, you have no life in you.' (John 6:53)

DAY
167

THE FRUITS OF HOLY COMMUNION (CCC 1391-1397)

'As the Father sent me, and I live because of the Father, so he who eats me will live because of me.' (John 6:57)

YOUCAT 221

Jesus said: 'He who eats my flesh and drinks my blood abides in me, and I in him' (John 6:56). In Holy Communion we know the most intimate union with Christ. We become the beneficiaries of every spiritual grace and blessing. In receiving the Eucharist God's grace is preserves but also increases and renews the grace of our Baptism. In receiving the Eucharist we are cleansed from past sins and preserved from future ones. The Eucharist restores our strength; strengthens charity and wipes away our venial sins. The Eucharist unites us in love, in solidarity with the poor, the sick and prisoners. Pope Pius X said: 'Receiving Holy Communion is the shortest and safest way to heaven.'

Lord God, just as earthly food and drink nourishes and feeds my body so too the heavenly food and drink of the Eucharist feeds my spiritual life.

THE EUCHARIST AND CHRISTIAN UNITY (CCC 1398-1401)

DAY 168

Jesus prayed that his disciples would be one as he and his Father were one (John 17:11). The Lord's prayer for unity suggests that this blessing is not simply a given but requires prayer and intercession. St Augustine said: 'If ever there was a race given to disunity it is the human race; if ever there was a race given to unity, it is the human race.' The unity of believers has been Jesus' prayer for the Church since the beginning. For St Augustine the Eucharist was a sacrament of unity: 'O sacrament of devotion! O sign of unity! O bond of charity!' The tragedy and pain of separation between churches is that it breaks our common participation in the table of the Lord.

'All the faithful should remember that the more effort they make to live holier lives according to the Gospel, the better will they further Christian unity and put it into practice.' (Unitatis Redintegratio 7)

YOUCAT 222

Lord God, the unity you desire will come through a 'spiritual ecumenism' rooted in a love and respect for each other, prayer and through our celebrating of the Eucharist - the sacrament of unity and love.

Day 169

The Pledge of Future Glory (CCC 1402-1405)

'O Sacred banquet in which Christ is received as food, the memory of his Passion is renewed, the soul is filled with grace and a pledge of the life to come is given to us.' (An ancient prayer)

YOUCAT 223

Blessed Cardinal John Henry Newman said: 'Love of heaven is the only way to heaven.' We tend not to feel comfortable thinking too much about the Second Coming of Christ, heaven or the life to come. We fear perhaps being too heavenly minded to be of any earthly good. Our vocation, however, invites us to fix our thoughts on heavenly things (Colossians 3:1). The Eucharist is an anticipation of the heavenly banquet and a pledge, a promise, of the glory to come. Christ is in our midst but his presence is veiled. The Spirit moves us to long for heaven and pray for Christ's return. On that day we will see God as he is. We will have some share in the divine nature and praise God forever.

Lord, we are a people who groan inwardly for the Second Coming of Christ, the blessed hope of the Church.

When we examine our hearts we find we are easily drawn to what is wrong and gravitate towards what is evil. Despite the gift of the new life of Baptism we remain wounded and weakened by sin. We find within us sometimes a refusal, a rebellion even, to acknowledge God as our source and we lose sight of our final destiny, to be with God. We are like St Paul who, acutely aware of this inner conflict and dichotomy cried out, 'What a wretched man am I! Who will rescue me from this body of death?' (Romans 7:24). He answers his own question: 'Thanks be to God - through Jesus Christ our Lord' (Romans 7:25).

'Stronger than all the evils in the soul is the Word, and the healing power that dwells in him.'
(Origen of Alexandria)

YOUCAT 224

Lord Jesus, you are the Physician of our souls, and through the sacraments of Penance and the Anointing of the Sick your work of healing and salvation continue.

DAY 171

THE NAME OF THE SACRAMENT (CCC 1422-1424)

'Be reconciled to God.' (2 Corinthians 5:20)

The sacrament of Penance has many different names: the sacrament of conversion, confession, forgiveness and reconciliation. Each one identifies an essential element of the grace available to us. We understand the need for confession, forgiveness and reconciliation but we don't always appreciate our need for conversion. Christ's call to conversion is ongoing and lifelong. This second conversion is our response to the Holy Spirit working in our lives. It is the movement of a contrite heart, drawn and moved by grace to respond to the merciful love of God who loved us first (CCC 1428).

YOUCAT 225

Lord, restore to me, through the Sacrament of Reconciliation, the joy of my salvation. Cleanse me and I shall be clean, purify me and I will be pure.

St Peter's treacherous betrayal was perhaps the culmination of other dark areas and shadows in his life which overflowed in this infamous act. We know he was rash, emotional, impulsive, and capable of violence. What moved him to repentance? What made him weep bitter tears of sorrow? St Luke tells us that it was Jesus' look and his recall of Jesus' warning that he would betray him (Luke 22:61). It was Jesus' look of infinite mercy which drew tears of repentance from St Peter (Luke 22:61). It was Jesus' overwhelming love and forgiveness for him which softened his heart and moved him to weep bitterly in repentance.

'To him who still remains in this world, no repentance is too late.' (St Cyrpian)

YOUCAT 226

Lord, through the waters of Baptism we were converted. Through the tears of repentance we are washed and cleansed by the blood of Christ and walk in the path of ongoing conversion.

Day 173

Interior Repentance (CCC 1430-1433)

'Let us fix our eyes on Christ's blood and understand how precious it is to his Father, for, poured out for our salvation, it has brought to the whole world the grace of repentance.' (St Clement of Rome)

YOUCAT 229

The Catechism gives us a beautiful definition of the meaning of interior repentance. Interior repentance is what the Scriptures and the Church mean by true and genuine repentance. Such repentance is deep, profound, heartfelt and changes our behaviour. Just as the first believers used to put to memory the Creed, we would do well to put to memory the following definition of true repentance: 'Interior repentance is a radical re-orientation of our whole life, a return, a conversion to God with all our heart, an end of sin, a turning away from evil. At the same time it entails the desire and resolution to change one's life' (CCC 1431).

Father, by looking upon Jesus, the One we have pierced with our sins, may we know and experience life-changing, interior and radical repentance.

Try as hard as we might, there is no escaping sin, repentance and conversion. Many have tried over the years, suggesting such things are negative and depressing. The truth is that sin is sin, repentance is necessary; conversion is at the heart of the gospel. Rather than seeing them as negative and depressing they are the way into a joy-filled, happy and fulfilled Christian life. In the Parable of the Prodigal Son, God the Father is full of mercy, compassion and forgiveness (Luke 15:20). The return of the prodigal son results in a party, a banquet and great happiness (Luke 15:22-24). We learn that heaven rejoices and celebrates when we repent (Luke 15:10).

'The beautiful robe, the ring and the festive banquet are symbols of the new life - pure, worthy, joyful - of anyone who returns to God and to the bosom of his family, the Church.' (CCC 1439)

YOUCAT 229

Father, today I put on the robe of the joy of repentance, the ring of forgiveness and the sandals of penance by being prepared to go the extra mile in love and service of my neighbour.

Day 175

The Sacrament of Penance (CCC 1440-1445)

'Jesus receives sinners at his table, a gesture that expresses in an astonishing way both God's forgiveness and the return to the bosom of the People of God.' (CCC 1443)

YOUCAT 230-231

Throughout history human genius has pushed back the frontiers of science, the arts, music, architecture and so on. It is as if there is no limit to what we can do and achieve. However, there is one thing we cannot do and that is forgive sin; only God can forgive sin (Mark 2:7). Only in the Sacrament of Reconciliation can we know God's forgiveness and be reconciled to God and to his Church. Jesus imparted the power to forgiven sins to his apostles. We receive the blessing of Christ's forgiveness in the Sacrament of Confession. Through this holy sacrament the Church is a sign and instrument of God's forgiveness, mercy and reconciliation.

Lord God, through the Sacrament of Reconciliation may I come to a new and fresh awareness of God's love, mercy and forgiveness.

Sometimes we can be tempted to think that God won't forgive our sin. We can think that what we have done is so terrible that we have put ourselves outside God's mercy. But no one, no matter how bad or heinous their sin, no matter how far they may feel they are beyond the reach of God's redemption, is not beyond the mercy of God, the source of all forgiveness. The prayer of absolution is a sacred moment in which we receive God's mercy; our sins are forgiven and we are cleansed and set free. Through the sacrament of Holy Orders the priest has the authority to absolve us in the name of the Father and of the Son and of the Holy Spirit.

'The Fathers of the Church present this sacrament as 'the second plank [of salvation] after the shipwreck which is the loss of grace'.' (CCC 1446)

YOUCAT 231

Through the ministry of the Church may God give you pardon and peace, and I absolve you from your sins in the name of the Father, and of the Son and of the Holy Spirit.

Day 177

Contrition (CCC 1450-1454)

'I live in a high and holy place but also with him who is contrite and lowly in spirit, to revive the heart of the contrite.' (Isaiah 57:15)

YOUCAT 232

King David's contrition after his adultery with Bathsheba is captured in Psalm 51. This hymn of repentance expresses his brokenness and sorrow but also his hope in God's mercy and forgiveness. King David prays: 'The sacrifice acceptable to God is a broken spirit; a broken and contrite heart, O God, you will not despise.' (Psalm 51:17). The Catechism draws on the definition of contrition given many centuries ago at the Council of Trent (1551): '..sorrow of the soul and detestation for the sin committed, together with the resolution not to sin again.' Contrition, then, is a blessing because it humbles and creates in us a meek spirit (Matthew 5:6).

Lord Jesus, you do not despise a broken spirit nor a contrite heart. For you are humble and gentle in heart and in you we find rest for our souls.

An essential part of the Sacrament of Reconciliation involves the confession, the disclosure and naming of our sins. This requires God's grace and not a little courage on our part. Confession of sin does not come easily or naturally to us. We are inclined to hide our sins, and, truth be told, we can be deeply ashamed and embarrassed by some of them. Our confessor, if he is compassionate and kind, will recognize the grace at work in us which has led us to this moment. However, we must bear in mind also the encouraging and consoling words of St John: 'If we confess our sins, God is faithful and just and will forgive us our sins and purify us from all unrighteousness' (1 John 1:9).

'Whoever confesses his sins...is already working with God.'
(St Augustine)

YOUCAT 233-235

I confess to almighty God... that I have greatly sinned in my thoughts and in my words, in what I have done and in what I have failed to do, through my fault, through my fault, through my most grievous fault.

DAY 179

SATISFACTION (CCC 1459-1460)

'It is better for us to confess our sins than harden our hearts.' (Pope St Clement I)

Penance is an important part of the Sacrament of Reconciliation. Why is penance necessary when we have already been forgiven? It is because, although absolution forgives and takes away our sin, it does not remedy all the disorders sin has caused. We recover our full spiritual health by doing penance of one kind or another. What kind of penance we are given is very much subject to the discretion and discernment of our confessor. He must take into account our personal situation and the gravity and nature of the sins committed. The types of penance are wide and varied: prayer, works of mercy, service of our neighbour and acts of self-denial.

Lord, help me to understand that penance helps to configure us to Christ. We are co-heirs with the risen Christ 'provided we suffer with him.' (Romans 8:17)

THE MINISTER (CCC 1461-1467)

DAY 180

By virtue of Holy Orders bishops and priests have the power to forgive sins 'in the name of the Father, and of the Son, and of the Holy Spirit.' Their holy office bestows on them a great honour and grace but also great responsibility. The priest, however, is the servant of God's forgiveness not its master. We pray for our priests because this high calling is challenging and demanding. Each confessor requires maturity and experience in many areas of life: knowledge of Christian behaviour, experience of life, sensitivity to the broken and fallen, a love of the Magisterium, the teaching authority of the church, and the ability to lead and guide penitents to maturity and healing.

'[the priest]... can make no use of knowledge that confession gives him about the penitent's lives. This secrecy, which admits of no exceptions is called 'the sacramental seal.' (CCC 1467)

YOUCAT 236

Lord, we give thanks and praise for the Sacrament of Confession, and we pray for our priests who are charged with dispensing the sacrament in love, wisdom and maturity.

DAY 181

THE EFFECTS OF THIS SACRAMENT (I) (CCC 1468-1470)

'In this sacrament, the sinner, placing himself before the merciful judgement of God, anticipates in a certain way the judgement to which he will be subjected at the end of his earthly life.' (CCC 1470)

YOUCAT 239

St Paul taught, 'Be reconciled with God.' (2 Corinthians 5:20). Reconciliation with God is the primary grace of the Sacrament of Forgiveness. Many blessings flow from it. We are reconciled with ourselves in our inner being and regain our innermost truth. We are reconciled with our neighbour and with those we may have hurt or wounded. We are reconciled with the Church and in a mysterious way we are also even reconciled with creation itself. Drawing on the wisdom of the First Vatican Council, the Catechism teaches that a good confession '..is usually followed by peace and serenity of conscience with strong spiritual consolation.' (CCC 1468).

Lord, I give you thanks and praise for the many graces and blessings you pour out in the Sacrament of Reconciliation. May I avail myself of this grace more frequently and know in deeper measure the joy of my salvation.

In the Sacrifice of Penance we place ourselves before the merciful judgement of God. This process of examining our lives and identifying ways we have sinned and offended the Lord anticipates in a certain way our own judgement at the end of our lives. Confessing ours sins can be hard enough but the idea of God's judgement can be a truly frightening one. There is no escaping that Jesus spoke a lot about judgement, teaching that God the Father had left 'all judgement, to the Son' (John 5:22). But he also comforted us with the promise that the Son of God did not come to judge but to save and to give his life that we may know the life he has in himself (John 3:17).

'In converting to Christ through penance and faith, the sinner passes from death to life and 'does not come under judgement'.' (CCC 1470)

YOUCAT 239

Lord, in the Sacrament of Penance may I grow in understanding of how sin grieves you but also grow in confidence in your love, mercy and forgiveness.

DAY 183

GOING TO CONFESSION (CCC 1480-1484)

'In failing to confess, Lord, I would only hide You from myself, not myself from You.' *(Saint Augustine)*

How long has it been since your last Confession? Our experience teaches us that the more we go, the easier it is to want to go. The less we go, the harder it is to go. The Church asks that we go to Confession at least once a year, ideally during Lent. The Church also encourages us to receive the Sacrament of Forgiveness frequently and often. In the sacrament Christ himself speaks to us personally: 'My son, your sins are forgiven.' (Mark 2:5). He is the divine physician who raises us up and brings healing, cleaning and purification. In Confession we grow in our knowledge and understanding of God's love, especially his mercy and forgiveness.

YOUCAT 224-239

Father, through the Sacrament of Reconciliation we come to know and rely on your love. In this sacrament in some way your love is made complete and so we have confidence in confessing our sins and in the judgement to come.

DAY 184

THE SICK PERSON BEFORE GOD (CCC 1499-1502)

'It can be said that each person in a special fashion becomes the way for the Church when suffering enters their life.' (Pope John Paul II)

YOUCAT 240

Sickness and illness bring us in touch with many harsh realities of our existence. We experience powerlessness; we understand our limitations, we touch our own frailty and we sense something of our own mortality. The Catechism says, 'Every illness can make us glimpse death' (CCC 1500). Sickness also creates its own special temptation. On the one hand we can be inclined to give into anguish, self-loathing, despair and even rebellion against God. On the other, suffering can make us more mature and patient with ourselves and with others. It also can create within us a search for God and be the cause for a deeper conversion - a turning back to God.

Lord God, we live our suffering in your presence for you are our shepherd who leads us beside quiet waters and restores our soul.

CHRIST THE PHYSICIAN (CCC 1503-1505)

God has a preferential love for the poor as well as a preferential love for the sick. Jesus' love is so profound, so intimate, that he identifies himself directly with the sick: 'I was sick and you visited me' (Matthew 25:36). Through his cross the Lord made their suffering his own. 'He took our infirmities and bore our diseases' (Isaiah 53:4). From the very beginning Jesus' ministry involved healing the sick and restoring those who suffer to health. He cured lepers, he opened the eyes of the blind, he restored the hearing of the deaf and he raised the dead. The healing miracles were signs pointing to the radical healing to come through his victory on the cross over sin and death.

'Human suffering evokes compassion; it also evokes respect.' (Pope John Paul II)

YOUCAT 241

Lord Jesus, through your Passion and death on the cross you have given new meaning to suffering and through it we are configured to you and are united with you in your redemptive Passion.

DAY 186

THE WORK OF HEALING (CCC 1506-1510)

'Is any among you sick? Let him call for the elders (presbyters) of the Church and let them pray over him, anointing him with oil in the name of the Lord.' (James 5:14-15)

Our faith gives us a new outlook on illness and sickness. We become partakers in Jesus' ministry of compassion and healing. We have received the commission to 'heal the sick' (Matthew 10:8) and the risen Lord confirmed this was essential to our calling: 'In my name they will lay their hands on the sick, and they will recover' (Mark 16:17-18). Some have received a special charism of healing. Despite our prayers healing does not always come. We learn from St Paul who, despite his own prayer, was not granted the healing he sought. The Lord consoled him, saying: 'My grace is sufficient for you, for my power is made perfect in weakness' (2 Corinthians 12:9).

YOUCAT 242

Lord, I give you thanks and praise for your life-giving presence and healing made available to us in the Sacrament of the Anointing of the Sick but also in the Eucharist.

THE SACRAMENT OF THE SICK (CCC 1511-1513)

DAY 187

The Sacrament of the Sick has its roots in a rite first practised in the early church. St James describes how the elders of the church prayed over the sick and anointed them with oil (James 5:14-15). The rite was underpinned by a lively hope and expectation that God would heal and restore the sick person to health. Tradition has recognized in this apostolic rite the Sacrament of Anointing. Over the centuries a tradition evolved in which the sacrament was primarily administered to those on their deathbeds and it became known as 'Extreme Unction.' However, despite this the Church has never failed to ask the Lord to heal the sick.

'In the sacrament Christ continues to 'touch' us in order to heal us.' (CCC 1504)

YOUCAT p.140-141

Through this holy anointing may the Lord in his love and mercy help you with the grace of the Holy Spirit. May the Lord who frees you from sin save you and raise you up.'

Day 188

Who receives and who administers this sacrament (CCC 1514-1519)

'The Anointing of the Sick completes our conformity to the death and resurrection of Christ, just as Baptism began it.' (CCC 1523)

YOUCAT 243

The Anointing of the Sick is not a sacrament only for those on their deathbeds. It is for those whose health is seriously impaired by sickness or old age, including before surgery because of serious illness. Only a bishop or a priest can administer the sacrament. We can be reluctant or a little reticent in asking for this blessing. Often this is because we don't want to bother the priest, but also because we identify it with the last rites and don't want to alarm the sick person. The sacrament however is a 'healing sacrament', a wonderful gift and we should not deprive ourselves, or indeed others, of its healing grace and touch.

Lord, in the Sacrament of Anointing you pour out your strength, peace and courage. This gift of grace renews our trust and faith in God and strengthens us against the temptation to despair and lose hope.

The effects of this Sacrament (CCC 1520-1523)

In the Sacrament of Anointing we are given the courage, strength and peace to face our trials with dignity and fortitude, sure in the knowledge of God's love. In the sacrament we also receive healing for our soul and forgiveness of our sins. If it is God's will we can also be healed in body and restored to health. Through the sacrament we are united to Christ's death and resurrection and participate in the saving work of Christ. It is also the sacrament of departure and the Catechism expresses this beautifully: 'This last anointing fortifies the end of our earthly life like a solid rampart for the final struggles before entering the Father's house'.

'His preferential love for the sick has not ceased through the centuries to draw the very special attention of Christians toward all those who suffer in body and soul.' (CCC 1503)

YOUCAT 245

Lord, in the Sacrament of Anointing we receive every spiritual blessing and an abundance of grace. You anoint us, Lord, in the joy and peace of the Holy Spirit.

The Eucharist when given to someone in the last moments of their lives is called Viaticum. The word Viaticum comes from the Latin and means literally 'provision for the journey.' The Viaticum is precisely that: food or nourishment for the journey, as we pass over from this life to the Father and eternal life. As Jesus himself promised: 'He who eats my flesh and drinks my blood has eternal life, and I will raise him up at the last day.' (John 6:54). The Sacrament of Reconciliation, the Sacrament of Anointing and Viaticum are the sacraments that prepare us for our heavenly homeland and complete our earthly pilgrimage.

'Only priests (presbyters and bishops) can give the sacrament of the Anointing of the Sick, using oil blessed by the bishop, or if necessary by the presbyter himself.' (CCC 1530)

YOUCAT 247

Before our Lord Jesus Christ passed from this world to return to the Father, he left us the sacrament of his Body and Blood. When the hour comes for us to pass from this life and join him, he strengthens us with this food for our journey and comforts us by this pledge of our resurrection.

SERVICE AND ORDER (CCC 1533-1538)

DAY 191

We have all received a common vocation as Christ's disciples which is grounded in the sacraments of Christian initiation: Baptism, Confirmation and Eucharist. The two other sacraments of Holy Orders and Matrimony involve our call to serve. The Sacrament of Holy Orders is directed towards the salvation and service of others as well as the building up of the Church. The Sacrament of Orders has three degrees: episcopate (bishop), presbyterate (priest), diaconate (deacon). At ordination the Holy Spirit is poured out upon the candidate giving him the grace to exercise 'sacred power' (*sacra potestas*), to be able to perform his priestly or diaconate ministry.

'No one can see Christ; but everyone sees the priest, and through him they wish to catch a glimpse of the Lord! Immense is the grandeur of the Lord! Immense is the grandeur and dignity of the priest!' (Pope John Paul II)

YOUCAT 248

Lord, you poured out the blessing of the Holy Spirit and the power of grace upon those called to Holy Orders. Renew and refresh them in their ministry and consecrate them in your presence and your word. We ask this through Jesus Christ our Lord. Amen.

Day 192

In Persona Christi (CCC 1539-1553)

'The Lord said clearly that concern for his flock was proof of love for him.' (St John Chrysostom)

Our priests by virtue of the sacrament of Holy Orders act *in Persona Christi*, in the person of Christ. St Thomas Aquinas explains: 'Christ is the source of all priesthood; the priest of the old law was a figure of Christ, and the priest of the new law acts in the person of Christ.' Furthermore, and in a beautiful turn of expression, St Ignatius of Antioch said that the bishop is *typos tou Patros*, 'the living image of God the Father.' This grace does not preserve the bishop or priest from human weakness, a spirit of domination or control, or from human error and sin. This is why we must pray for them because with great grace and blessing comes great responsibility.

YOUCAT 250

Lord God, when you call a man to serve you as a priest you call him to lay down his life for the Church and for God's people.

Our bishops hold an office that goes right back, in an unbroken succession, to the apostolic times. The bishops are successors of the first apostles and 'the transmitters of the apostolic line' (*Lumen Gentium* 20). Just as the apostles received the Spirit poured out upon them by the laying on of hands, so today bishops receive the same anointing. The office of bishop is the high priesthood, the acme (*summa*) of the sacred ministry. The bishop receives the fullness of the sacrament of Holy Orders and is made a true and authentic teacher of the faith. Again, we pray for our bishops because with great grace, blessing and anointing comes great responsibility.

'Let everyone revere the deacons as Jesus Christ, the bishop as the image of the Father, and the presbyters as the senate of God and the assembly of the apostles. For without them one cannot speak of the Church.' (St Ignatius of Antioch)

YOUCAT 251-253

Lord God, we pray for our bishops that, strengthened by your grace and fortified by the Spirit, they may serve us as teachers, shepherds and priests and feed their flock.

'Nothing means more to me or gives me greater joy that to celebrate Mass each day and to serve God's people in the Church. That has been true ever since the day of my ordination as a priest. Nothing has ever changed this, not even becoming Pope.' (Pope John Paul II)

YOUCAT 254

Priests are ordained to be the co-workers of the bishop. Through the grace of the sacrament of Holy Orders they are anointed with a special character which configures them to Christ and enables them to act in the person of Christ. They are united to their bishop in a spirit of trust and generosity and depend on him in the exercise of their priestly office. At the moment of ordination each priest promises obedience to their bishop and, in a moving gesture at the end of the ordination liturgy, they receive a kiss of peace from him. The kiss is a sign that the bishop considers his priests co-workers, sons, brothers and friends. They in turn give him their love and obedience.

Father, we give you thanks for the gift of the priesthood. For by their consecration priests receive the grace to preach the gospel, shepherd God's people and celebrate divine worship as true priests of the New Testament.

At the Second Vatican Council the ministry of the permanent diaconate was restored. At an ordination to the diaconate only the bishop lays hands on the deacon, signifying his special attachment to the bishop. The deacon is called to a ministry of service (*diakonia*). The sacrament of Holy Orders marks them with a special indelible imprint (character) and configures them to Christ. They are ordained to perform many tasks, functions and roles. They assist the bishop in celebrating the Eucharist. They can bless marriages, preside over funerals, read the Gospel at Mass, preach, teach and serve in many charitable ways in the parish and in the diocese to which they are assigned.

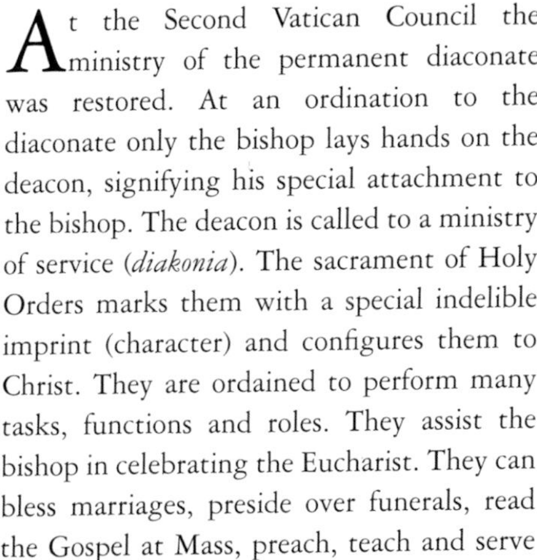

'Let them be merciful, and zealous, and let them walk according to the truth of the Lord, who became the servant of all.' (St Polycarp)

YOUCAT 255

Lord, help me to come to know you more and more. Help me to be ever more at one with your will. Help me to live my life, not for myself, but in union with you, to live it for others. Help me to become ever more your friend.

DAY 196

WHO CAN RECEIVE THIS SACRAMENT? (CCC 1577-1580)

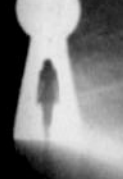

'The vow of celibacy is a matter of keeping one's word to Christ and the Church. A duty and a proof of the priest's inner maturity; it is the expression of his personal dignity.' (Pope John Paul II)

YOUCAT 256

The New Testament confirms that Christ chose men to be part of the college of the twelve apostles. The Church has always understood that she is bound by this choice, which is why the ordination of women is not possible. Celibacy is an ordinary Church requirement for Holy Orders, except for those called to the permanent diaconate who can be married. The gift of celibacy, whilst a 'sign of contradiction' and often misunderstood, is a sign of the new life of Christ. Those called to the priesthood renounce the joys and blessings of marriage for the kingdom of God. Celibacy, when accepted with a joyful and generous heart, is a living and radiant sign of the reign of God.

Lord, we pray for all those who feel called to test their vocation to the priesthood. Give them courage to step forward and respond to your invitation with joyful and generous hearts.

THE EFFECTS OF THIS SACRAMENT (CCC 1581-1589)

DAY 197

Our priests are often simple, ordinary men, and often, on their own admission, unworthy, yet they are called to respond to Christ's invitation: 'Follow me.' Despite their weakness and shortcomings, by virtue of the sacrament of Holy Orders they are configured by a special grace to act as Christ's representative. They receive an indelible spiritual character and a special grace from God to fulfil their vocation. The bishop receives the strength to govern with wisdom and prudence. The priest receives the gift to proclaim the gospel and celebrate the mysteries of faith. The deacon receives the charism to lay down his life and serve others in charity and love.

'The priest continues the work of redemption on earth. If we really understood the priest on earth, we would die not of fright but of love. The priesthood is the love of the heart of Jesus.' (St John Vianney, Cure of Ars)

YOUCAT p.143-148

Lord, you know all our hearts and through the sacrament of Holy Orders you bless and anoint chosen men to serve you as ordained ministers. Your call and grace are irrevocable and for this we give you thanks and praise.

DAY 198

MARRIAGE IN GOD'S PLAN (CCC 1601-1611)

'For God himself is the author of matrimony, endowed as it is with various benefits and purposes.' (Gaudium et Spes 48)

YOUCAT 260

Marriage has a central role in God's plan. The Bible begins with the creation of man and woman in the Garden of Eden (Genesis 1:26-27) and finishes with 'the wedding feast of the Lamb' (Revelation 19:7). The Second Vatican Council affirmed the centrality of marriage in God's plan: 'The well-being of the individual person and of both human and Christian society is closely bound up with the healthy state of conjugal and family life' (*Gaudium et Spes* 47). Within the sacrament of marriage we realize and live out our vocation to love. We are created in the image and likeness of God who is love and who calls us to love.

Lord, we give thanks and praise for the beautiful vocation of marriage. May those called to this holy state be fruitful and multiply the gifts and fruits of the Spirit.

Christian Marriage and Virginity (CCC 1612-1620)

Day 199

St Paul urged husbands, '....love your wives, as Christ loved the Church and gave himself up for her, that he might sanctify her' (Ephesians 5:25-26). The entire Christian life is very much connected to the spousal love between Christ and his Bride, the Church. Baptism itself is a nuptial mystery, a nuptial bathing, if you like, before the wedding feast - the Eucharist. From the very beginning men and women have renounced the blessing and great good of marriage for the kingdom of heaven. Those who embrace this vocation through their consecration are married to Christ. Christian Marriage and virginity are esteemed and honoured among us because they both come from Christ himself.

'Whoever denigrates marriage also diminishes the glory of virginity. Whoever praises it makes virginity more admirable.' (St John Chrysostom)

YOUCAT 265

Lord, we give you thanks and praise for the grace of marriage and virginity. For marriage is a sign of your presence and virginity a sign of the world to come.

DAY 200

THE RITE OF MARRIAGE (CCC 1621-1624)

'Thus a man and a woman, who by their union of conjugal love 'are no longer two, but one flesh' (Matthew 19), render mutual help and service to each other through an intimate union of their persons and of their actions.' (Gaudium et Spes 48)

YOUCAT 266

It is the couple themselves who are the ministers of God's grace to each other in the Sacrament of Marriage. It is the couple themselves who confer the grace of the Sacrament. They are ministers of the new covenant of marriage. They do this by expressing their consent to a lifelong communion of love and fidelity. After giving their consent the priest or deacon declares: 'You have declared your consent before the Church. May the Lord in his goodness strengthen your consent and fill you both with his blessings. What God has joined, man must not divide.' The priest or deacon is there to formally witness the marriage, bless the rings and bless the couple.

Lord, we ask for the grace of the Holy Spirit to be poured out on all married couples. For it is the Spirit who is the seal of their covenant, source of their love and strength of their fidelity.

Consent (CCC 1625-1632)

Day 201

Consent is a vital component in many areas of life. Indeed, where there is no consent we find abuse, manipulation and wrongdoing. The Church considers consent to be the indispensable element that makes the marriage. With consent there is a marriage; without it there is not. Consent is given when the spouse says in the wedding ceremony: 'I take you to be my wife' and the bride says, 'I take you to be my husband.' In this act of consent the spouses fulfil the promise from the book of Genesis and confirmed by Jesus in his teaching (Mark 10:8): 'becoming one flesh' (Genesis 2:24).

'Marriage should be honoured by all, and the marriage bed kept pure, for God will judge the adulterer and all the sexually immoral.' (Hebrews 13:4)

YOUCAT 261

Lord, through the 'I do' of marriage the spouses declare their love and commitment to each other. In their 'I do' to you and the Church may they live lives worthy of the high and noble calling they have received.

'For the unbelieving husband is consecrated through his wife, and the unbelieving wife is consecrated through her husband.' (1 Corinthians 7:14)

YOUCAT 267

A mixed marriage is a marriage between a Catholic and a baptized non-Catholic. In the case of a marriage between a Catholic and non-baptized person there is a 'disparity of cult'. Marriages between couples from different Christian denominations or from different religions have their own trials and challenges. Both require formal approval - a mixed marriage needs express permission and 'disparity of cult' express dispensation. The Catholic party must preserve his or hers faith and ensure that their children are baptized and educated in the Catholic Church. God's grace is poured out in a special way upon such marriages.

Lord, through reverence for each person's faith may mixed marriages be richly blessed. Lord, through the grace of prayer may a non-believing spouse be led to the grace of Baptism and conversion.

The Effects of This Sacrament (CCC 1638-1642)

Day 203

Married couples receive many graces and blessings and are anointed with every spiritual gift. They are consecrated and strengthened in their duties and in the dignity of their calling. The blessing of their covenant is mysteriously caught up with the divine covenant and the love of the Blessed Trinity. Marriage is a real partnership, a union of sanctity and holiness. The grace of marriage has its source in Christ himself, who gives the strength for couples to forgive each other, bear with each other and love one another. The joys, blessing and privilege of marriage are, in some way, a foretaste of the wedding feast of the Lamb.

'How can I ever express the happiness of a marriage joined by the Church, strengthened by an offering, sealed by a blessing, anointed by angels and ratified by the Father?' (Tertullian)

YOUCAT p.149

Lord, through the Sacrament of Marriage a bond exists between the couple which is exclusive and perpetual. Although separated by death, may they be united once again in the joy and happiness of everlasting life.

'Children are the supreme gift of marriage and contribute greatly to the good of the parents themselves.' (Gaudium et Spes 50)

YOUCAT 262

In marriage two people united in love become one flesh (Matthew 19:6). This sacred union makes demands of indissolubility, faithfulness and openness to fertility. The grace and strength to live like this is confirmed, purified and completed day by day as the couple live in communion with Jesus Christ. The Catechism, as if recognizing how hard a life long commitment to marriage can be, says: 'It can seem difficult, even impossible, to bind oneself for life to another human being' (CCC 1648). However, each couple is sustained and supported by God's grace. The fundamental task and crowning glory of marriage is the procreation and education of children.

Father, the fundamental task of marriage is to be at the service of life. We praise you for the sacred gift of life and of children. We pray especially for spouses not blessed with children that their marriage may radiate a fruitfulness of love and service to others.

The Domestic Church (CCC 1655-1658)

The church has always esteemed the family and the home. The Second Vatican Council, drawing on an ancient yet ever new expression, referred to the family as '*Ecclesia Domestica*' (the domestic church). In the family we minister the priesthood of our Baptism in many ways: by receiving the sacraments, family prayer, personal prayer, Scripture reading, *lectio divina*, thanksgiving, grace before meals, the witness of a holy life, self-denial and active charity. The family home is where we learn to put into practice: forgiveness, long-suffering, endurance, hard work, perseverance, patience, kindness, good manners and, the greatest of all, love.

'With parents leading the way by example and family prayer, children, and indeed everyone gathered around the family hearth, will find a readier path to human maturity, salvation and holiness.' (Gaudium et Spes 48)

YOUCAT 271

Lord, we give you thanks and praise for our homes which are rightly called domestic churches, communities of grace and prayer, schools of human virtues and of Christian love.

DAY 206

SACRAMENTALS (CCC 1667-1670)

'God is more anxious to bestow his blessings on us than we are to receive them.' (St Augustine)

YOUCAT 272

Sacramentals are objects or actions in which a blessing is given and which bear some resemblance to the sacraments. The most common Sacramentals, and two we are perhaps most familiar with, are the sprinkling of holy water (this recalls Baptism) and making the sign of the cross (common to all the sacraments). Sacramentals do not confer the grace of the Holy Spirit but prepare us to receive God's grace and dispose us to co-operate with the Spirit. They bring God's blessing into our lives. For example, having a small bottle of holy water means that we can bless ourselves and others when making a long journey or embarking on a difficult challenge (exams, a job interview, etc).

In the name of the Father and of the Son and of the Holy Spirit. Amen

Blessings (CCC 1671-1673)

Day 207

By virtue of our Baptism not only are we called to be a blessing but we are called to bless. This could perhaps be the basis of an examination of conscience. Have I been a blessing to others? Have I witnessed to God's blessing in the way I live my life? We are encouraged to call upon God's blessing in many areas of our lives. In asking for God's blessing we receive grace and protection from evil. Many situations and circumstances call for this in our lives. Some, for example, on moving into a new house can ask that a priest or deacon bless it, sprinkling holy water and asking, in the name of Jesus, that their home and all who dwell in it be protected from the Evil One.

'Watch thou, O Lord, with those who wake, or watch, or weep tonight, and give thine angels charge over those who sleep. Tend thy sick ones, O Lord Christ. Rest thy weary ones. Bless thy dying ones. Soothe thy suffering ones. For thy love's sake.' (Blessing of St Augustine)

YOUCAT 273

Blessed be God the Father, the Father of all Blessings, who pours out on us his children every spiritual blessing, grace and gift.

DAY 208

THE ROSARY AND DEVOTIONS (CCC 1674)

'If you say the Rosary faithfully unto death, I do assure you that, in spite of the gravity of your sins, 'you will receive a never-fading crown of glory.' (Saint Louis de Montfort)

YOUCAT 274

The Rosary is probably the most popular of all the sacramentals. The saying of the Rosary is experiencing something of a new springtime, especially among young people. Pope Benedict said recently: 'The Rosary is one of the most eloquent signs of love that the younger generation nourish for Jesus and his mother.' Indeed, prison chaplains say that Rosary beads are even in demand inside prison. Prisoners wear them around their necks as a blessing and for God's protection. Praying the Rosary is really a meditation on the most important moments in salvation history. Let us renew our devotion to this most holy and sacred of prayers.

Lord, we lift up our minds and hearts to you in prayer and seek you through the many forms of piety devotions available to us: the veneration of relics, visits to sanctuaries, pilgrimages, processions, stations of the cross and medals.

If you have ever had the experience of being part of, for example, the torchlit procession at Lourdes or taken part in a walk of witness on Good Friday you will appreciate how faith-affirming they can be. The sense of being united in faith, in harmony with the Church and joined in pilgrimage, is truly a great gift of our faith. Such prayers and devotions do not replace the liturgy but rather strengthen it, enrich it and lead us more deeply into its riches. We are grateful to our priests for encouraging the many varied expressions of piety available to us, because they lead us to the liturgy of the Eucharist, the source and summit of our faith, and the fount of all blessing and grace.

'Popular devotions of the Christian people are to be highly commended, provided they accord with the laws and norms of the Church, above all when they are ordered by the Apostolic See.' (Sacrosanctum Concilium, 13)

YOUCAT 274

Lord God, we give you praise and thanks for the gift of prayer, the variety of devotions and piety so richly available to us, as through them you lead us to Christ made real and present to us in the Eucharist.

DAY 210

A HAPPY DEATH (CCC 1680-1683)

'Holy Mary, Mother of God, pray for us sinners, now and at the hour of our death. Amen' (Hail Mary Prayer)

YOUCAT p.159

The Church is our Mother. We are the children of her womb, born a new creation through the new life of Baptism. She accompanies us throughout our lives through the Sacraments. The goal of our lives is directed towards our last Passover, when we pass from this life into the life to come. As we pray, so we live: 'I look forward to the resurrection of the dead, and the life of the world to come.' (Nicea-Constantinopolitan Creed). The day of our death marks the end of our sacramental life and the fulfilment of our Baptism. The Church is with us right until the very end of our lives, even until our last breath, when she surrenders us into the Father's hands.

O my Lord, support me in my last hour by the strong arms of your sacraments, and the fragrance of your consolations. Let your absolving words be said over me, and the holy oil sign and seal me; and let your own body be my food. (Blessed John Henry Newman).

The funeral liturgies offer us comfort and consolation and strengthen our hope and faith at a time in our life when we are numb with grief and vulnerable. There are three parts to the liturgy: the Vigil, the Mass of Christian Burial and the Rite of Committal or Graveside Service. The Mass of Christian Burial is at the heart of the funeral liturgies. The emphasis is on the hope of the resurrection, the promise of eternal life and the peace of heaven. In this Eucharist we learn to live in communion with our loved one who has fallen asleep in Christ. The Eucharist unites us to the living but also those who have gone before us marked with the sign of faith.

'I am the resurrection and the life, says the Lord. If anyone believes in me, even though he dies, he will live. Anyone who lives and believes in me, will not die.' (John 11:25)

YOUCAT 278

Father of mercies, God of compassion, you have given us sure and certain hope that, together with all who have died in Christ, we will rise again with Christ on the last day. Grant them eternal rest, O Lord, and let your perpetual light shine upon them.

LIFE IN CHRIST

SOME OF THE MOST memorable and striking encounters with Jesus in the Gospels are with those caught up in one way or another with the darkness and confusion of living a life outside of God's plan.

A number of examples spring to mind. The women at the well at Sychar in Samaria (John 4:1-26). The woman caught in the act of adultery (John 8:1-11). Matthew the tax collector (Matthew 9:9-13). Zaccheus, who had become rich and wealthy through exploitation and cheating others (Luke 19:1-10).

Jesus' teaching and his embrace was radical and shocking; it caused scandal, upset and moral indignation. Jesus always held out the hope and promise of God's mercy, acceptance and forgiveness.

Each of these encounters teaches us how God's mercy, compassion and love reaches out to us, despite our moral failings, weaknesses or sin.

However, there is another encounter the Lord had with a rich young man who was in fact, living a very moral, righteous and upright life. He was, if you like, from the other end of the moral spectrum. We learn as much from this encounter as we do from the others.

The rich young man was clearly attracted to Jesus and asked him a profoundly important question: 'Teacher, what good deed must I do, to have eternal life?' (Matthew 19:16-17). Jesus' responded, 'If you would enter life, keep the commandments' (Matthew 19:16-17).

He had striven to keep the commandments and live a good and holy life. Despite this, however, he knew that something was missing or lacking in his life. 'All these I have kept,' the young man said, 'what do I still lack? (Matthew 19:20).

The Lord challenged him to follow him and sell all his possessions and give to the poor. The Lord promised him treasure in heaven and fullness of life. The rich young man went away sad and downcast because he could not relinquish the hold his possessions had on him. He could not take leave of them and follow the Lord.

Part 3 of the Catechism is essentially exploring the aspiration and hope of the rich young man whereby we all have to live a good, holy and happy life and inherit the promised eternal life. This section of the Catechism helps us to consider: What it means to be good? How do we live moral lives, pleasing to God and pleasing to one another? Furthermore, how do we inherit eternal life and live with God forever?

The tragedy of the fall of the human race was that the life of holiness became impossible for us because of the damage and the wound to our human nature caused by sin. Through the Incarnation and Paschal Mystery of Jesus Christ a new relationship, a new Covenant has been established between God and us, through baptism we become a new creation, born anew of the Holy Spirit.

The Risen Jesus is the first of this new creation, the first of a new human race. But by union with Christ through the Sacrament of Baptism, each of us begins to share in the relationship Jesus enjoys with the Father; each of us has become a new creation and is made capable of living a life of holiness, which previously the wound of sin had seriously hindered.

To put it quite simply: living the Christian life and following the commandments is very much the fruit of what Jesus has accomplished through his death and resurrection and the fruit of the grace of Christ communicated to us through the sacraments.

Without Christ and the power of his grace present to us through the Liturgy, we would be in the same position as the people of the Old Testament, who had received the commandments from God, but were powerless, because of fallen human nature, to put them into practice.

The commandments were a blessed gift from God; they revealed God's great desire for us to a life worthy of beings created in his image and likeness. However, as we shall see over and over again in *Doorway to Faith*, we fall short, we are weak and often incapable of really living out our true vocation because of the wound and effect of sin.

We needed an action of God that would bring healing to our wounded nature and set us free from the slavery of sin. In God's great mercy, and in the fullness of time, this healing came with the coming of Christ.

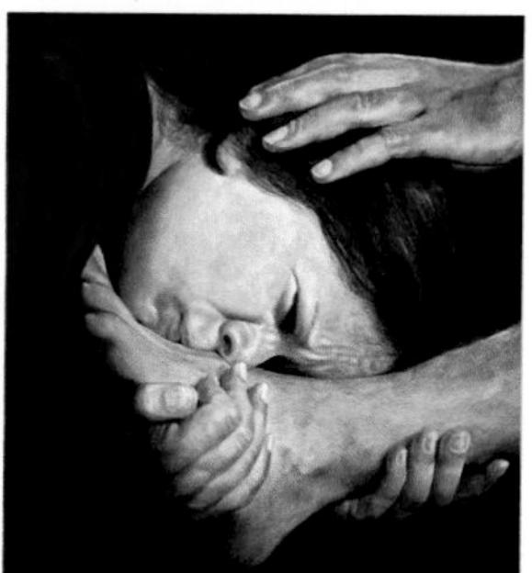

Christ identified himself with us; and by offering his life as an act of perfect obedience and worship to the Father, he was raised from the dead to become the beginning of a new human race that could now live as Jesus himself lived in the power of the Spirit.

It is of immense significance that Part 3 of the Catechism begins with a quotation from Pope Leo the Great:

'Christian, recognise your dignity and, now that you share in God's own nature, do not return to your former base condition by sinning. Remember who is your head and of whose body you are a member. Never forget that you have been rescued from the power of darkness and brought into the light of the Kingdom of God' (CCC 1691).

What could be clearer? Living a moral life and obeying the commandments is really only possible as we take hold of all that Christ has done for us.

Let us keep this beautiful text of Pope Leo the Great in mind as we explore all that the Catechism teaches us about our vocation about the various elements of our moral and social nature and finally, about the power of the grace of Christ enabling us to love God and our neighbour.

'Christian, recognise your dignity and, now that you share in God's own nature, do not return to your former base condition by sinning' (St Leo the Great, CCC 1691)

YOUCAT 279

It is made abundantly clear that living the Christian life is first and foremost a matter of receiving and cooperating with the grace of God at work within us. Living a life 'worthy of our calling' depends utterly upon all that we have been seeing in the first two parts of the Catechism. In the Creed we confess our belief in the most holy Trinity and in the plan of God to grant us a share in the Trinitarian life through the Paschal Mystery of Christ's death and resurrection. The grace of what God has promised and has accomplished for us in Christ is communicated to us through the sacraments. It is the work of the Holy Spirit in us to conform us to the likeness of Christ.

Because Christ is our head, all of his faculties and virtues are communicated to us. Teach me, Holy Spirit, to make use of these to serve, love and glorify God.

MADE IN GOD'S IMAGE (CCC 1701-9)

When the words of Genesis 1:26 described the human person as being made 'in the image and likeness of God', the amazing mystery of what was being revealed could barely have been glimpsed. Only with the coming of Christ is Genesis 1:26 unveiled. Christ, the second person of the Trinity, is the true image of God, and who, in every respect, bears God's likeness. Because of the original sin of humanity, or the Fall, no other human person was truly 'in God's image and likeness'. Humanity was disfigured on account of sin, but healed in Christ. We are endowed with reason, freedom, an immortal soul and, transformed by the grace of Christ, we can live in a way that reflects God's holiness.

'Christ ... in the very revelation of the mystery of the Father and of his love, makes man fully manifest to himself and brings to light his exalted vocation.' (Gaudium et Spes 22, CCC 1701)

YOUCAT 280

Lord Jesus, may I become ever more closely united to you and by your grace be transformed into your likeness. Our true glory is to be fully formed in you.

'The Beatitudes ... shed light on the actions and attitudes characteristic of the Christian life; they are the paradoxical promises that sustain hope in the midst of tribulations.' (CCC 1717)

YOUCAT 282

We are created by God and redeemed by the saving work of Christ. Everything about our redeemed nature points to a vocation or a call to live a life of beatitude or blessedness. The Catechism describes the Beatitudes from Matthew 5:3-12 as the heart of Jesus' preaching and also sees them as revealing the face of Christ himself. They describe the blessed life Jesus himself lived, but they also summarise the vocation of all those who are united to Christ through faith and the sacraments. They contain both promises of what we shall become and a revelation of what we have begun to be, albeit in perhaps a dim or somewhat hidden way for the moment.

Lord Jesus, help us to take the Beatitudes to heart both as our calling and as your promised blessings - already manifest in the lives of Mary and the saints.

THE DESIRE FOR HAPPINESS (CCC 1718-19)

DAY 215

There is in the heart of every human being the desire for happiness. Although there are many things that make us happy, it is primarily the goodness found in these things that is the cause of happiness. But ultimately, all goodness derives from God, who is goodness itself. Every created thing shares in God's goodness. In the end, the human heart seeks the ultimate goodness that is found only in God, even though at times we can temporarily be satisfied with lesser goods. We can even be blinded by the lesser goods and fail to seek the face of God. The Beatitudes enable us to recognise and pursue the true good in our lives and eventually enjoy the glory of heaven.

'We all want to live happily; in the whole human race there is no one who does not assent to this proposition, even before it is fully articulated.' (St Augustine, CCC 1718)

YOUCAT 281

I thank you, Father, for everything that gives me happiness. I ask you to purify my heart so that your blessings in this life may lead me to you.

'Because of God's love and goodness toward us, ... he goes so far as to grant those who love him the privilege of seeing him.' (St Irenaeus, CCC1722)

YOUCAT 285

The word 'beatitude' is rich in meaning. It captures the joy, happiness and fullness of what God is calling us to. The New Testament has several expressions which describe what beatitude really is – the coming of God's kingdom; the vision of God; entering into the joy of the Lord and into God's rest. All of these hold out to us the mystery of our true dignity and, therefore, our ultimate vocation. We are called to enter into the glory of Christ and into the joy of the Trinitarian life. However, the challenge of life is full of choices. We are confronted daily to choose life or death, good or evil, God or that which falls short of God's love and goodness. Blessed are we when we choose God.

Holy Spirit, open my mind and my heart to the mystery of sharing in the Trinitarian life. Through you I can know the Father and the Son ever more fully.

Freedom and Responsibility (CCC 1730-38)

The fact that we can make moral choices introduces us to the notion of freedom. We are not programmed or predetermined to act in one way or another. Because we have the gifts of reason and will, we are able to shape our own lives so that we can take responsibility for our actions. When we do not bind ourselves to the ultimate good, which is God, there is the possibility of choosing either good or evil. The more our human choices move in the pursuit of good, the freer we become. The more our choices take us in the direction of evil, the less free we become. In fact we become enslaved. Scripture calls this the slavery of sin. Blessed are we when we choose God.

'Man is rational and therefore like God; he is created with free will and is master over his acts.' (St Irenaeus, CCC 1730)

YOUCAT 286-289

Help me, Lord, to understand that my true freedom lies in choosing the good and in living according to the truth that you have revealed.

'By his glorious cross Christ has won salvation for all men. He redeemed them from the sin that held them in bondage. 'For freedom Christ has set us free'.' (Gal 5:1) (CCC 1741)

YOUCAT 289

We have always experienced difficulty in understanding the difference between genuine human freedom and the licence to do whatever we wish. Since the original sin of humankind, there is a disorder within us – a certain slavery to sin. What we want to do and what we desire is not always good and the right thing. At times what we desire is harmful to ourselves and to the good of others. We need the salvation that Christ has won for us. He has set us free from the slavery of sin and sinful desires. By the Cross we can know a putting to death of the sinful drive within us, thereby setting us free to follow the promptings of the Holy Spirit and of divine grace.

Lord Jesus, I understand that there is a drive in me to do wrong and to act selfishly. May the power of your Cross put this drive to death.

The Sources of Moral Action (CCC 1749-54)

Day 219

We are moral agents, the father of our acts if you like and responsible for our actions. The Catechism distinguishes between the object of an act and the intention behind it. It is often said today 'the ends justify the means.' But this is not true, for example, if we lie in order to help our neighbour this good act does not justify the lie. Or, conversely, if we give to charity, a good act, of course, but broadcast our giving in a vainglorious way and for personal gain, our giving becomes wrong and disordered, it could be said to be evil. The circumstances and consequences surrounding an evil act can mitigate or explain it, but they cannot make an evil act good, or a wrong action morally right.

'The object, the intention, and the circumstances make up the 'sources' or constitutive elements of the morality of human acts.' (CCC 1750)

YOUCAT 291

Holy Spirit, please purify my conscience so that I may always recognise whether my chosen actions are really good or bad, even when my intentions are good.

'A morally good act requires the goodness of the object, of the end (my intentions), and of the circumstances together.' (CCC 1755)

YOUCAT 292

Today truth is considered something shifting, like the sand, subject to the ebb and flow of opinion and relative to the situation and circumstances we find ourselves in. The Catechism teaches us that an action is morally wrong regardless of the circumstances or situation. For example, sex before marriage is considered the norm today but fornication is always wrong. A basic moral teaching of the Catechism is this: one may not do evil so that good may result from it (CCC 1756). Murder is always murder. Adultery is always adultery. Perjury is always perjury. Fornication is always fornication. But also the thirst for praise and recognition corrupt the good action of something good like prayer or fasting.

Lord God, when I am faced with moral dilemmas and feel the pressure to perform a bad action, give me grace always to choose to do good.

The Passions (CCC 1762-70)

Day 221

The term 'passions' refers to the affections or the feelings. The Catechism (CCC 1772) lists the principal passions as love and hatred, desire and fear, joy, sadness and anger. Ideally, the passions are all in some way related to the good. Love, desire and joy are aroused and attracted by the good; hatred, anger and sadness are aroused by evil. However, our nature has become disordered by sin so that our passions can also become disordered – inclining us to evil actions. Hence the passions need to be governed by our reason and our will – directing them in the right direction. Christ heals our disordered passions.

'To love is to will the good of another.' (St Thomas Aquinas)

YOUCAT 293

Heal me, Lord Jesus, that my desire and love may be truly directed towards godly things, and my fear and sadness be aroused by sin and its consequences.

'Deep within our conscience we discover a law which we must obey. Its voice ever calling us to love and to do what is good and to avoid evil.' (CCC 1776)

YOUCAT 295-296

The great teacher on the subject of conscience was Blessed John Henry Newman. The Catechism draws on his insight to help us understand this interior law which resides in our most secret core and inner sanctuary. Conscience does not dictate nor is it a harsh taskmaster of duty and responsibility, it does not threaten or intimidate or force us. Rather, as Blessed John Henry Newman says, 'Conscience is a messenger of him, who both in nature and in grace, speaks to us behind a veil, and teaches and rules us by his representatives.' For Newman conscience was the aboriginal 'Vicar of Christ' living in us, guiding, leading, prompting and urging us to choose the good and reject what is evil.

Lord God, teach me to create the space and quiet within me so that I may be able to hear and listen to the voice of my conscience.

Formation of Conscience (CCC 1783-85)

Day 223

The critical issue for our conscience is that it must be well formed. While it is a natural gift that we possess, without formation and education its voice can become dulled and even corrupted. We are subjected to so many influences from the world around us and our disordered fallen nature can rebel against the voice of conscience as we can also rebel against the teaching of legitimate authority, especially that of Christ's Church. Therefore, the Catechism speaks of the lifelong task of educating the conscience. This begins in our earliest years and helps us to practice virtue and overcome selfishness, pride, complacency and our human weaknesses and faults. The Holy Spirit helps us to form our conscience.

'The education of the conscience guarantees freedom and engenders peace of heart.' (CCC 1784)

YOUCAT 297

Teach me, Holy Spirit, to examine my conscience each day, to discern the true moral nature of my actions. Help me to use Scripture and Church teaching wisely.

Day 224

Moral Choice (CCC 1786-89)

'It is prudence that immediately guides the judgment of conscience. The prudent person determines and directs their conduct in accordance with this judgment.' (CCC 1806)

YOUCAT 297

Day by day we are continually faced with moral choices. We can make good judgements in accordance with reason and God's law or erroneous judgements when we turn away from these. Sometimes the moral choices are difficult or unclear. This is when we need the help of the virtue of prudence, of wise teachers and the Holy Spirit. The Catechism also offers three rules which always apply: Never do evil that good may result; do unto others what you would wish them to do to you; and follow the law of charity, which proceeds by way of respect for one's neighbour and his conscience - never 'do anything that makes your brother stumble'. We pray to the Holy Spirit for guidance.

My dear Lord, have mercy on me. How often do I act wrongly and how seldom rightly. Grant me your forgiveness and the wisdom and strength to do better.

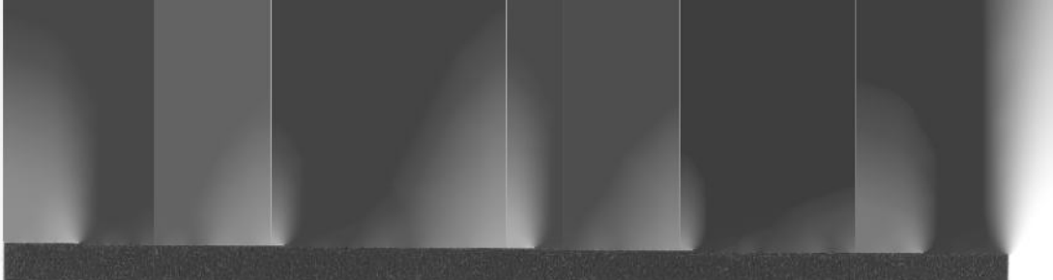

It is possible for the moral conscience to be in ignorance and therefore to make false or erroneous judgments about acts which are about to be or already have been carried out. But it is not enough to say 'my conscience is clear'. We are responsible for educating our conscience, for taking the time and trouble to inform ourselves about right and wrong. We need also to understand that our conscience may be in ignorance because it has become dulled simply by the habits of sin. A lively and informed conscience is a gateway to God. Not only can we learn to hear God's voice within us, we also open ourselves to his love and his mercy. Key to a good conscience is learning to examine our lives.

'The more a correct conscience prevails, the more do persons and groups turn aside from blind choice and try to be guided by objective standards of moral conduct.' (Gaudium et Spes 16, CCC 1794)

YOUCAT 298

I thank you, Father, for the gift of conscience – the very first way that you are present to me. Teach me to treasure my conscience by educating and examining it.

WHAT IS A VIRTUE? (CCC 1803)

'A virtue is an habitual and firm disposition to do the good' (CCC 1803)

So far we have seen that the Catechism is building up a picture of the various elements that contribute to our living our life in accordance with God's call to us. We have seen that we are created in the image of God and now by the power of the Spirit we are enabled to live in his likeness so as to live a life of blessedness. This life is made up of free moral choices, even in the midst of struggle against our own disordered nature. The passions and our conscience play a part, but this week we shall also consider the role of the virtues. The virtues are to the moral life what habits and skills are to a craftsman or artist. It is a lifelong task to master the virtues and produce the fruit of the Holy Spirit (Galatians 5:22).

YOUCAT 299

Lord Jesus, help me not only to do good, but also create in me the dispositions that will lead me to seek and desire the good with all my heart, mind and will.

Anyone who wants to master a certain skill has to build up a number of habits. A pianist needs to be able to play a musical scale almost without thinking about it. Typing or texting usually involves a similar habit. In the Christian life, making good moral choices is rendered so much easier if we have developed the habit of choosing the good rather than the habit of choosing the wrong or bad thing. Developing a habit takes effort and practice and also involves the whole person – the intellect, the will and the desires all working together. The more we consistently and consciously make good moral choices and act in a good way, the more the habits or virtues will be formed.

'Human virtues are firm attitudes, stable dispositions, habitual perfections of intellect and will that govern our actions, order our passions and guide our conduct according to reason and faith.'
(CCC 1804)

YOUCAT 300

Holy Spirit, help me to be aware of the times in the day that I make moral decisions, so that I may more consciously develop the habit of choosing the good.

'Prudence is the virtue that disposes practical reason to discern our true good in every circumstance and to choose the right means of achieving it.' (CCC 1806)

YOUCAT 301

Based on the teaching of Scripture (Wisdom 8:7) and a long tradition in the Church, there are four virtues that are recognised as central and around which all other virtues can be grouped. They are the Cardinal Virtues – Prudence, Justice, Fortitude and Temperance. Prudence has been described as 'the charioteer of all virtues'. It is the virtue which guides the judgment of conscience and drawing upon practical reason seeks to apply moral principles to particular situations where a moral decision or choice is required. Prudence means that we are consciously trying to discern what is right and wrong, rather than simply acting unthinkingly.

Lord, the image of the charioteer is a great help. The gift of prudence enables me to hold together all the various virtues and passions and leads me forward.

The Scriptures, especially the Old Testament, speak many times of 'the just man'. The New Testament reveals that the whole law of God can be summed up in two commandments – love God and love your neighbour. Justice is that moral virtue or basic habit of heart and mind that points us in the direction of God and neighbour. With regard to God, justice is sometimes called the 'virtue of religion'. It leads us to give God his due worship and obedience. With regard to our neighbour, this virtue leads us to respects the rights, conscience and good of others, including what is called the common good, thus promoting equity and harmony.

'Justice is the moral virtue that consists in the consistent and firm will to give their due to God and to neighbour.' (CCC 1807)

YOUCAT 302

'This is what the Lord God asks of you: only this, to act justly, to love tenderly and to walk humbly with your God.' (Micah 6:8)

Day 230

The Cardinal Virtues – Fortitude (CCC 1808)

'Fortitude is the moral virtue that ensures firmness in difficulties and constancy in the pursuit of the good.' (CCC 1808)

YOUCAT 303

In the world in which we live, moral choices can be very difficult. We experience, first of all, a battle within ourselves because we are often drawn, by our fallen nature, to actions that are immoral or wrong. We also experience the temptations of the evil one. From the world we are also subjected to various pressures to conform to popular opinion and common practice. We fear being different or persecuted. In extreme situations, our faith and way of life could even lead to the threat of imprisonment or death. Fortitude is the virtue that enables us to be strong against all of these forces. Our own fortitude is greatly strengthened by our union with Christ, who was victorious over every difficulty.

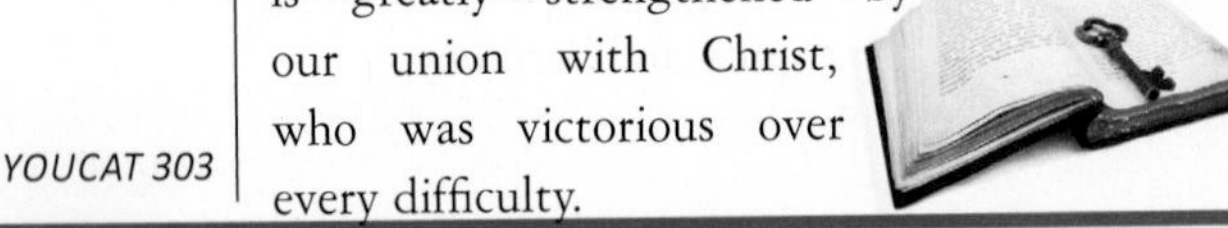

'I was pressed down and was falling, but the Lord came to my help. The Lord is my strength and my song, he has become my saviour'. (Psalm 118:13-14)

THE CARDINAL VIRTUES – TEMPERANCE (CCC 1809)

The world is full of things that give us pleasure and bring us happiness. The world and humanity is created by God, and as Genesis 1 tells us 'He saw that it was good' (Genesis 1:10). At the same time, the fall of humanity into sin has had a profoundly damaging effect upon us. Our nature has become disordered and our appetites and desires don't always function as God intended them. We sometimes allow our desires to become excessive, we indulge them too much. As a result, we can do harm to ourselves or to others. We can turn God's good gifts into gods that become the centre of our lives. Temperance is the habit of keeping these things in order and balance and moderation.

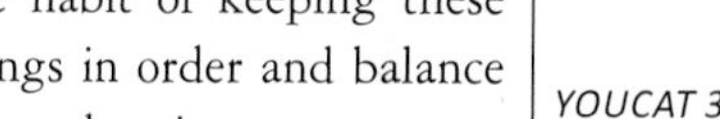

'Temperance is the moral virtue that moderates the attraction of pleasures and provides balance in the use of created goods.' (CCC 1809)

YOUCAT 304

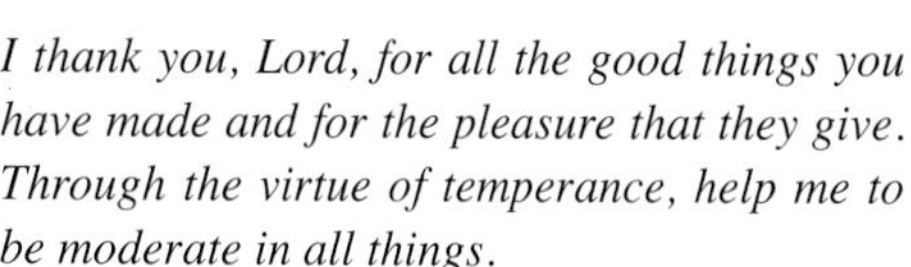

I thank you, Lord, for all the good things you have made and for the pleasure that they give. Through the virtue of temperance, help me to be moderate in all things.

'It is not easy for us, wounded by sin, to maintain moral balance. Christ's gift of salvation offers us the grace necessary to persevere in the pursuit of the virtues.' (CCC 1811)

YOUCAT 305

The human virtues are the natural possession of every human being. Every person can make progress in fostering and nurturing them, by constantly seeking to put them into practice. As with any habit, it is practice that enables them to be formed. Nevertheless our human nature has become damaged by sin and by the fall of humanity (Original Sin). It is not easy to foster virtues and this always involves a struggle. As we have seen, there are forces at work against our full human development and progress. The work of Christ's redemption is needed if we are to persevere in the pursuit of virtues. We should therefore seek the help of grace to strengthen the virtues within us.

Father, I want to live a moral life that is pleasing to you. I thank you for the grace you give me through the Holy Spirit and the sacraments.

This week we look at the theological virtues. We know them as Faith, Hope and Charity. There is a close connection between the moral virtues and the theological virtues, although there is a significant difference also. We saw that the human moral virtues are natural, a gift to everyone. However, because we are wounded by sin, we still need God's grace even for the natural virtues to be developed. The theological virtues, on the other hand, are a particular gift to those who are baptised. Their aim is to enable us, to give us the capacity, to share in the life of the Trinitarian God. These virtues are principally directed to God and cultivated within by grace.

'The theological virtues relate directly to God. They dispose Christians to live in a relationship with the Holy Trinity.' (CCC 1812)

YOUCAT 306

How great are your gifts, O Lord. By Faith, Hope and Charity I can rise to the greatest of heights – to know you as a son or daughter.

DAY 234

THE THEOLOGICAL VIRTUES – FAITH (CCC 1814-16)

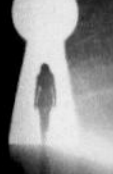

'Faith is the theological virtue by which we believe in God and believe all that he has said and revealed to us, and that the Holy Church proposes for our belief ...' (CCC 1814)

YOUCAT 307

The first of the baptismal virtues is the gift of Faith. As a virtue or a habit it is the ability and the activity of accepting God's revelation of himself and his salvation in Christ. To receive God and his salvation is to give ourselves to God to grow in our knowledge of him and commit ourselves to doing his will. But if our faith is to be a living faith we must be willing to express and consciously live by it through remaining in union with Christ and his Body, the Church. As the whole Catechism teaches us, Faith is to be professed, celebrated in the sacraments and in prayer, and also expressed in the life we live and the moral choices we make.

Lord, like the father of the epileptic boy who cried out to you, 'Lord, I believe, help my unbelief' (Mark 9:24).

Hope relates to our ultimate vocation to eternal happiness in heaven. Hope enables us to rise above our earthly goals and ambitions and to order our whole lives towards what God has promised in the life to come. The Catechism refers to Abraham as both the origin and model of hope. God's promise to him was really the promise of a completely new creation of humanity in which the wound of sin is healed. This promise, symbolised by Isaac, became a reality in Jesus' resurrection. While we do not yet see the final reality of God's new creation in heaven, hope gives us a glimpse and a share in what is to come and also strengthens us in the face of present trials and discouragements.

'Dream that the more you struggle, the more you prove the love that you bear your guard, and the more you will rejoice one day with your Beloved, in a happiness and rapture that can never end.' (St Teresa of Avila)

YOUCAT 308

Almighty God, relying on your promises and your great mercy, I trust that with the help of your grace I may attain the final glory of life in heaven.

DAY 236

THE THEOLOGICAL VIRTUES – CHARITY (CCC 1822-29)

'Charity is the theological virtue by which we love God above all things ... and our neighbour as ourselves for the love of God.' (CCC 1822)

YOUCAT 309

The gift and virtue of charity resides first and foremost in Jesus Christ himself. Indeed, Jesus speaks of his own love as being the love with which the Father loves him. It is this same love between Jesus and the Father that is infused into us – the greatest fruit of our baptism. We can see here most clearly that the theological virtues give us the capacity to share in the very life of the Trinity. But just as the love of the Father in Jesus led him also to love his disciples and even his enemies, so also the virtue of charity in us must have its expression in our love for others. Love inspires every virtue. This is why St Augustine famously said, 'Love and do what you will.'

Lord Jesus, you said: 'As the Father has loved me, so have I loved you; abide in my love.' Grant that knowing your love for me, I might grow in love for others.

In fidelity to the Sacred Scriptures, the Catechism finally mentions the gifts and fruits of the Spirit. These are all listed in the writings of St Paul. There is a distinction between them. The seven gifts of the Spirit –wisdom, understanding, counsel, fortitude, knowledge, piety and fear of the Lord – are all virtues that properly belong to Christ himself. The Spirit conforms us to Christ's likeness by sharing Christ's virtues. The Holy Spirit also forms in us what St Paul calls 'fruits'. They are perfections of the glory to come which are being formed in us now – charity, joy, peace, patience, kindness, goodness, generosity, gentleness, faithfulness, self-control, modesty and chastity.

'For all who are led by the Spirit of God are sons of God ... If children, then heirs, heirs of God and fellow heirs with Christ.' (Romans 8:14, 17; CCC 1831)

YOUCAT 310-311

Teach me, Holy Spirit, to embrace your living presence in my life. Grant that the gifts and fruits of your presence may shine ever more clearly in me.

'The Gospel is the revelation in Jesus Christ of God's mercy to sinners ... to receive his mercy we must admit our faults.' (CCC 1846-1847)

YOUCAT 314

'Like a physician who probes the wound before treating it, God, by his Word and by his Spirit casts a living light on sin' (CCC 1848). The Catechism reveals in these words a great truth about the mercy and salvation of God. During the previous days we have seen again and again the truth about our nature being wounded by sin. But in order for true conversion to take place in us, we need to be convinced that sin is a reality in us. This is not in order to weigh us down with guilt, but is the first sign of the Spirit's work in us – a double gift – it is a confirmation that our conscience is working properly, and is the beginning of the work of our redemption.

Holy Spirit, help me to recognise sin in my life, both mortal and venial. May this recognition be a joy because it means that you are at work in me, leading me to salvation.

Mortal and Venial Sin and The Vices (CCC 1849-69)

Day 239

Sin is described as an offence against right reason, truth and right conscience; a failure in genuine love for God and neighbour; an utterance, a deed, or a desire contrary to the eternal law. As such, it is therefore an offence against God. There are a variety of ways of listing and classifying sins and the Catechism provides several examples from the Scriptures. The Church distinguishes between mortal and venial sin. We would want a doctor to tell us the gravity of our condition if we were sick or ill, so too we welcome this teaching concerning the elements that make up the gravity of sin and the vices that develop through repetition of sin, because it brings clarity and healing.

'Mortal sin, by attacking the vital principle within us – that is, charity – necessitates a new initiative of God's mercy and a conversion of heart which is normally accomplished within the setting of the Sacrament of Reconciliation.' (CCC 1856)

YOUCAT 315-316

Lord Jesus, I ask you to show me where there is mortal sin in my life. I need to know the truth so that I can seek your remedy in the Sacrament of Reconciliation.

Day 240

Community (CCC 1877-89)

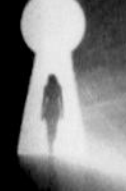

'The human person is and ought to be the principle, the subject and the end of all social institutions.' (Gaudium et Spes 25, CCC 1881)

YOUCAT 321-322

We are called to fellowship, friendship and fraternity. Our vocation invites us to live in harmony and communion with one another. Human society exists for the well being and flourishing of the human person and especially the human family. State or societal systems that do not care for the human person in their physical, intellectual and spiritual dimensions diminish first the person and then the state. The human person is never a means to a collective goal. Subsidiarity is the Church's understanding that a higher social order (eg. the state) should not take over the rights and duties of a lower social order (eg. the family).

I thank you, Father, for civil society and the family, and all other groupings that promote the good and growth of human persons. I pray for the reformation of groups that have become ends in themselves.

St Paul exhorted the first believers to be subject to the governing authorities and to live good and law-abiding lives (Romans 13:1-2). The rule of law, legitimate authority and wise government deserve respect and obedience. However, those who abuse power, create unjust laws and trample on human dignity and human rights, do not. Dietrich Bonhoefer opposed the Nazis and Pope John Paul II worked alongside the trade union Solidarity in Poland by resisting the oppression of their communist masters. Authority that seeks the common good and employs morally acceptable means should be obeyed. Those who do not must be resisted; their authority is not binding on conscience.

'Every human community needs an authority to govern it. The foundation of such authority lies in human nature. Its role is to ensure the common good of the society.' (CCC 1898)

YOUCAT 325-326

Today I pray especially for all civil authorities. May they recognise their double responsibility: to the society of persons who chose them and to God from whom their authority derives.

DAY 242

THE COMMON GOOD (CCC 1905-1917)

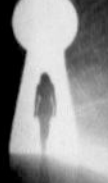

'The common good is ... 'the sum total of social conditions which allow people, either as groups or as individuals, to reach their fulfilment more fully and more easily'.' (Letter of Barnabas, CCC 1906)

YOUCAT 327

The quotation to the left provides a definition of the common good. The Catechism then delineates three essential elements: respect for the person - his or her fundamental and inalienable rights, which include freedom to fulfil his/her vocation, the right to act according to conscience, privacy and freedom of religion; the social well-being and development of the group itself – the Catechism here lists the things needed for a truly human life (CCC 1908); and, the common good requires peace – the stability and security of a just order, and legitimate personal and collective defence. In these matters the political community and its structures have a key role to play.

Turn my heart, Lord, from merely selfish concerns to a desire for the common good of all. May I recognise your call in the plight of others.

'It is necessary that all participate, each according to his position and role, in promoting the common good.' (1913)

YOUCAT 328

We are encouraged to participate at some level in serving the common good. Our very human dignity calls for this. In the first place, we can serve the common good by faithfully carrying out the personal responsibilities of our own state in life, especially with regard to the family (e.g. educating our families), and to conscientiousness at work. However, there is a further dimension of serving the common good and that is through various forms of participation in public life according to one's time and gifts. It is also important to consider ways in which the common good is undermined and eroded: fraud, greed, tax evasion, tax avoidance and huge bonuses.

It belongs to my human dignity to pursue the common good. Help me Lord, to recognise the ways that I might do this. Bless all who serve in public life.

Everything with regard to civil society, civil authority and social justice is rooted in respect for the dignity of the human person. This dignity is something transcendent. It is not primarily defined by us but derives from the good Creator. Social life and order must always recognise the true worth of the person as its ultimate goal. A number of human rights arise from our dignity as children of God, rather than simply from particular philosophies of society. In the Gospels we are commended to see others as 'another self' and have the responsibility of making ourselves a neighbour to others and actively serving them. In the end it is the love of Christ within us, rather than legislation, that makes this possible.

'Social justice can be obtained only in respecting the transcendent dignity of man. The person represents the ultimate end of society, which is ordered to him.'(CCC 1929)

YOUCAT 329

Lord Jesus, you taught us in the Parable of the Good Samaritan that it was you who were first a 'neighbour' to me. Help me by your grace to become a neighbour to others.

DAY 245

EQUALITY AND DIFFERENCE (CCC 1934-38)

'I have willed that one should need another and that all should be my ministers in distributing the graces and gifts they have received from me.' (St Catherine of Siena, CCC 1937)

YOUCAT 330-331

We derive our dignity from being created in the image of God, and also, through redemption in Christ. We each share equality of dignity and equality of rights. Therefore, every form of discrimination 'must be curbed and eradicated as incompatible with God's design' (CCC 1935). However, it is also clear that, in God's design, not all persons are equally equipped with everything they need for developing their physical and spiritual life. In God's plan, we are dependent upon one another and are obliged to share our gifts with those who need (lack) them. Some inequalities (economical and social disparities) are sinful and call for repentance both as individuals and as nations.

Lord God, you have blessed me with many gifts and talents. Help me not to claim them selfishly but place them at the service of my fellow human beings.

The Polish trade union 'Solidarity' appeared on the international scene in the context of the struggles of the workers in Gdansk but had its origins in the teaching of Pius XII. Solidarity does not just mean simply a means of organising workers against oppressive regimes, but is rather a call to a change of mindset in all of us. Pope Pius XII said that the law of human solidarity is 'dictated and imposed both by our common origin, and by the equality in rational nature of all peoples, whatever nation they belong to' (CCC 1939). Solidarity is a way of thinking about each other and can become effective in overcoming the conflicts and tensions of various groups and nations.

'Solidarity is an eminently Christian virtue. It practises the sharing of spiritual goods even more than material ones.' (CCC 1948)

YOUCAT 332

Lord, teach us to respect the rights of all who are created in your image. Inspire us to love all people, to recognise our equality, and to act in solidarity for the common good.

'The natural law, the Creator's very good work, provides the solid foundation on which we can build the structure of moral rules to guide our choices.' (CCC 1959)

YOUCAT 333

We have been seeing all along that although we are called as human beings to live a life of happiness and blessedness, we are, in fact, wounded by original sin and the effects of personal sin. As a result, in order to live as we should we need God's help. This comes in two ways, as indicated by the title to this section in the Catechism: through the law (natural and revealed) and through God's grace. The Natural Law is what we are able to perceive as rational beings – the need to do good and avoid evil. We are able, even if we do not always do so, to use our reason to understand the principles that govern right and wrong. The Ten Commandments express these principles.

Father, you have given to us the gift of reason so that we can truly discern right from wrong. All laws have their basis in reason and your eternal law.

The Old Law (CCC 1961-64)

Day 248

While the natural moral law can, and to some extent is, known naturally by us through reason, it is the plight of humanity, because of sin, that our reason does not always work properly. For the sake of humanity, God chose Israel and made known to them, by a special revelation, the truths about right and wrong that can be the foundation for the vocation of every person made in the image of God. In spite of being God's gift to Israel, the Law of Moses is imperfect. It can make known right and wrong but it cannot help us to do it. Rather it reveals our need for God's salvation in Christ. We treasure the Old Law as a tutor and as a prophecy of Christ.

'The Law of Moses expresses many truths naturally accessible to reason.' (CCC 1961)

YOUCAT 334

Thank you Father for the Ten Commandments and the universal principles they teach us. Grant us the grace of Christ to understand and apply them in our lives.

'The New Law is called a law of love because it makes us act out of the love infused by the Holy Spirit ... a law of grace, because it confers the grace to act ...' (CCC 1972)

YOUCAT 336

Today we reflect on the great crown of all laws – the law of the Gospel. This Law expressed in the Sermon on the Mount (Matthew 5-8) is the fullness and the fulfilment of all our ways of coming to know the right way to live. First of all, the Law of the Gospel reveals fully what the Old Law only imperfectly revealed. Second, the Holy Spirit imprints this New Law interiorly in our hearts along with the gift of charity and thereby enables us in the living of this law, which up to that point no law had been able to do – even when we could read the moral law in our conscience. In Christ, the New Law becomes the gift of grace and this is not from ourselves or our own effort but is a free gift.

Teach me, Holy Spirit, to meditate on the Sermon on the Mount and imprint its precepts in my heart, so that I may become conformed to Christ.

'Justification' is the summit of God's work of salvation as it becomes a reality in each one of us. From the beginning, God created us to live in his presence and live a life worthy of his calling. Sin has disrupted this, and although we could still read the moral law in our minds and consciences and in the Decalogue, the problem of sin remained. In Christ a new work of God has taken place. His death is a remedy for sin both as a barrier between us and God and as a corrupting power within us. By the gift of the Spirit, justification is made a reality in each of us, reconciling us to God and empowering us in Christ to live the New Law.

'The grace of the Holy Spirit has the power to justify us, that is, to cleanse us from our sins and to communicate to us the righteousness of God ...' (CCC 1987)

YOUCAT 337

I am filled with gratitude that through baptism I have received the grace of Christ, by which I am freed from sin and made a new creation - to live a godly life.

GRACE (CCC 1996-2004)

'The grace of Christ is the gratuitous gift that God makes to us of his own life, infused by the Holy Spirit into our soul to heal it of sin and to sanctify it.' (CCC 1999)

YOUCAT 338-340

'Grace' has really been the subject of the whole Catechism. Grace is about God's action and help in our lives. While we do not feel it, we can see its fruit. Ultimately, it is God's gift of himself to us, enabling us to know God as Father, to become united with Jesus in his death and resurrection and to receive the infusion of the Holy Spirit and the gift of charity to inspire all our actions. Grace creates in us a permanent disposition to live and act in accord with God's call. It also refers to special moments of God's help in our lives – the sacraments, charisms and grace for our particular state in life. An essential element however, is that we learn to cooperate with God's grace.

Lord Jesus Christ, your grace is an awesome and overwhelming gift. I can hardly begin to appreciate it. Help me to trust in and to cooperate with your grace.

With so much talk of God's grace, is there anything we can do that merits reward? This is the problem of merit. We do not earn our salvation or indeed do anything that puts God under some sort of obligation towards us. However, another aspect of the great love and mercy of God is that he 'has freely chosen to associate man with his work of grace' (CCC 2008). In other words, after the initial pure grace of forgiveness and justification, God invites us to cooperate with him and he rewards our cooperation. We can thereby merit graces and blessings for ourselves and others, through our prayers and good works. Grace is always at the root of our merits – something the saints were always aware of.

'Grace, by uniting us to Christ in active love, ensures the supernatural quality of our acts and consequently their merit before God and before men.' (CCC 2011)

YOUCAT 341

Lord, there is nothing I can do to earn salvation – it is entirely your gift. Yet you permit me to use your grace and your inspirations to merit further graces for myself and others.

'... all the faithful, whatever their condition or state, ... are called by the Lord to that perfection of sanctity by which the Father himself is perfect,' (CCC 825) (Lumen Gentium II)

YOUCAT 342

We are called to holiness. The Dogmatic Constitution on the Church (*Lumen Gentium*) describes holiness as essentially union with Jesus Christ, and through him participation in the mystery of the Holy Trinity. It is significant that holiness is presented as progress in union with Christ rather than simply as a certain kind of behaviour. It emphasises once again that our actions and moral choices arise from the grace of Christ in us and the love infused by the Spirit. The way of holiness also involves union with the Cross of Christ, because it includes both renunciation (of sinful ways) and spiritual battle (against our fallen nature and the evil one).

Give me, Lord Jesus, the courage and strength to embrace the call to holiness. Keep me united to you and grant me perseverance in spite of trials and failures.

The Church as Moral Guide (CCC 2030-2040)

Day 254

Today we look at the role of the Church and our response to the Church with regard to our living the Christian life and the day-to-day moral choices we make. The Church is presented under the images of both Mother and Teacher – emphasising her care for all who are baptised and also the responsibility Christ gave her, through the Apostles, for teaching the faithful. The Church's teaching, including the teaching about morality, has the authority of Christ himself, and brings the light of God's revelation to various questions of a moral nature. For this reason, each of us has the duty to allow the Church's teaching to shape our consciences according to God's truth.

'It is in the Church, in communion with all the baptised that the Christian fulfils his vocation. From the Church he receives the Word of God containing the teachings of 'the law of Christ'.' (CCC 2030)

YOUCAT 343-344

I thank you, Father, for the Church; for her care and fidelity to your truth. Help me to receive her teachings as the truth willed by you for my salvation.

'The precepts of the Church are set in the context of a moral life bound to and nourished by the liturgical life.'
(CCC 2041)

YOUCAT 345

The precepts of the Church were established in view of the fact that living the Christian life and making good moral choices is only made possible for us through the work of God's grace in us. This has been the consistent theme throughout this section of the Catechism. The moral life is the fruit of our union with Christ and the salvation he has given to us. It is the fruit also of the Holy Spirit dwelling within us. It is clear, therefore, that the life of prayer and the sacraments are essential if we are going to live our lives in the power of God's grace. This translates into five precepts which ensure at least a minimum of contact with the sources of grace.

Help me Lord, to attend Mass each Sunday; to confess and to receive Holy Communion at least once a year; to observe days of fasting and abstinence and support the Church's needs.

We have now reached the final few paragraphs of the first section of Part 3 of the Catechism. The next section will reflect upon the moral law as it is contained in the Ten Commandments. Today, these few paragraphs remind us that each of us can make a significant difference by striving to be faithful to living a good moral life in accordance with the teachings of Christ, that the Church lovingly makes known to us. The Church's mission is to proclaim the Gospel and manifest its truth and beauty before the world. If this mission is to succeed, the life and witness of every individual member of the Church is an essential element.

'The fidelity of the baptised is a primordial condition for the proclamation of the Gospel and for the Church's mission in the world.'
(CCC 2044)

YOUCAT 347

Holy Spirit, grant that my own life may contribute to the building up of the Church and of enhancing its mission, rather than being a hindrance or a scandal.

DAY 257

CHRIST THE RABBI – TEACHER (CCC 2052-55)

'Jesus acknowledged the Ten Commandments, but he also showed the power of the Spirit in their letter.' (CCC 2054)

YOUCAT 348

The second section of the Catechism's teaching on 'Life in Christ' is going to look in detail at the Ten Commandments. However, the opening few paragraphs immediately indicate that we shall be looking at the commandments only in the light of Christ. In the Gospel, a young man asks Jesus 'what must I do to have eternal life?' (Matthew 19:16). Jesus replies that he must keep the commandments. However, he goes on to say that, if he wished to be perfect, the young man should become Jesus' disciple. In Jesus we find the perfection of obedience to the commandments – both in the sense that Jesus alone perfectly lives them, and in the sense that Jesus reveals their true meaning and interpretation.

Lord Jesus, you have called me to be your disciple and to see you as my supreme good. Fill me with your love and open to me the true meaning of the commandments.

The Catechism wants us first of all to understand the original context in which the Ten Commandments were given. It was the time of the Exodus, when Israel was delivered from its slavery in Israel and was invited into the freedom of a covenant relationship with God. From the way that the giving of the Commandments is described in Scripture, it is clear that they represent God's revelation of himself (to Moses) and his revelation of a way of life that is free of the slavery of sin. To embrace the commandments is to embrace God himself and to be drawn into the covenant with him. They are the initiative of God, they open us up to his grace, leading us into God's freedom.

'The Ten Commandments take on their full meaning within the covenant.' (CCC 2061)

YOUCAT p.192-193

Lord God, the Ten Commandments are first and foremost a revelation of your love and your loving plan to call me to freedom from sin. May I respond to, and love the commandments.

DAY 259

Love of God, Love of Neighbour (CCC 2064-68)

'In fidelity to Scripture and in conformity with the example of Jesus, the tradition of the Church has acknowledged the primordial importance and significance of the Decalogue.' (CCC 2064)

YOUCAT 350

The Ten Commandments provide a statement of what is required in the love of God (first three commandments) and the love of neighbour (last seven commandments). From the time of St Augustine onwards, the Ten Commandments have formed a central part in the catechesis of people preparing for baptism and in the teaching of the faithful – especially in the basic formation of children. Memorising them has held an important place also. The commandments form an organic unity. Each commandment refers to each other one and to all of them. Thus, honouring mother and father is incomplete without loving and honouring God above all things. And loving God also includes the obligations to our neighbour.

Lord, I see through the commandments that my faith in you and my social responsibilities are not in two separate compartments. Help me to express my faith by loving my neighbour.

Although the Ten Commandments have come to us through God's revelation, in fact, they simply state the natural law that lies in the hearts of all and is accessible by the use of reason. As has been said many times throughout this booklet, the heart of men and women and our reason have been affected by sin so that we do not always clearly see what is natural for us to see. Therefore, God has also revealed the natural law in the Ten Commandments. Because they represent both the natural law of man and the revealed will of God, the Ten Commandments are a grave obligation for us all. But the presence of Jesus in us enables us to live the commandments in holiness.

'From the beginning, God had implanted in the heart of man the precepts of the natural law. Then he was content to remind him of them. This was the Decalogue.' (St Irenaeus, CCC 2070)

YOUCAT 351

To live the Ten Commandments is to be most fully human. Lord Jesus, may I live in close union with you so that I may become what God made me to be.

DAY 261

WORSHIP THE LORD YOUR GOD (CCC 2083-2086)

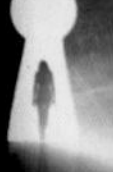

'To serve God first.' *(St Joan of Arc)*

The first commandment, 'You shall worship the Lord your God and him only shall you serve' is the most important one, the cornerstone if you like, of all the others. Our vocation is to make God known, to witness to his truth and so bear testimony that we are created 'in the image and likeness of God' (Genesis 1:26). The first commandment invites us to examine, pray and reflect on the question: Who is God? God is unchanging, constant, faithful, just and without evil. God is mighty, all-powerful, kind and compassionate to all he has created. As the Catechism says: 'Who could not love him when contemplating the treasure of goodness and love he has poured out on us?'

YOUCAT 352

You are the Lord our God, teach me to worship you in faith, hope and love, and place all my trust in you.

Our vocation is an invitation to love God with all our heart, mind, soul and strength. This was confirmed in the Old Testament, 'Choose to love the Lord your God and to obey him and to commit yourself to him for he is your life' (Deuteronomy 30:20). And confirmed in the New Testament: 'Love the Lord your God with all your heart and with all your soul and with all your mind. This is the first and greatest commandment' (Matthew 22:27-28). Our love for God is the litmus test, the benchmark, of our walk with God. As C S Lewis said, 'Every Christian would agree that our spiritual health is exactly proportional to our love for God.' God thirsts for our love; and we thirst for God.

'Late have I loved thee, O beauty, so ancient, so new. For behold, thou were within me and I outside.' (St Augustine of Hippo)

YOUCAT 352

Lord, teach me to seize every day, each opportunity, and every moment, to see you more clearly, follow you more nearly and love you more dearly, day by day.

'If anyone serves, he should do it with the strength God provides, so that in all things God may be praised through Jesus Christ.' (1 Peter 4:11)

YOUCAT 353

What does it mean to serve God? It means that we possess an attitude or disposition which is directed towards giving God our adoration, our prayer and our sacrifice. To adore God is to be prepared to fall on our knees confessing our 'nothingness', acknowledging that we are beggars in need of God's grace, mercy and forgiveness. We cannot serve God unless we pray - in prayer, through praise, thanksgiving, intercession and petition, we give God the gift of worship he deserves. The only true sacrifice we can offer to God is that of a humble, contrite, repentant and broken spirit (Psalm 51:7) which sincerely prays: 'Lord, have mercy on me a sinner.'

Lord, I promise to serve you with all my heart, soul and strength and I vow today to devote myself to serving your Church by striving to be a loyal and faithful servant.

A foundational human freedom is religious freedom. This freedom is rooted in our very dignity of being human and is at the core of our human rights. This understanding informs our respect for other religions recognizing in them the light of truth. We treat with love, prudence and patience those who oppose or reject the faith through error or ignorance. Today we raise our voice on behalf of those who suffer through loss or infringement of their religious freedom: the Coptic Christians in Egypt; the Chaldean Christians in Iraq; and the plight of the Palestinian Christians, who are subject to many restrictions, forcing many to leave the Holy Land.

[Human freedom requires], '....the priority of ethics over technology, the primacy of persons over things, the superiority of spirit over matter.' (Redemptor Hominis, 16)

YOUCAT 354

Lord God, united in a communion of faith, hope, and love, let us live the truth in freedom and love so as to open wide the doors to Christ!

'Therefore, my dear friends, flee from idolatry.' (1 Corinthians 10:14)

GK Chesterton said, 'When we cease to worship God we do not worship nothing but we worship everything.' We don't tend to think of ourselves as idolaters. However, Origen, the early Church Scripture scholar, taught that an idolater is: '[someone]....who transfers his indestructible notion of God to anything other than God.' We bow down to wealth, money and celebrity. We pay these temporal and fleeting things an instinctive homage arising from a profound faith. We continue to look to horoscopes, astrology, clairvoyance and the wearing of charms for comfort and guidance. Our faith rejects such superstitions, magic and divination, and we put our lives in the hands of God and his loving Providence.

YOUCAT 355-356

Lord, we reject the idols of our day and cling to you the living God who gives life to the world and intervenes in history.

ATHEISM AND AGNOSTICISM (CCC 2123-2128)

DAY 266

Atheism and agnosticism have many forms but essentially an atheist rejects or denies the existence of God whereas an agnostic does not deny God's existence but finds it impossible to affirm or deny. In truth, as the Catechism says, 'Agnosticism is all too often equivalent to practical atheism' (CCC 2128). A certain form of aggressive or militant atheism is very much in vogue today. Its proponents seize every opportunity to make their dogmatic case. However, God's existence and loving plan for us is in harmony with the deepest desires, aspirations and longings of the human heart. We pray for atheists and agnostics that they would come to a knowledge of the living God.

'Believers when careless about their instruction in the faith, or present its teaching falsely, or even fail in their religious, moral, or social life, [believers] must be said to conceal rather than to reveal the true nature of God and of religion.' (Gaudium et Spes 19)

YOUCAT 357

Lord, today, we give you thanks and praise for the gift of faith and of reason, which together, working in harmony, lead us to acknowledge you as the Living God.

'..The honour rendered to an image passes to its prototype and whoever venerates an image venerates the person portrayed in it.' (St Basil)

YOUCAT 358

The first commandment says, 'You shall not make for yourself a graven image' (Exodus 20:3). However, throughout the Old Testament it became clear that, progressively and over time, God permitted or ordained the making of images that pointed towards our salvation by the incarnate Word, Jesus of Nazareth, the Word among us (John 1:14). We see this in the bronze serpent (Numbers 21:4-9) the ark of the covenant (Exodus 25:10) and the cherubim (1 Kings 6:23). By becoming man, Jesus ushered in a new economy of images, and since the Seventh Council of Nicea (787 AD) the Church has justified and permitted the veneration of icons - of Christ, of Mary the Mother of God, of angels and saints.

Lord, you are the author of beauty and greater than all your works. By contemplating, praying and venerating the icons of our faith we learn to come into the presence of your transcendence and worship the living God.

The second commandment, although specific in relation to God's name, in a wider sense refers also to our attitude and speech towards all sacred things. What revelation makes clear to us is that God is not anonymous and has a name. Jesus' mission was to reveal his Father's name. 'I have revealed your name to those whom you took from the world to give me' (John 17:6). We must not abuse God's name in speech or gesture or by our actions, but rather bless, praise and glorify it. The Israelites, out of respect for God do not pronounce his name (CCC 209). By giving his life to free us from sin, Jesus reveals that he bears the divine name. We adore and give thanks and praise the name of Jesus.

'To disclose one's name is to make oneself known to others; in a way it is to hand oneself over by becoming accessible, capable of being known more intimately and addressed personally.' (CCC 203)

YOUCAT 359

At the name of Jesus, every knee will bow, every tongue confess that Jesus Christ is Lord and King, to the glory of God the Father in the power of the Holy Spirit.

'The divine name is mysterious just as God is a mystery.' (CCC 206)

YOUCAT 359

Just as we have lost something of a sense of sin in our culture perhaps we also have lost a sense of the sacred. We can rather effortlessly fall into referring to God in a way that falls short of the sense of the reverence we owe his holy name. This sense of awe and respect is not because of servile fear but rather it is rooted in a profound love, gratitude and adoration for the very mystery of God. We must strive to resist speaking in a way which is casual or even overly familiar about God. When we do this we can easily cause scandal, give offence and undermine our own witness. The Spirit helps us to turn away from and repent of ways we have disrespected the Lord's name.

Lord, may my witness, my sharing of the gospel and my testimony be permeated with a living and real sense of my respect and reverence for God's holy name.

The legal process in every country takes the swearing of an oath very seriously indeed. If called as a witness we are asked to swear on the Holy Bible that we shall tell the truth, the whole truth and nothing but the truth. The wheels of justice depend on truthfulness; without it the scales of justice risk falling off. This is why if it has been proven that a witness has lied under oath this is considered to be a serious crime inviting a custodial sentence. Perjury (lying under oath) has resulted in destroyed careers, falls from grace and for some a lengthy prison sentence. Perjury is both a legal crime and also an offence against God and contrary to the holiness of the divine nature.

'But when he, the Spirit of truth, comes, he will guide you into all truth.' (John 16:13)

YOUCAT 359

Lord, may I always have a great respect for the legal process and be always prepared to tell the truth, the whole truth and nothing but the truth.

'God's name is great when spoken with respect for the greatness of his majesty. God's name is holy when said with veneration and fear of offending him.' (St Augustine)

YOUCAT 359

Jesus' name, the name that is above all other names (Philippians 2:10), is often used as a swear word when expressed in a defiant, contemptuous and hateful way. This misusing of Jesus' name in this way is downright blasphemous. Why does Jesus' name get singled out and abused in such a shocking and disrespectful way? This is hard to answer but we know that during his days on earth the Lord was 'despised and rejected by men' (Isaiah 53:3) and people hardened their heart against him. So too today there is always the danger of a hardening of heart towards the One who loved us and died for us. The root of blasphemy and scorn for the sacred can be despair and a cry for help.

Lord God, we revere and honour your name because you are God and your name is holy. Protect us from misusing your name and thus taking the holy name of Jesus in vain.

The swearing of false oaths was prevalent in the ancient world. In the Sermon on the Mount Jesus condemned the practice because God's name was being called upon to witness to dishonesty and untruthfulness. Jesus said: 'But I say to you, do not swear at all…let what you say be simply 'Yes' or 'No'; anything more than this comes from the evil one' (Matthew 5:33-34). We can, of course, swear on oath in a court of law because it is made for grave and right reasons. The second commandment is about honouring, reverencing and cherishing God's name in speech. With the help of the Holy Spirit we tame our tongue and our speech and strive to avoid blasphemy, cursing and making false promises.

'Do not swear, whether by the Creator or by a creature, except truthfully, of necessity and with reverence.' (St Ignatius of Loyola)

YOUCAT 359

Lord, your name is holy and sacred. Teach me to keep your name holy in all I say and do. May I seek your forgiveness through the Sacrament of Reconciliation should I fall.

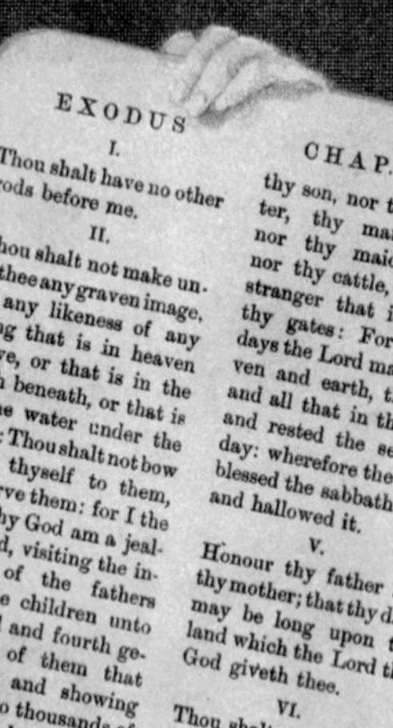
EXODUS
CHAP. XX
I.
Thou shalt have no other gods before me.
II.
Thou shalt not make unto thee any graven image, or any likeness of any thing that is in heaven above, or that is in the earth beneath, or that is in the water under the earth: Thou shalt not bow down thyself to them, nor serve them: for I the Lord thy God am a jealous God, visiting the iniquity of the fathers upon the children unto the third and fourth generation of them that hate me; and showing mercy unto thousands of them that love me, and keep my commandments.
III.
Thou shalt not take the name of the Lord thy God in vain: for the Lord will not hold him guiltless that taketh his name in vain.
IV.
Remember the sabbath-day, to keep it holy. Six days shalt thou labour, and do all thy work: but the seventh day is the
abbath of the Lord thy
in it thou shalt not
do
work, thou, nor
thy son, nor thy
ter, thy
nor thy
nor thy cattle, nor
stranger that is
thy gates: For in
days the Lord made
ven and earth, the
and all that in them is,
and rested the seventh
day: wherefore the Lord blessed the sabbath-day, and hallowed it.
V.
Honour thy father and thy mother; that thy days may be long upon the land which the Lord thy God giveth thee.
VI.
Thou shalt not kill.
VII.
Thou shalt not commit adultery.
VIII.
Thou shalt not steal.
IX.
Thou shalt not bear false witness against thy neighbour.
X.
Thou shalt not covet thy neighbour's house, thou shalt not covet thy neighbour's wife, nor his man-servant, nor his maid-servant, nor his ox, nor his ass, nor any thing that is thy neighbour's.

THE CHRISTIAN NAME (CCC 2156-2158)

DAY 273

Names are very important in terms of our faith. Both God's name, which is holy but also our own has immense significance for us. We are baptized 'in the name of the Father and of the Son and of the Holy Spirit.' (Matthew 28:19). We receive our own individual name at baptism in the name of the Church. The Church encourages parents and godparents to choose a name which ideally should be the name of a saint and one that is not foreign to Christian sentiment. This is because in the mystery of faith, the saint whose name we chose for our own becomes for us our intercessor though the course of our lives.

'The Sign of the Cross strengthens us in temptations and difficulties.' (CCC 2157)

YOUCAT 361

Lord God, I dedicate each and every day to your name and make the sign of the cross. In the name of the Father, and of the Son and of the Holy Spirit. Amen.

'To him who conquers...I will give a white stone, with a new name written on the stone which no one knows except him who receives it.' (Revelation 2:17)

YOUCAT 361

God calls each of us individually, personally and intimately by name. God spoke through the prophet Isaiah: 'Fear not, for I have redeemed you; I have summoned you by name; you are mine' (Isaiah 43:1). Jesus invites us to follow him personally and by name: 'He calls his own sheep by name and leads them out' (John 10:3). Our names are an icon, a sign of our dignity as children of God, created in the image and likeness of God (Genesis 1:26). We retain our baptismal name and identity even after death and in the blessing of eternity it takes on a new splendour. Our baptismal name has a unique, mysterious and personal character and is special to us forever.

Lord, you have given us so many things to rejoice and praise your name for. But I rejoice most of all that my name is written in heaven (Luke 10:20).

Recalling both the creation of the world (Exodus 20:11) and Israel's liberation from Egypt (Deuteronomy 5:15), the Sabbath has always been a holy day for the Jewish people. Sunday is holy for us too, and our faith finds its fulfilment in Jesus Christ who is Lord even of the Sabbath (Mark 2:27-28). Today many forces are at work to prevent Sunday from being a holy day or a day of rest. Commercial demands and the pursuit of wealth mean that Sunday trading is now part and parcel of our cultural landscape. God rested on the seventh day and we too should seek out this day as one on which we recover, pray, enjoy our families and seek some respite from the busyness and pace of our lives.

'This is the day which the Lord has made; let us rejoice and be glad in it.' (Psalm 118:24)

YOUCAT 362

Lord, by your grace teach me to keep Sunday as a holy and sacred day upon which I can retreat, pray, recharge my batteries and be refreshed and renewed in body, soul and spirit.

DAY 276

THE LORD'S DAY (CCC 2174)

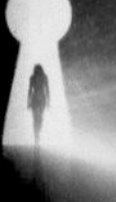

'Sunday is the day of the Resurrection, it is the day of Christians, it is our day.' (St Jerome)

YOUCAT 364

Sunday is a day at the very heart of the Christian life. It is the first of all days and the first of all feasts. As the first day of Christ's resurrection we remember the first creation and celebrate the birth of the new creation, the new humanity won for us by Jesus' Passion, Death and Resurrection. Sunday is the joy of Easter Sunday returning week by week, celebrating Christ's victory over sin and death, the fulfilment in him of the first creation and the dawn of 'the new creation' (2 Cor 5:17). Keeping Sunday special is a challenge. The Spirit helps us to be creative, adaptive and responsive so that we can reap the blessing and graces of keeping Sunday special and holy.

Lord, each Sunday, may I relive something of the experience of the disciples on the road to Emmaus when their hearts burnt as you opened the Scriptures to them and at the breaking of bread revealed yourself as the Risen Lord.

SUNDAY, FULFILLMENT OF THE SABBATH (CCC 2175-2176)

DAY 277

Sunday worship or going to Mass has replaced, for us the Sabbath. Sunday is our Sabbath. As Pope Gregory the Great said, 'For us, the true Sabbath is the person of our Redeemer, our Lord Jesus Christ.' What our faith makes clear is that the mystery of Christ was hidden in the Old Testament but fully revealed in the New. Jesus is not the abolishment of the Sabbath but its fulfillment. Sunday then is a blessed and holy day upon which in the celebration of the Eucharist, the fellowship we enjoy with one another and the opportunity to recreate, we enter into the rest of the Lord.

'For the Christian, Sunday is above all an Easter celebration, wholly illumined by the glory of the Risen Christ. It is the festival of the new creation.' (Pope John Paul II)

YOUCAT 364

Lord God teach me that Sunday Mass is a wonderful opportunity to come into your presence and give praise and thanks for your universal beneficence and goodness to all you have created.

'.....[the Christians]... gather together on a set day before sunrise and singing among themselves a hymn to Christ as to a God'. (Pliny the Younger)

YOUCAT 365

The Sunday celebration of the Eucharist is at the very heart of the Church's life. Sunday is our most important holy day of obligation. The author of the Letter to the Hebrews reminds his readers, '…not to neglect to meet together, as is the habit of some, but to encourage one another' (Hebrews 10:25). In the Sunday Eucharist we receive so many graces and blessings which give us strength and fortify us for the week to come. Like every obligation or duty, attending Sunday Mass requires a special grace from God and a special effort from us to be committed and faithful. God richly blesses and rewards us and pours out, by the power of the Spirit, his love and joy.

Lord God, thank you for the gift of the Sunday Eucharist. This day is given to us for prayer and rest. This is the day that the Lord has made; let us rejoice and be glad in it.

It is a remarkable fact that every Sunday, in every Catholic Church around the world, Mass is celebrated for the world's 1.2 billion Catholics. On this sacred and holy day we are united together in virtually every country on the planet. We share the same Sunday obligation, the same Sunday liturgy and the same Sunday Eucharist. The Catechism says of this global act of solidarity and communion: 'Participating in the communal celebration of the Sunday Eucharist is a testimony of belonging and of being faithful to Christ and his Church' (CCC 2182). Our Sunday worship then is a 'testimony of belonging' and through this we testify to God's holiness and goodness but also strengthen and support one another.

'Blessed is Sunday, for on it creation began... on Sunday heaven and earth rejoiced and the whole of creation was filled with light. Blessed is Sunday, for on it were opened the gates of paradise so that Adam and all the exiles might enter without fear.' (Syriac Office of Antioch)

YOUCAT 365

Heavenly Father, may I rediscover with new intensity the meaning of Sunday: its mystery, its celebration, and its significance for my life.

DAY 280

A Day of Grace and Rest from Work (CCC 2184-2187)

'The charity of truth seeks holy leisure; the necessity of charity accepts just work.' (St Augustine)

YOUCAT 365

Even God rested on the seventh day from the work of creation (Genesis 2:2). If God rested then so should we. There is a natural rhythm and cycle to human life which combines work and rest. We understand this readily enough whether believer or non-believer. The popular maxim says, 'All work and no play makes Jack (or Jill for that matter) a dull boy (or girl).' For the sake of our spiritual, mental and physical health and well-being we need to find time to rest and recreate. But how do we make Sunday special in our 24/7 hectic and busy culture? By deciding to carve out time and set it aside to devote to the things which bring us peace of mind, heart and body.

Lord, teach me to cherish and protect my Sunday rest. May it be a time for renewal and prayer but also of refreshment and enjoyment of the good gifts you have given me.

Our society has changed tremendously over the last 25 years. Society as a whole used to have a reverence and respect for Sunday as a day of rest which no longer exists. Sunday trading, the thirst for profit combined with consumer demand, has undermined Sunday as a day of respite but also as the Lord's day. The danger we face is that Sunday can seem just like any other day. We must resist this and be prepared to play our part in defending the right to keep Sunday special, sacred and holy. Be prepared to lodge your concerns with your MP, the local or even national government. Keeping Sunday holy and special is a precious contribution to the spiritual life and well-being of every society and culture.

'The celebration of the Christian Sunday remains..... an indispensable element of our Christian identity.' (Pope John Paul II)

YOUCAT 366

Lord, thank you for the blessing of Sunday. May I celebrate it as a special day of faith, lived in such a way that it bears witness to the joy, peace and love of the Risen Lord.

DAY 282

LOVE YOUR PARENTS (CCC 2196-2200)

'This week we explore the fourth commandment, which begins the 'second table of the Decalogue.' (CCC 2197)

The first three commandments ('the first table') focuses on our obligations toward God; the second table, on our duties towards our neighbour. It is fitting that the call to love of our neighbour begins first with the command to love our parents. After God, we should honour our parents because we owe them our life, our very existence. The fourth commandment is the only one which comes with a promise attached: '….that it may be well with you and that you live long on the earth' (Ephesians 6:3). There is a profound link between our relationship with our parents and the well being of society. This is because it lays the foundation for all our other relationships both personal but also in wider society.

YOUCAT 367

Lord, thank you for my parents and for the way they gave freely and generously of themselves to love and care for me. May I always be aware of the debt of love and service I owe them.

Where do you go to church? We rightly think of our parish church as our place of worship and fellowship. God and his Church however recognize in each Christian family a special and unique revelation of what the Church is. The Church has, from the very beginning, recognized that the family can and should be called a 'domestic church.' Each and every Christian family is to be esteemed and treated with great respect and honour because it is in itself a community of faith, hope and love. In the rich teaching of the Church the family is also a sign, an image or icon, if you like, of the Blessed Trinity; of the communion of love which exists between the Father, the Son and the Holy Spirit.

'Keep the joy of loving God in your heart and share this joy with all you meet especially your family. Be holy – let us pray.' (Blessed Mother Teresa of Calcutta)

YOUCAT 368

Lord, we praise you for the dignity you have bestowed upon the privileged community of the family, called to share in the Father's work of creation and the prayer and sacrifice of Christ.

'Sometimes I used to wake up in the middle of the night and find my father on his knees. We never spoke about a priestly vocation but my father's example was a first home seminary.' (Pope John Paul II)

YOUCAT 369-370

The family is the spiritual womb from which we are all born. The family is the 'school of Christ' where we learn to become responsible members of society and fruitful members of the church. Our parents are our first educators. From them we lay the foundation of our spiritual lives and the lessons we learn should stand us in good stead for the rest of our lives. Pope John Paul II, whose mother died when he was nine and who was raised by his father, said that he would often wake to see his father on his knees in the early hours praying earnestly and sincerely. This left a profound and long-lasting impression on the future Pope. His vocation was nutured in the womb of his family home.

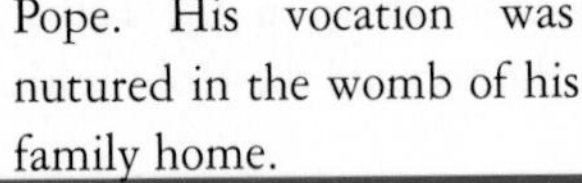

Lord, teach me to live in such a way in my family that we all learn to care for each other but also to reach out beyond to serve the young, the old, the sick, the handicapped and the poor.

We owe our parents a great debt because they have given us the gift of life. They bring us into the world and through their love, devotion and care throughout our early years we grow and mature into adulthood. They are the first to hand on to us the gift of faith. However, no parent is perfect, as indeed is no child, but the bond between them remains the most natural, deepest and powerful of all human affections. This debt towards our parents creates in us a number of virtues which we are called to nourish and cultivate. Respect (filial piety), gratitude and obedience serve to remind children of their responsibilities towards their parents as they grow older.

'Whoever honours his father atones for sins, and whoever glorifies his mother is like one who lays up treasure.' (Sirach 3:12)

YOUCAT 371

Lord, with all my heart I honour my mother and my father. They gave me the gift of life and the gift of faith and in respecting, obeying and serving them, I serve you.

Day 286

The Duties of Parents (CCC 2221-2231)

'We take care of our possessions for our children. But of the children themselves we take no care at all. What an absurdity this is! Form the soul of thy son aright and all the rest will be added hereafter.' (St John Chrysostom)

YOUCAT 372

Pope John XXIII said, 'It is easier for a man to have children than for children to have a real father.' Parents, not the Church or the nursery or the school, are the first educators of their children. This is their primordial and inalienable right. However, as we know, with rights comes responsibility and duty. Parents must create a home where tenderness, forgiveness, respect, fidelity and true love and service prevail. Parents must also set an example in the way they witness to the gifts, graces, blessings and fruits of the Holy Spirit. They must also be prepared to humbly acknowledge their faults and failings to their children and in doing so teach them the grace of *metanoia*, of repentance and true contrition of heart.

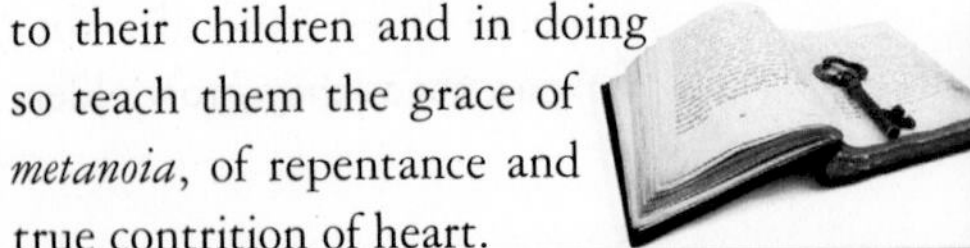

Lord, may all parents come to know the great dignity and treasure of their holy vocation. Give them strength, courage and wisdom in living out their calling.

The fourth commandment extends to those who hold positions of authority in society. However, there has been something of a crisis of confidence in those we once revered and respected. The banks with the financial crisis, politicians with the expenses scandal and the corporations BBC or Shell (to name only two), all who have proven to have been negligent or untrustworthy. Sadly, the Church itself loses credibility and terrible scandal ensues when safeguarding practices are abused or hypocrisy has had free reign. Those who hold positions of power or authority are called to serve, not exploit. As Jesus said: 'Whoever would be great among you must be your servant' (Matthew 20:26).

'Refusing obedience to civil authorities, when their demands are contrary to those of an upright conscience, finds its justification in the distinction between serving God and serving the political community.' (CCC 2242)

YOUCAT 374

Lord, we pray for those who are in positions of authority that they would be worthy of our respect and reverence, and uphold both the natural law and the Law of the Gospel.

Day 288

The Church and Politics (CCC 2244-2246)

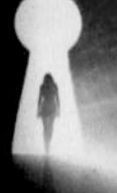

'The Church respects and encourages the political freedom and responsibility of the citizen.' (Gaudium et Spes 76)

YOUCAT 376

Throughout history the Church has resisted totalitarian political regimes. Be it communism or fascism or similar closed systems. The hallmark of such regimes is the power the state seeks to have total control over every aspect of society and the lives of its citizens. To achieve this it resorts to violence, terror and intimidation in order to subjugate its people. Such ideology is rooted in a godless, hostile vision of the human person and of a society without God and without hope. The Church teaches however that our origin, dignity and destiny are all within the loving plan of God, the good Creator and our Redeemer, our Lord Jesus Christ.

Lord, may our faith inform our politics such that we always strive to uphold the inalienable right and dignity of the human person created in the image and likeness of God (Genesis 1:26).

We understand that murder is, to quote, Shakespeare, 'most foul' (Hamlet) and, of course, a crime. Human life is sacred, God is its author and Lord. No human being has the right to claim for themselves the right to directly destroy an innocent human being. In the murder of Abel in the Bible's first chapters we learn a profound yet disturbing insight into the act of murder and the condition of the human heart - for in the heart dwell anger and envy and these dark forces are at work in every murderous act (Genesis 4:10-11). Human history and the covenant between God and us is interwoven with tragic and frightening examples of our capacity for murder, genocide and holocaust.

'For your lifeblood I will surely required a reckoning... whoever sheds the blood of man, by man shall his blood be shed; for God made man in his own image.' (Genesis 9:5-6)

YOUCAT 378

Lord God, we thank you for the holy teaching of the Church that cherishes, protects and holds human life as sacred, from the cradle to the grave, from the womb to the tomb.

'The right to life does not depend and must not be declared to be contingent, on the pleasure of anyone else, not even a parent or a sovereign.' (Blessed Mother Teresa of Calcutta)

YOUCAT 383

'A woman who deliberately destroys the foetus is answerable for murder. And any fine distinction as to its being completely formed or unformed is not admissible among us' (St Basil). The Church teaches that from the moment of conception a human being exists. The embryo, foetus or baby in the womb is a human person. The Church has always taught that human life is sacred from the womb to the tomb and this will never change; in fact, it is unchangeable. Within the womb grows a human being who is entitled to dignity, protection and the inalienable right to life. 'Before I formed you in the womb I knew you, and before you were born I consecrated you' (Jeremiah 1:5).

O Lord, my God, my frame was not hidden from you, when I was made in secret, intricately wrought in the depths of the earth (Psalm 139:15).

The Catechism never retreats from difficult, contentious or controversial moral issues. She is the guardian, protector of life and has always upheld the sanctity and right to life of every human being. Euthanasia and recently assisted suicide are understood as relative - neither right or wrong - but informed by circumstance, emotions, and subjective experience. There is a growing sense that a person who is seriously sick, critically ill or disabled, is a burden. This can lead those who are afflicted in this way or suffering to contemplate ending their lives. Any action that leads to the ending of a sick or dying person's life is a great evil and morally unacceptable. Human life belongs to God alone.

'It is never licit to kill another; even if he should wish it, indeed if he request it hanging between life and death..nor is it licit even when a sick person is no longer able to live.'
(St Augustine)

YOUCAT 382

Lord, teach me to raise my voice in a society which promotes a 'culture of death' to promote through witness and proclamation a 'culture of life.'

DAY 292

SCANDAL (CCC 2284-2287)

'Have mercy on your Church... You stood up, you arose and you can also raise us up. Save and sanctify your Church. Save and sanctify us all.' (Pope Benedict XVI)

YOUCAT 386

Scandal is very damaging, undermining faith and confidence. The politicians' expenses scandal undermined our faith in politicians. The bankers' bonuses scandal weakened our confidence in banks. The hacking scandal has made us even more mistrustful of the media. The Church is holy but her sons and daughters are not immune from scandal. The clerical child abuse crisis in the Church has caused great hurt, offence and scandal. Pope Benedict, clearly deeply distressed said: 'How much filth there is in the Church, and even among those who, in the priesthood, ought to belong entirely to him! How much pride, how much self-complacency!'

'Lord, your Church often seems like a boat about to sink. The soiled garments and face of your Church throw us into confusion. Yet it is we ourselves who have soiled them! It is we who betray you time and time again.'

The Catechism teaches us that we are a composite of body and soul. Bodily health and fitness are precious gifts to be cherished. There exists today however a 'cult of the body' in which bodily perfection and physical beauty are pursued at all costs. We see this in our celebrity culture which denies the natural process of ageing and focuses on intervention and enhancement. Teeth whitening, plastic surgery, extreme diets, excessively toned bodies and a dress size zero are pursued at all costs. This has a damaging effect, especially on young people. This idea of bodily beauty, status and achievement favours the rich and the strong and marginalizes the poor and the weak.

'The Church permits cremation, provided that it does not demonstrate a denial of faith in the resurrection of the body.' (CCC 2301)

YOUCAT 388-394

Lord God, help me to care and respect my body appropiately because although mortal and corruptible we will be raised, body and soul, to the eternal life in Christ.

'Lord, make me an instrument of thy peace. Where there is hatred, let me sow love; where there is injury, pardon.' (St Francis of Assisi)

YOUCAT 395

On hearing Jesus' teaching on the Eucharist some disciples complained: 'This is a hard teaching. Who can accept it?' (John 6:60). The same is true of the Lord's teaching on anger and revenge. It is a hard teaching. It is easy to be angry and hard to be patient and seek peace and reconciliation. Anger and resentment can fester in us and, when nursed, overflow in damaging and destructive ways. We all stumble and fall in many ways but by God's grace we can resist deliberate and intentional hatred of those who have hurt or offended us. 'But I say to you, love your enemies and pray for those who persecute you, so that you may be sons of your Father who is in heaven' (Matthew 5:44-45).

Lord Jesus, you reconciled us to the Father. Teach me to be a peacemaker, because blessed are those who seek peace, forgiveness and reconciliation in your name.

War is an ancient bondage; it is always a defeat for humanity. Peace is ultimately rooted in the human heart. True peace between nations cannot be secured without 'safeguarding the goods of persons, free communication, respect for the dignity of persons and peoples and the assiduous practice of fraternity' (CCC 2304). Despite the many wars and conflicts around the world, we are living through a time of relative peace and stability. We pray for peace because war is so awful, so high a price to pay and so destructive to human flourishing and well-being. War is a great evil. 'From famine, pestilence, and war, O Lord, deliver us. (CCC 2327)

'Today the scale and horror of modern warfare - whether nuclear or not - make it totally unacceptable as a means of settling differences between nations.' (Pope John Paul II)

YOUCAT 397

Lord God, make me an instrument of peace, a sign of reconciliation, a channel of love, a peacemaker not a warmonger.

DAY 296

God's Gift of Sex (CCC 2331-2336)

'Therefore a man leaves his father and his mother and cleaves to his wife, and they become one flesh.' (Genesis 3:12)

YOUCAT 400

The sixth commandment is far-reaching and includes many things: 'respect for life, marriage, the aptitude for forming bonds and communication with others' (CCC 2332). The sixth commandment is a signpost showing us how to live according to God's plan as sexual beings and how to love. Human sexuality is one of God's greatest gifts. Sex is willed by God, within marriage, between a man and a woman, for procreation, union between spouses and pleasure. So precious a gift is sex that tradition has always seen in the Song of Songs a unique expression of human love and a reflection of God's love - a love as strong as death that many waters cannot quench (Song of Songs 8:6-7).

Lord God, you created the human race male and female and placed within us an innate, fundamental and holy vocation to be fruitful, multiply and love.

Sex is everywhere in our culture. In a society obsessed with sex the idea of chastity and living a chaste, holy life, goes against the grain. We tend to think of chastity as living without sex. However, this is not so as married people have received a vocation to chastity also. So what is chastity? Chastity is a process, often life-long, of self-mastery and temperance in which we learn to integrate our sexuality and (with God's help and strength) govern our desires such that we are not a slave to them but master. In this sense the virtue of chastity is a training in freedom through which we are liberated to serve the living God and love and serve our neighbour.

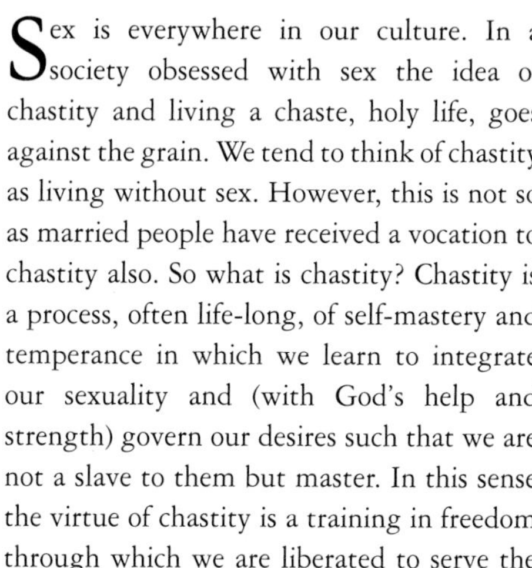

'Indeed it is through chastity that we are gathered together and led back to the unity from which we were fragmented into multiplicity.' (St Augustine)

YOUCAT 404

Lord, pour out upon me the grace and blessing of chastity and through the power of the Holy Spirit received at baptism enable me to imitate the purity of Christ.

DAY 298

OFFENCES AGAINST CHASTITY (CCC 2351-2356)

'According to contemporary scientific research, the human person is so profoundly affected by sexuality that it must be considered as one of the factors which give to each individual's life the principal traits that distinguish it.' (Persona Humana 1)

YOUCAT 405-411

The Catechism identifies the following as offences against chastity: lust, masturbation, fornication, pornography, prostitution, as well as the serious sexual crime of rape. All of these involve the isolation or separation of sex from its original procreative and unitive purpose within the covenant of marriage. Each has the effect of reducing the human person to an object or a means of sexual pleasure as an end in itself. This kind of thinking, very much prevalent in our culture, undermines the dignity of the human person at its deepest core. Sexual sins and crimes are profoundly damaging because they offend against the respect, freedom, physical and moral integrity which is both our right and our very dignity.

Lord, through the grace of the Sacrament of Reconciliation may I come to know your mercy and forgiveness for ways that I have sinned against chastity.

The Church distinguishes between homosexual acts and a homosexual orientation. The tradition of the Church has been consistent from the very beginning that homosexual acts are intrinsically disordered. Such acts are against the natural law and close the sexual act to procreation and the gift of life. The Catechism upholds God's original plan of sexual complementarity in creating the human person as both male and female (Genesis 1:27). However, a homosexual orientation is not in itself sinful and those with this orientation are to be treated with respect, compassion and sensitivity. We are all equally loved by God.

'The Church... refuses to consider the person as a 'heterosexual' or a 'homosexual' and insists that every person has a fundamental identity: the creature of God, and by grace, his child and heir to eternal life.' (Pastoral Care of the Homosexual Person 16)

YOUCAT 415

Lord, our sexuality is always in need of grace and healing. We thank you that in Christ our dignity is rooted in being sons and daughters of God, heirs of eternal life.

DAY
300

CONJUGAL LOVE (CCC 2360-2365)

'Young husbands should say to their wives: 'I have taken you in my arms, and I love you, and I prefer you to my life itself. My most ardent dream is to spend it with you in such a way that we be assured of not being separated'.' (St John Chrysostom)

YOUCAT 417

We celebrate sex as one of the great goods of marriage. Sexual intercourse between two spouses is honorable, noble, and a sign and pledge of their spiritual communion. Their bodily union is an act of total self-giving and the source of great joy, gratitude and mutual pleasure. This union is not merely biological or physical but reaches profoundly and deeply into the heart of their relationship. In their sexual union the spouses witness to the twofold end of marriage which is the enriching of each other and the transmission of life. The vocation and sacrament of marriage invites the couple to witness to their faith through faithfulness, fidelity and fecundity.

Father, we give thanks and praise to you for those called to marriage who through their unique, indissoluble union bear witness to the mystery of Christ's love and fidelity to the Church.

THE GIFT OF A CHILD (CCC 2366-2379)

DAY 301

A child is the supreme gift of marriage but not a right or an accessory. Children are the supreme good of marriage, its fruit and fulfilment. Married couples share in the creative power and fatherhood of God. It is their natural mission to bring life into the world and co-operate with the creative, life-giving nature of the Creator. Couples who are unable to have children suffer deeply. As Rachel cried out in her anguish to Jacob: 'Give me children, or I shall die' (Genesis 30:1). On exhausting legitimate medical options open to them they often foster or adopt. Others choose to remain childless but produce great spiritual fruit by giving themselves to a life of love and service of others.

'It is easier for a father to have children than for children to have a real father.' (Pope John XXIII)

YOUCAT 418

Father, we thank you for the vocation of marriage through which children are brought into the world and by handing on the faith, parents once again give birth to Christ.

DAY 302

OFFENCES AGAINST MARRIAGE (2380-2391)

'The adulterer is a more grevious offender than the thief.' (St John Chrysostom)

YOUCAT 425

The Catechism identifies the following as offences against marriage: adultery, divorce, polygamy, incest, free union and trial marriage. We do not live in a perfect world and we are fallen and imperfect. Jesus insisted on God's original plan of the Creator for marriage. This has been the bedrock and foundation of the Church's teaching and vision for marriage. The Lord taught that Moses permitted divorce because of a hardness of heart among the people (Matthew 19:7-9). The Church is committed to upholding God's standard for marriage until the end of time but holds out loving pastoral care, forgiveness and mercy to those who fall short, repent and turn back to the Lord.

Lord, we thank you for the gift of the sacrament of marriage and commit ourselves to defending its sanctity and upholding the dignity of this holy and sacred vocation.

The seventh commandment, 'You shall not steal' (Exodus 20:15), prohibits unjustly taking or keeping goods belonging to another. The commandment is not merely about the moral failing and the criminal act of theft. It shines God's light on our attitude, our way of thinking and acting in many areas of our lives: respect for the destination and distribution of goods, private ownership, respect for persons, respect for property and even creation itself. The commandment goes to the heart of the Church's social doctrine because it teaches us how to live and act in a righteous, good and holy way in the complex, economic, social and political world in which we live.

'The bread which you hold back belongs to the hungry; the coat which you guard in your locked storage-chests belongs to the naked; the footwear mouldering in your closet belongs to those without shoes. The silver that you keep hidden in a safe place belongs to the one in need.' (St Basil)

YOUCAT 426

Lord, we are stewards of creation entrusted with the resources of the earth. We strive for truth, justice and solidarity, promoting equality, the distribution of wealth and the common good.

'Christian revelation... promotes deeper understanding of the laws of social living.' (Gaudium et spes 23)

YOUCAT 428

What is theft? The Catechism gives us a clear and precise definition: 'Theft ...is..usurping another's property against the reasonable will of the owner' (CCC 2408). However, the Church recognizes, of course, that in the case of urgent and obvious necessity when the need for food, shelter or clothing is acute, or desperate even, those in such predicaments have no other choice available to them but to put the property or goods of another at their disposal. At times of war or famine or natural disaster such exceptional circumstances often prevail and the needs of our common humanity and the care of the person are paramount and take precedence.

Lord Jesus, teach me to respect the property, goods and dignity of my neighbour and to always give generously to those in need or distress.

THE CHURCH'S SOCIAL DOCTRINE (CCC 2419-2425)

The Church is not a political organization. However, she concerns herself in economic and social matters 'when the fundamental rights of the person or the salvation of souls requires it' (*Gaudium et Spes* 76). She raises her voice on behalf of the poor and the oppressed of the world. In the nineteenth century and the ensuing industrial revolution the world's economy changed from being agrarian to industrial. The Church has always spoken up for workers and their rights in relation to: proper working conditions, a just wage and the right to own private property. When state and corporations exploit their workforce they commit a form of theft - robbing them of dignity, value and their human rights.

'For the poor will never cease out of the land: therefore I command you. 'You shall open wide your hand to your brother, to the needy and to the poor in the land.' (Deuteronomy 15:11)

YOUCAT 438

Lord, teach me to make the Church's social doctrine better known and esteemed, because it is a jewel and treasure of wisdom, light and grace.

'Whatever you do, work at it with all your heart, as working for the Lord, not for men.' (Colossians 3:23)

YOUCAT 442

We are living through a time of recession and economic hardship. Many are suffering through redundancy and unemployment. The Church raises her voice on behalf of all those who suffer in this way. Through the generosity of parishes, charities and organizations we reach out to those among us in need. Work is a duty but it also confers great dignity. Jesus, the carpenter of Nazareth worked with his hands and sanctified human work and labour. We are called to remind state governments, but also society as a whole, of the moral duty to provide and create employment, ensuring that the economic fabric of society holds together and human beings flourish.

Lord, we pray for all those who struggle during these difficult economic times. We pray for governments and entrepreneurs that they will create jobs and new opportunities even in a time of austerity.

INTERNATIONAL JUSTICE (CCC 2437-2442)

DAY 307

Blessed John Henry Cardinal Newman observed that all bow down to wealth and pay it homage. This has always been true but is perhaps never so true as it is today. The Times newspaper publishes each year a Rich List naming individuals whose net worth runs into millions and billions of pounds. There are also rich countries and prosperous nations. The Church reminds rich nations of the grave moral responsibility they have towards their poorer neighbours. The lay faithful are called to work tirelessly for peace and justice and to raise their voice on behalf of the poor and downtrodden, at home and in other countries. Justice, solidarity and love teach us that we are our brother and sister's keeper.

'To renounce wealth is the beginning and sustaining of virtues.' (St Ambrose of Milan)

YOUCAT 444-448

Lord Jesus, the poor are very dear to you and for them your love is preferential. Grant me a special love for them for it is more blessed to give than to receive.

DAY 308

LOVE FOR THE POOR (2443-2446)

The Catechism's teaching on the seventh commandment covers many areas of economic and social life. We might ask, 'What has all of this got to do with the act of theft?' St John Chrysostom sheds light on this question: 'Not to enable the poor to share in our goods is to steal from them and deprive them of life. The goods we possess are not ours, but theirs.' This is quite a challenging teaching isn't it? Perhaps we haven't thought like this before. St Gregory the Great elaborated on this challenging teaching: 'When we attend to the needs of those in want, we give them what is theirs, not ours. More than performing works of mercy, we are paying a debt of justice.'

'When her mother reproached her for caring for the poor and the sick at home, Rose of Lima said to her, 'When we serve the poor and the sick, we serve Jesus. We must not fail to help our neighbours because in them we serve Jesus'.' (P Hansen, Vita mirabilis (Louvain, 1668)

YOUCAT 449

Lord, we are profoundly and deeply committed to the poor of the world. They are, if you like, our other selves. Teach us to reach out and give generously to them the goods, graces and blessings we have received in our own lives.

St John Chrysostom said, 'Do you wish to receive mercy? Show mercy to your neighbour.' There are spiritual and corporeal works of mercy. Spiritual works of mercy involve instructing, advising, consoling, comforting, forgiving and bearing wrongs patiently. Corporeal works of mercy consist of, feeding the hungry, sheltering the homeless, clothing the naked, visiting the sick and those in prison and burying the dead. Giving generously to the poor and those in need has always been especially encouraged because it is pleasing to God (James 2:14-15). God hears the cry of the poor. The Church has a preferential love for the poor and works tirelessly for their relief, defence and liberation.

'Two works of mercy set a person free: forgive and you will be forgiven; and give and you will receive.' (St Augustine)

YOUCAT 450-451

Merciful Father, teach me to show mercy and kindness to my neighbour. First by my actions, secondly by my words and thirdly by my prayer.

DAY 310

TRUTHFULNESS (CCC 2264-2270)

'We could not live with one another if there was not mutual confidence that we were being truthful to one another.' (St Thomas Aquinas)

YOUCAT 452

The eighth commandment, 'You shall not bear false witness against your neighbour' (Exodus 20:16) prohibits misrepresenting or abusing the truth in our relationships with others. This commandment flows from our vocation to bear witness to God who is the source of all truth. Jesus is truth made incarnate. Jesus is the One who is full of grace and truth; he is '....the way, the truth and the life' (John 14:6). What does it mean to live by the truth? It means that we strive for an uprightness in word and deed, reflected in a sincerity and candour. It guards against duplicity, deception, hypocrisy, lying and slander; it promotes honesty and straightforwardness but also wisdom, sensitivity and discretion.

Lord, we stumble and fall in many ways and especially in what we say. For out of the overflow of our mouths flow our hearts. I repent for the ways that I do not live by the truth nor speak the truth.

St Francis of Assisi famously said, 'Preach the gospel, if necessary use words.' We, for our part are called to witness to Chirst and to the truth by our words and deeds. It can be difficult and challenging to stand up for our faith and the truth, but has it not always ever been so? To give a reason for our hope, joy and love means that some will be attracted and others repelled; some will embrace what we say, others reject it. We are not ashamed of the gospel; rather we are ashamed if we do not share our faith. We do so always with respect and reverence for others but also with courage, creativity and conviction. Woe to us if we do not share or witness to Christ.

'I seek him who died for us; I desire him who rose for us. My birth is approaching.' (St Ignatius of Antioch)

YOUCAT 454

Lord, the blessed martyrs are the supreme witnesses of faith. We stand on their shoulders and hand on the precious faith they died for.

'But now you must rid yourself of all such things as these: anger, rage, malice, slander, and filthy language from your lips.' (Colossians 3:8)

YOUCAT 455

It is sobering and striking that offences against the truth involve speech, words and the tongue: false witness, perjury, detraction, calumny, flattery, adulation, boasting and lying. St James observed that the tongue although only a small part of the body makes great boasts (James 3:5). He compared it to a dangerous spark capable of creating a blaze leaving chaos and destruction in its wake (James 3:6). Through baptism 'we have put on the new self created after the likeness of God in true righteousness and holiness.' (Ephesians 4:24). We take to heart St Paul's exhortation: '...put away all malice and all guile and insincerity and envy and all slander' (Ephesians 4:25).

Lord, I repent of the ways I have offended against the truth through my words, attitudes and actions. Pour out your Spirit that I may be transformed and renewed in mind, body and spirit.

Lying (CCC 2482-2487)

Day 313

St Augustine gave a succinct definition of lying: 'A lie consists in speaking a falsehood with the intention of deceiving.' 'Do not lie' proclaims the Torah (Leviticus 19:11). The Lord denounces lying as a work of the devil. 'When he lies, he speaks according to his own nature, for he is a liar and the father of lies.' (John 8:44). Lying is linked to gossip because both violate the virtue of truthfulness. Lying and gossip therefore do real violence to a person's integrity and dignity. Lying is a direct offence against the truth and destructive at many levels. The Holy Spirit leads us into all truth, helps us examine our conscience and leads us to repentance and healing.

'Jesus teaches the unconditional love of truth: 'Let what you say be simply 'Yes' or 'No'.' (Matthew 5:37)

YOUCAT 456

Lord, help me to understand more profoundly how grevious and offensive lying, dishonesty and gossip are, and lead me in the path of integrity and truthfulness of speech.

DAY 314

RESPECT FOR THE TRUTH (CCC 2488-2492)

'Keep thy tongue from evil, and thy lips from speaking guile.' (Psalm 34:13)

British Army Intelligence has two phrases relating to careful speech. The first, a slogan from World War II warned against the dangers of spies and said, 'Loose talk costs lives.' The second, an urban warfare dictum: 'On a need to know basis.' Maturity, discretion, privacy and confidentiality relate to careful speech and a respect for the truth. Privacy and confidence are vital in many aspects of professional life and also in the Church. The seal of the Sacrament of Reconciliation is inviolable and can never, under any pretext, be violated or abused. The priest can never break the seal of the confessional by word or in any other manner, or for any reason.

YOUCAT 457

We pray for our priests who hear confessions, that they may exercise this pastoral responsibility strengthened by God's grace and wisdom, never breaking the sacramental seal.

The first casualty of war is the truth. Wartime propaganda's goal is to subvert, disinform, confuse and manipulate the enemy. Whether in war or peacetime the media is always a force to reckon with. Perhaps, sadly, the casualty of the media today is also the truth. The closure of the News of the World and the findings of the Leveson enquiry confirm the public perception that '....you can't believe what you read in the newspapers.' The Catechism calls on all those involved in the work of social media to observe the highest moral and ethical standards. It reminds them of their obligation to publish or broadcast the truth in keeping with the dignity and sacred nature of the human person.

'The Church recognizes, too, that we can employ the media contrary to the plan of the Creator and to our own loss. Indeed, the Church experiences maternal grief at the harm all too often done to society by their evil use.' (Inter mirifica 1)

YOUCAT 459

With the help of the Holy Spirit may my heart, mind and conscience be enlightened, formed to discern the truth and to resist what is unwholesome and undermining of human dignity in the media.

DAY 316

TRUTH, BEAUTY AND SACRED ART (CCC 2500-2503)

'The function of all art lies in fact in breaking through the narrow and tortuous enclosure of the finite, in which we are immersed while living here below, and in providing a window on the infinite for our hungry souls.' (Pope Pius XII)

YOUCAT 461

Michelangelo said, 'The true work of art is but a shadow of the divine perfection.' St Thomas Aquinas echoed this saying, 'The beauty of all things is derived from the divine beauty.' And on his conversion St Augustine of Hippo lamented: 'Too late I loved you, O beauty so ancient yet ever new.' God, the Holy One is the source and fount of all beauty, truth and goodness; before God we humbly bow, worship and adore the true Beauty, ever ancient, ever new. The Catechism encourages us to seek out the good, the true and the beautiful and to see in sacred art a means through which our minds and hearts can be lifted up to give glory and praise to the transcendent mystery of God.

By God's grace may I seek out works of sacred art which are inspired by the wisdom and truth of God and reflect something of the beauty of the Creator and love of the Saviour, and the motherhood of the most Holy Virgin Mary.

Over the next few days we reflect on the ninth commandment: 'You shall not covet your neighbour's house; you shall not covet your neighbour's wife, or his manservant, or his maidservant, or his ox, or his ass, or anything that is your neighbours' (Exodus 20:17). The tenth commandment, as we shall see, focuses also on coveting, but of our neighbour's goods and material possessions. Jesus taught that we covet our neighbour's wife, commit adultery, by merely looking upon her with lustful desire in our hearts (Matthew 5:28). With the help of the Holy Spirit, examining our conscience and seeking God's forgiveness in the Sacrament of Reconciliation, we can live pure and holy lives.

'I thought that continence arose from one's own power, which I did not recognize in myself. I was foolish enough not to know that no one can be continent unless you grant it.' (St Augustine of Hippo)

YOUCAT 462

Lord God, by your grace and the promises of Christ teach me to purify myself from everything that contaminates body and spirit, perfecting holiness out of reverence for you.

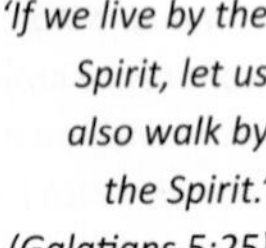

'If we live by the Spirit, let us also walk by the Spirit.' (Galatians 5:25)

YOUCAT 462

Concupiscence is not a word we hear or indeed use every day. It is however a very important one in understanding our human condition. Concupiscence can be best understood as an intense human desire or appetite which can consume and overpower us. To be precise and to give its more formal definition, concupiscence is: 'the movement of the sensitive appetite contrary to the operation of the human reason.' We recognize it in sexual lust or in an overpowering desire for food or alcoholic drink. When in its grip it creates within us compelling, overwhelming and intense desires, seemingly beyond our control. Such desires involve us in a certain interior struggle, a tension between the 'spirit' and the 'flesh.'

Lord, in the daily experience of the spiritual battle help me to overcome by resisting temptation in its many forms and by your grace live a self-controlled and disciplined life.

The Catechism teaches that the heart is the seat of the moral personality. The prophet Jeremiah observed: 'The heart is deceitful above all things' (Jeremiah 17:9). Jesus taught that the heart is the place within us from which evil flows: 'Out of the heart come evil thoughts, murder, adultery, fornication' (Matthew 15:19). The Lord also proclaimed in the Beatitudes, 'Blessed are the pure in heart for they shall see God' (Matthew 5:8). The pure in heart are those who by God's grace and the virtues of temperance and self-control are able to attune their intellects and wills to the call of God's holiness.

'To my God a heart of flame: to my fellow men, a heart of love; to myself, a heart of steel.' (St Augustine)

YOUCAT 463

Lord Jesus, you promised that the pure in heart will see God. Teach me to uphold the dignity of my neighbour by recognizing that their body is the temple of the Holy Spirit.

DAY 320

THE BATTLE FOR PURITY (CCC 2520)

'Since then we are a holy portion, let us accomplish all that pertains to holiness; fleeing from slander, vile and impure embraces, drunkenness and rebellion and filthy lusts, detestable adultery and foul arrogance.' (St Clement of Rome)

YOUCAT 463

St Augustine of Hippo famously prayed, 'Lord, make me chaste, but not just yet.' He struggled with chastity, recognizing in himself the desire for purity, but of being powerlessness to attain it. After his conversion and reflecting on this he realized that God's grace could have given him the resolve and power he needed to change: 'For you would surely have granted it if my inner groaning had reached your ears and I with firm faith had cast my cares on you.' The grace of baptism purifies us from all our sins. However, we face a constant, ongoing and lifetime struggle against concupiscence of the flesh and the disordered desires of our appetites.

Lord, grant me the virtue and gift of chastity, purity of intention and vision, and recourse to prayer, recourse to your grace, that I may be among the pure in heart who will see God.

Modesty is a dying art in our society. Of course, modesty is not an art or even a fashion but rather a virtue. Indeed it is one that is increasingly absent in our brash and loud culture. There is a hunger fuelled by the media and a thirst created by the consumer for a certain exhibitionism and a cult of the body beautiful, resulting in its worship. This has the effect of crudely debasing and violating human dignity. Modesty, on the other hand, means refusing to unveil what should remain hidden and is related to the virtue of purity. Modesty has to do with our whole person, our feelings, our clothing, how we dress, present ourselves and relate to other people.

'I never look at them and neither does anyone else, because they are all looking at me to see how I am reacting.' (Blessed Angelo Roncalli, later Pope John XXIII, as papal nuncio in Paris he was asked whether plunging necklines embarrassed him)

YOUCAT 464

Lord, teach me the virtue of modesty. Help me to be reserved, discreet in dress, speech and manner and to seek always to uphold the nobility of the human body and the dignity of the human person.

DAY 322

MORAL PERMISSIVENESS (CCC 2525-2526)

'True freedom is not advanced in the permissive society, which confuses freedom with licence to do anything whatever and which in the name of freedom proclaims a kind of general amorality.' (Pope John Paul II)

YOUCAT 4

What are the signs of a morally permissive society? Promiscuous sex, the practice of homosexuality, abortion, artificial contraception, euthanasia and assisted suicide, to name a few. Everything is permissible. 'Live and let live; do what you want; we are not hurting anybody' is the cry. The teachings of the Church are not obstacles to human freedom but rather facilitate and encourage it. The gospel paradox is that in dying to self, living self-controlled lives and seeking to obey God's commandments, we come to know true freedom and are liberated from the shackles of selfishness and self-gratification. In Christ we live no longer for ourselves but for him who died for us.

Lord Jesus, you are the Son who sets us free from the bondage and darkness of selfishness and self-indulgence, so that we can live as children of God, free indeed.

THE GOOD NEWS OF CHRIST (2527)

DAY 323

Jesus caused scandal during his public ministry, by associating with 'public sinners.' Tax collectors, prostitutes and many on the margins of society came to him. Holiness attracts; it does not judge or condemn. Jesus said, 'Come to me all you who are weary and heavily burdened and I will give you rest' (Matthew 11:27-29). Both as individuals and as a society we are wearied and burdened by sin. The 'Good News' is not merely a moral message but one of God's lavish, abundant grace, poured out upon us. Through the Paschal Mystery, sin and death are conquered, the new humanity is revealed and by God's grace we can live a new life in the power of the Spirit.

'The rivers of time sweep on, but there, like a tree planted in the water, is Our Lord Jesus Christ. He became man, willing to plant himself beside the river of time. If you feel yourself drifting down to the rapids, lay hold of the tree; if you are caught up in the love of the world, hold on to Christ.' (St Augustine)

YOUCAT p.252

Heavenly Father, the Good News of Christ renews every aspect of the life and culture of fallen humanity. Christ makes everything new and so we pray with confidence: 'Send forth your Spirit and renew the face of the earth.'

DAY 324

THE INTE[illegible]IONS OF THE HEART (CCC 253[illegible]

'Would you like to see God glorified by you? Then rejoice in your brother's progress and material advancement and you will immediately give glory to God. We declare ourselves members of one and the same organism, yet we devour one another like beasts.' (St John Chrysostom)

YOUCAT 465

The tenth commandments is: 'You shall not covet...anything that is your neighbour's. You shall not desire your neighbour's house, his field, or his manservant, or his maidservant, or his ox, or his ass, or anything that is your neighbour's (Exodus 20:17). St John the Evangelist identified three kinds of covetousness: lust of the flesh, lust of the eyes and the pride of life (1 John 2:16). The tenth commandment addresses an interior attitude of the heart, an avarice and inordinate desire to possess our neighbour's goods, property and material possessions.

Lord Jesus, set me free from the sadness of envy whose dark desire is to possess and own the goods which belong to my neighbour. Grant me the great grace of contentment and joy, the fruit of knowing your love.

In the film Wall Street, Gordan Gekko a hedge fund manager, coined the phrase, 'Greed is good.' The comedian Harry Enfield parodied the boastful rich with the character Stavros, who shouted out whilst adorned with a wad of pound notes in his hand, 'Loads of money.' Greed is not good; it is evil. 'Loads of money' is the slogan of the prideful and arrogant. Pope Francis condemned 'the cult of money' and urged world leaders to consider the words of St John Chrysostom who said 'Not to share one's goods with the poor is to rob from them.' The problem with money is we will never have enough of it and greed and avarice impoverish and diminish our human dignity.

'The worship of the golden calf of old has found a new and heartless image in the cult of money and the dictatorship of an economy which is faceless and lacking any truly human goal.' (Pope Francis)

YOUCAT 465

Lord, preserve and protect us from falling into the unsatiable hunger of greed and the unquenchable thirst of avarice.

'From envy are born hatred, detraction, calumny, joy caused by the misfortune of a neighbour, and displeasure caused by his prosperity.' (St Gregory the Great)

YOUCAT 466

Envy is an exhausting vice. It saps us of energy and creates within us a sadness of heart. The sage taught that it was through the devil's envy that death entered the world (Wisdom 2:24). St Augustine referred to it as ...'the diabolical sin.' When envy intends grave harm to a neighbour it becomes a mortal sin (CCC 2539). Some are more prone to it than others and it can be for many of those afflicted a lifelong and intense struggle. How do we conquer envy? How do we resist it? By keeping the commandments. By showing good will towards our neighbour and rejoicing in their achievements. As St John Chrysostom taught, '....conquer envy by rejoicing in the merits of others, God will be praised.'

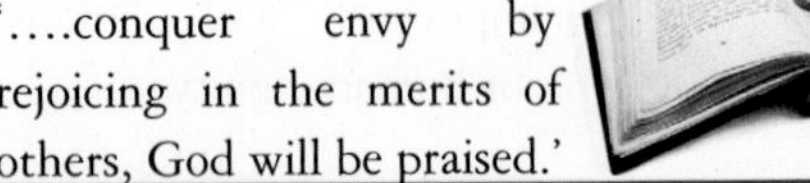

Lord God, help me to resist and overcome the sin of envy by giving praise and thanks for all the good gifts, blessings and graces I have received, and by extending the hand of charity and good will to my neighbour.

St Paul struggled with obeying the ninth and tenth commandments. 'For I would not have known what coveting really was if the law had not said, 'Do not covet.' (Romans 7:6). He writes powerfully and eloquently of his own interior fight. Rather than preventing him from coveting, the commandment opened him up to, 'every kind of covetousness desire' (Romans 7:8). In other words, although he had the desire to obey the commandments, he could not (Romans 7:18). What was the remedy, the solution? He cried out, 'Who will rescue me from this body of death? (Romans 7:24). And he answered his own question: 'Thanks be to God - through Jesus Christ our Lord' (Romans 7:25).

'But now the righteousness of God has been revealed apart from law, although the law and the prophets bear witness to it, the righteousness of God through faith in Jesus Christ for all who believe.' (Romans 3:21-22)

YOUCAT p.254

Lord, we have crucified the flesh with its passions and desires and we are led by the Spirit and now follow the desires of the Spirit.

'For your sake he became poor.' (2 Corinthians 8:9)

'Who being in very nature God, did not consider equality with God something to be grasped.' (Philippians 2:6)

YOUCAT 467

It is a lifelong battle to prevent greed, avarice and envy poisoning the soul. How do we win the battle and conquer such foes? Jesus shows us the way in the first Beatitude, 'Blessed are the poor in spirit.' (Matthew 5:3). To understand what it means to be truly 'poor in spirit' we need a grace of revelation, an insight into the mind of God. To be poor in spirit is to realize how naked and abject the creature is before the good Creator (Revelation 3:20). To be poor in spirit is to realize our utter dependence on and need of God. Through this insight of wisdom, the shine and glare of possessions, status, position, wealth and riches fade and grow dim and pale.

Lord, help me to be attentive to the witness of the poor widow of Jerusalem and strive to be poor of spirit and generous of heart. For she gave to God out of her poverty all she had to live on.

I WANT TO SEE GOD (CCC 2548-2549)

DAY 329

The goal of the Christian life, the purpose of our pilgrimage, is to behold the face of God. In short, to see God. This is our hope that spurs us on but only after death can we truly behold God. The Ten Commandments are simply signposts, guideposts to that end. They help us live happy and fulfilled lives. As St Clement of Alexandria said, 'Happiness is the practice of the virtues.' True, the commandments are handed down to us in the form of prohibitions but they serve to keep us on the path of righteousness, the road to salvation. The Catechism in its opening paragraph explains why this is our goal, purpose and mission: 'God is infinitely perfect and blessed in himself' (CCC 1).

'God alone satisfies.' (St Thomas Aquinas)

YOUCAT 468

Heavenly Father, help me to keep the Ten Commandments, practise the Beatitudes and witness to the goodness, truth and beauty of the Gospel.

'God himself will be the goal of our desires; we shall contemplate him without end, love him without surfeit, praise him without weariness. This gift, this state, this act, like eternal life itself, will assuredly be common to all.' (St Augustine)

YOUCAT 468

Our vocation invites us to walk the Highway of Holiness called the Way of Perfection. The Spirit and the Bride, the Church, constantly summon us to live holy lives. To be perfect as the Father is perfect is in essence the Christian calling (Matthew 5:48). In short, God wants us to be saints. As St Thérèse of Lisieux said, 'You cannot be half a saint. You must be a whole saint or no saint at all.' God chose us in him before the foundation of the world to be holy and blameless in his sight (Ephesians 1:3-4). Through baptism we are made holy, because baptism unites us to Jesus and his Paschal Mystery, but we also need to become holy by conforming ourselves ever more closely to Christ.

Lord Jesus, you are the treasure, and where our treasure is, there our hearts are also (Matthew 6:21). Teach me to take up the call to be holy, as God is holy, and to be a saint, as God calls us to be saints.

PART FOUR

CHRISITIAN PRAYER

Here we are at Part Four of the Catechism, entitled Christian Prayer. When the Catechism was first published, many people claimed that this section on prayer was the most beautiful part of the Catechism. However, it is important to understand that the Catechism's teaching on prayer does not stand as something separate from the rest of the Catechism. Indeed, the key to its richness and beauty is the way that it is integrated with each of the other three sections of the Catechism.

There are four threads or themes that run through the whole Catechism and that tie the four parts together. The first of these is the centrality of the Trinity. Every element of the Catechism is entirely Trinitarian, and this is especially true of Part Four.

The second theme is the person of Christ. Christian prayer is essentially a sharing in the prayer of Christ – this theme draws upon the Vatican Council Constitution on the Sacred Liturgy *(Sacrosanctum Concilium)*.

The third theme is the Paschal Mystery of Jesus' death and resurrection. At the time of his death, Jesus most fully reveals that prayer is the response to the thirst of God to draw humanity to himself and, at the same time, reveals the perfect human response – the sacrifice of worship and obedience to the Father on behalf of all people.

Finally, a key theme, is that of the dignity of the human person. God reveals our true dignity by creating humanity in his own image and likeness, and even more through redeeming and reconciling us through Jesus and holding out to us an eternal and heavenly destiny. In fact, all of these themes relate directly to the Constitution on the Sacred Liturgy.

We could summarise the whole teaching of Part Four under four headings:

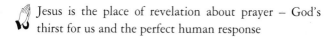

 Jesus is the place of revelation about prayer – God's thirst for us and the perfect human response

 Jesus invites us to drink at the wellsprings of prayer

 Prayer issues from the new heart – the place where we have become united with Jesus

 Jesus teaches us to pray the Lord's Prayer: the summary of the whole gospel

Revelation about Prayer

The truth about prayer begins with God himself. In the person of Jesus Christ God reveals his thirst for human beings to come into a relationship with him. Perhaps surprisingly, the Catechism refers to the incident at the well of Samaria, where Jesus expresses his thirst to the woman, who herself had come seeking water. This same thirst is expressed by Jesus on the Cross. Jesus is giving voice to something much more than a physical thirst. He is revealing, making incarnate, the very thirst of God for the human race, which itself is thirsting for God but is largely ignorant of where the living water of eternal life is to be found.

At the beginning of Part One of the Catechism we saw through the words of St Augustine that 'our hearts are restless, until they find their rest in you' (CCC 30). This restlessness has its origin in creation because God has made us so that we could come to know him. In Jesus the thirst of God for humanity and the cry of humanity for God become united.

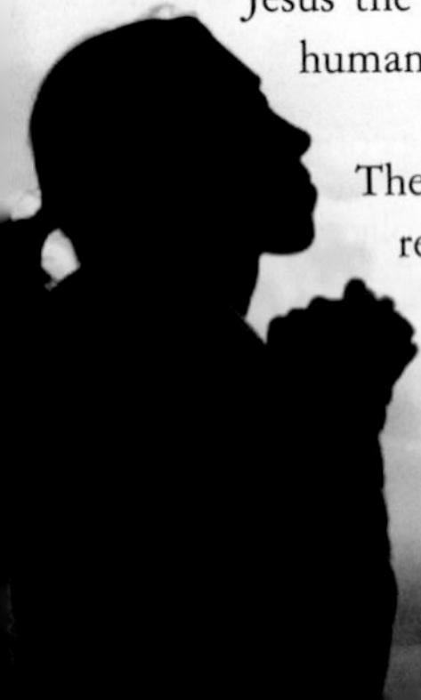

The revelation of God about prayer, about the relationship of God and humanity in prayer, began with creation and reaches its fullness in Jesus. The whole Old Testament is also a rich source of teaching about prayer. The various events and persons of the history of Israel are shown in the Catechism to

highlight a variety of elements of prayer which have now become the tradition of Christian prayer.

But most of all, the very person of Christ – his own personal prayer to the Father and his teaching on prayer – is the essence of the Catechism's teaching. We shall see throughout Part Four that Christian Prayer is essentially a participation, a sharing in the filial prayer of Jesus to the Father.

JESUS INVITES US TO DRINK AT THE WELLSPRINGS OF PRAYER

Jesus told the woman at the well of Samaria that he is the one who will give us living water. He was referring to the gift of the Holy Spirit, whom the Catechism names as 'the interior Master of Christian Prayer'. It is the Holy Spirit within us who joins us to the prayer of Jesus. The Spirit is present also in other wellsprings from which our prayer can be nourished: the Sacred Scriptures; the Liturgy; the gifts of faith, hope and charity, infused in us at Baptism; the Spirit is also active in the events of our lives drawing us into prayer.

PRAYER ISSUES FROM THE NEW HEART, WHERE WE ARE UNITED WITH JESUS

Christian prayer is activity that arises from the new heart, the new spirit, that God has created within us since our baptism. The Catechism encourages us to discover this new heart through personal conversion to Christ and through spiritual exercises – establishing a rhythm of prayer – daily, weekly in the Sunday Eucharist, and annually through the Church's feasts and seasons.

Jesus Teaches Us to Pray the Our Father – the Summary of the Whole Gospel

The final section of Part Four of the Catechism is a focus on the Lord's Prayer. The Our Father is the climax and summary of all that Sacred Scripture, and that Jesus himself, teaches us about prayer. The more that each of the proclamations of faith and petitions of the Lord's Prayer truly become an expression of our own heart and will, the more we can be sure that we are being transformed and conformed to the image of Jesus.

The second section of Part Four of the Catechism explores at length the meaning of the proclamations of faith and petitions of the Our Father. We shall discover the amazing richness of this prayer which is so familiar to us, but perhaps so little understood.

Christ with the Woman of Samaria by Paolo Veronese

'Prayer is the encounter of God's thirst with ours. God thirsts that we may thirst for him.' (CCC 2560, St Augustine)

YOUCAT 469

The Catechism describes prayer first of all as a vital and personal relationship with the living and true God. Then, referring to the writings of St Thérèse of Lisieux and St John Damascene, it speaks of prayer as 'a surge of the heart', 'a simple look towards heaven' and 'the raising of one's heart and mind to God, or the requesting of good things from God'. But the wonder of prayer is that it is really a response to the thirst of Jesus, who also reveals the thirst and desire of God, that we would come into a relationship with him. Even our prayer of petition is initiated by God. It is God who gives us the instinct to ask him for what we need, because he wants to give us himself.

Lord Jesus, help me to understand that your cry of thirst on the Cross was really the expression of your deep longing for me to come to you in prayer. Each time I choose to pray I am really responding in love to your call.

Prayer: A Covenant of Communion with God (CCC 2562-2565)

Day 332

A key concept used to help us understand the deepest mystery of prayer is that of the Covenant. It expresses a solemn joining together of two parties. The Covenant of prayer is the deep union between us and God. The Catechism speaks of the heart of man, not referring to the organ that pumps our blood, but rather our spiritual centre, where the very Spirit of God touches our being. It is the place where we become united to the Father through union with his Son, Jesus. We see once again that the Trinity is at the very centre of our Christian life and faith. This awesome truth of our relationship with the Trinity has its origin in our baptism.

'The life of prayer is the habit of being in the presence of the thrice-holy God and in communion with him.' (CCC 2565, St Gregory of Nazianzus)

YOUCAT 469

Holy Spirit, you dwell in my spirit. Help me to know how to enter into my deepest self in order to be in communion with the Father. Draw me into the same experience of sonship that belongs to Jesus and that he longs to share with me.

'In creating us God has made an indefectible covenant with every living creature and has always called people to prayer.' (CCC 2569)

YOUCAT 470

The instinct to pray lies in the very core of our being. We are created by God or as the Catechism puts it: 'God calls every being from nothingness into existence'. We are in the image of God, and in spite of original sin, we retain deep within us the desire for God. God, who called us into existence, continues to call us into 'that mysterious encounter known as prayer' (CCC 2567). In the history of mankind, and especially in the history of salvation, there is a great drama of our search for God and God's call to us. The revelation of this drama gradually unfolds in the history of the Old Testament and the following paragraphs of the Catechism will show this.

Lord God, I know that because of original sin the will and the desire to pray can be weakened in me. But I recognise that you are constantly calling all of us back to our true relationship with you. Help me to be restored to your likeness by turning my heart towards you.

We now turn to the revelation of prayer throughout the Old Testament – focusing principally on Abraham (and Jacob), Moses, Elijah, David and the Psalms. Several elements of prayer are highlighted from the life history of Abraham and his grandson, Jacob. Abraham is revealed as a man who responded in faith to God and who trusted in God's fidelity. God's visitation to Abraham foreshadows the coming of God among us in the Son, Jesus Christ. In his call to sacrifice his son, Isaac, Abraham becomes conformed to the likeness of God the Father – who will not spare his own Son.

'The spiritual tradition of the Church' has retained from Jacob's wrestle with God 'the symbol of prayer as a battle of faith and as the triumph of perseverance.' (CCC 2573, Genesis 32:24-30, Luke 18:1-8)

YOUCAT 471

Father, through our forefather Abraham you first began to reveal the lengths to which you would go in order to re-establish a covenant relationship of love with humanity. Help me to follow his example of faith.

'The king lifts his hands' in prayer on behalf of all, 'that the nations may know that he is the only God and that the heart of his people may belong wholly and entirely to him.' (CCC 2580, 1 Kings 8:10-61)

YOUCAT 472

Moses is the great model for intercessory prayer. He prays not for himself but for the people whom God has made his own. This ability and call derive from his experience of God revealing himself as a God who wishes to save his people. But Moses' experience only gradually attunes his will to that of God. Through his resistance to God, his excuses and most of all his questions, he converses with God. In response God confides to Moses his holy Name (God's reality). God spoke 'face to face' with Moses – a foreshadowing of Jesus. Through this intimacy God draws Moses into his work of salvation through intercession.

Today, like Moses, I intercede for all people, especially those closest to me or for whom you have given me a special care and responsibility.

ELIJAH, THE PROPHETS AND CONVERSION OF HEART (CCC 2581-2584)

DAY 336

In Israel the Temple became the principal place of experience and practice of prayer. The Temple and all that took place within it were signs of God's holiness and closeness. The danger, however, was that the people's practice would become mere ritual. Elijah and the prophets realised that people needed formation and conversion of heart – not unlike the present day. Elijah's story reveals the great power of intercessory prayer – he is able to call down fire from heaven and to raise the child of the widow of Zarephath back to life. He experiences, as did Moses, the presence and revelation of God on the mountain – a foreshadowing of the Transfiguration.

'Elijah foreshadows Jesus, who brings the fire of divine compassion and mercy and restores life to the human race.' (Pope Benedict XVI, Jesus of Nazareth, pp.196-7)

Lord Jesus, at Mass and at prayer, help me always truly to seek your face and to be transformed, so that, like Elijah, my prayer also will be powerful and effective in helping to make present the fire of God.

Day 337

The Psalms and the Prayer of the Church (CCC 2585-2589)

'The Psalms proclaim God's deeds and man's response. Christ will unite the two in himself. We pray the psalms as fulfilled in Christ.' (CCC 2587, Constitution on Divine Revelation, paragraph 39, Constitution on the Sacred Liturgy, paragraph 83)

YOUCAT 473

These next few paragraphs on the Psalms are very powerful and very beautiful. They express the great richness of what the Catechism calls 'the masterwork of prayer in the Old Testament'. Such is their richness that the Church continues to use them as its principal expression of prayer, in the Mass and the Divine Office. The rest of the Old Testament is largely a record of God's mighty deeds in history, bringing to light the mystery they contain. The Psalms, however, both express and proclaim God's great works, and, at the same time, put into words our own response (essentially Alleluia – Praise the Lord!).

Teach me, Holy Spirit, to treasure the Psalms. Not only were they the prayers on the lips of Christ, but they all have their fullest meaning and fulfilment in him. Open my eyes always to see and pray them in the light of Christ.

God's revelation about prayer is made known to us in Jesus himself. We approach Jesus as he engages in prayer, and hearing what he has to say about how we might share in his prayer. The key teaching of these paragraphs is that Jesus has made present and real in our humanity true filial prayer. For the first time ever, the Father receives from humanity the prayer which he has awaited from his children. It is prayer in which his human heart completely adheres to the will of the Father and in which his constant petition is always made with confident thanksgiving.

'In the loud cry of Jesus on the Cross, he sums up all the troubles of sinful humanity and all the petitions and intercessions of salvation history. The Father accepts them and answers them by raising his Son.' (CCC 2605-2606)

YOUCAT 474

Jesus, Lord, you came into the world to reveal to us all the mystery of your relationship with the Father. Moreover, you revealed in practice a human life lived out in complete union with the Father.

'In this new covenant the certitude that our petition will be heard is founded on the prayer of Jesus.'(CCC 2614)

YOUCAT 477

In the Gospels Jesus also gives explicit teaching on prayer, leading us progressively to the Father. This movement to the Father through Jesus in the Holy Spirit is the heart of our prayer. At Mass and in prayer he takes and leads us to the Father. Prayer requires a filial conversion entirely directed to the Father, and calls for a faith that is completely adhering to the Father. This faith is confident and bold because he himself is the door and the way. Jesus introduces his disciples and us, through his teaching and parables, into the Kingdom of God. If we practise, in union with Jesus, the characteristics of prayer that he teaches, the Father will deepen in us the Holy Spirit.

Jesus, you have taught us to 'ask in your name'. This is not a formula but an entrance with you, the Son of God, into the same filial union with the Father.

Today we reflect on the prayer of Mary. Her prayer is revealed at certain key moments of her life. First to be mentioned are the Annunciation and Pentecost. At each of these moments Mary's prayer cooperates in a unique way with the Father's plan – first for the conception of Christ and then for the conception of the Church, Christ's body. Mary's prayer is a *fiat* – let it be done to me according to your word. At Cana Mary intercedes for the needs of the guests – a sign of the Church asking for the gift of his Body and Blood; at the foot of the Cross, Mary's prayer is her silent union with her Son as he accomplishes the Father's will.

'The Canticle of Mary, the Magnificat ..., is the song both of the Mother of God and of the Church.' (CCC 2619)

YOUCAT 479 - 480

Hail Mary, full of grace, the Lord is with thee. Blessed art thou amongst women, and blessed is the fruit of thy womb, Jesus.

Day 341

The Spirit teaches the Church to pray (CCC 2623-2628)

'The prayer of blessing is man's response to God's gifts. Adoration is homage of the spirit to the 'King of Glory'.' (CCC 2626, 2628, Psalm 24:9-10)

YOUCAT 482-485

Since the day of Pentecost, the Holy Spirit has brought to mind everything that Jesus said and taught and forms the Church in the life of prayer. Through Acts 2:42, the Catechism shows that the Church's prayer is founded on the truth handed on by Jesus to the apostles, on their fellowship of love, and the nourishment of the Eucharist. The Spirit forms us in prayer through Scripture and through prayers in the Liturgy and the Church's spiritual traditions. The prayer of blessing is the basic twofold movement of Christian prayer – in the Spirit, through Christ we bless the Father; the Father blesses us with the gift of the Spirit through his Son.

Holy Spirit, teach me to bless the Father, because he has first blessed me with your presence as the supreme gift in my life.

Our prayers of petition and intercession are very human and natural because they arise from our utterly dependent nature and need for God. We did not choose our own coming into existence; neither are we 'the master of adversity' nor do we determine our final end. We all stand before God as fallen sinners asking for mercy and forgiveness. This prayer re-establishes our relationship with the Father – the very relationship shared between the Father and the Son – and into relationship with one another. After this, petition becomes our expression of desiring all that God wills and desires. As we pray for the coming of the kingdom, we co-operate with its coming.

'Christ ... is glorified by what we ask the Father in his name.' (CCC 2633, John 14:13)

'The intercession of Christians knows no boundaries.' (CCC 2636, 1 Timothy 2:1)

YOUCAT 486-487

Father, I pray that your kingdom will come in all the world and that all of humanity turn their hearts to you.

'The thanksgiving of the members of the Body participates in that of their Head.' (CCC 2637, Constitution on the Sacred Liturgy, paragraph 48)

YOUCAT 488

The Catechism speaks of the prayer of thanksgiving as a particular characteristic of the prayer of the Church. Thanksgiving acknowledges what God has already done, especially the great work of salvation in Jesus Christ. In Christ, we have already received everything and we are utterly convinced of the Father's love and care. It is this spirit of thanksgiving that provides the basis for confident petition. The Catechism states that every event and need in our lives can become an offering of thanksgiving. Even on the Cross Jesus' heart was full of thanksgiving as he commended himself into the Father's hands.

I thank you, Father, for opening my eyes to see that every aspect of my prayer is really a sharing in the very prayer of Christ, your Son.

Praise is the most self-less of all prayer. Praise is to recognise and worship God for who he is, rather than what he has done. 'Praise embraces the other forms of prayer and carries them toward him who is its source and goal' (CCC 2639). Praise of God was often the spontaneous reaction of the crowds to the words and actions of Jesus, especially in Luke's Gospel. In the Acts of the Apostles, wonder and praise are seen as the work of the Holy Spirit. To express praise, the Church from the beginning looked to the psalms – reading them in and with Christ. And under the inspiration of the Spirit, the Church composed hymns and canticles to God and joined with the song of the saints in heaven.

'The Eucharist contains and expresses all forms of prayer ... it is the sacrifice of praise.' (CCC 2643, Constitution on the Sacred Liturgy, paragraph 10)

YOUCAT 489

Glory be to the Father, and to the Son, and to the Holy Spirit. As it was in the beginning, is now, and ever shall be, world without end Amen.

DAY 345

THE WELLSPRINGS OF PRAYER - THE WORD OF GOD (CCC 2650-2654)

'The Church forcefully and specially exhorts all the Christian faithful ... to 'learn the surpassing knowledge of Jesus Christ' (Philemon 3:8) by frequent reading of the divine Scriptures.' (CCC 2653, St Ambrose)

YOUCAT 491

The Catechism teaches us, through the power of the Spirit, how to pray. In particular, we discover the principal resources that should be used to nourish our prayer and then we shall see once again how our prayer, if it is to be truly Christian prayer, must be entirely Trinitarian – also uniting us in the Church with Mary, the Mother of Jesus (as it has been from the beginning – Acts 1:14). The work of the Spirit in teaching us to pray is to lead us to 'the wellsprings of prayer'. The first of these is the Sacred Scriptures. Prayer and Scripture go together because in Scripture – the Word of God – God reveals himself and speaks to us, and in prayer we respond to him.

Holy Spirit, give me the courage and the will to open the Scriptures. Open the ears of my heart to be sensitive to the silent voice of God revealing himself and his plan of salvation.

The Wellspring of the Liturgy (CCC 2655)

Day 346

The second great source or wellspring for our prayer is the Sacred Liturgy. Here the Catechism has a side reference back to the beginning of Part Two of the Catechism (on the Liturgy or celebration of the Christian Mystery) – 'The liturgy is also a participation in Christ's own prayer addressed to the Father in the Holy Spirit' (CCC 1073). Our prayer is always a participation in Christ's prayer. This is a wonderful and enriching way to understand our own sharing in the celebration of Mass (the Eucharist) and the other sacraments. If we allow Christ to unite us in his prayer to the Father at Mass, we shall find that the effect and experience carries over into our daily lives.

'Prayer is always prayer of the Church; it is a communion with the Holy Trinity.' (CCC 2655)

YOUCAT 492

Father, help me to recognise that, every time I participate in the Holy Mass, I am being united with Christ in his prayer; and that, through him and with him, I enter into your presence and into communion with you.

Day 347

In Faith, Hope and Love (CCC 2656-2658)

'I love you, O my God, and my only desire is to love you until the last breath of my life.' (St John Vianney, CCC 2658)

YOUCAT 493

In baptism we receive the 'theological virtues' of faith, hope and love (CCC 1266). These gifts are to be activated and allowed to grow through a conscious and daily exercise. Without this they remain dormant in us. We can only enter prayer by 'the narrow gate of faith' (CCC 2656). By faith we take hold of Christ and all that he has revealed. To pray in hope means that we pray both privately and in the liturgy in expectation of Christ's return and also that we trust that God will hear and answer our cries. Finally, love is the source of prayer. God's love is poured into our hearts and this love enables us to love him in return.

Most Holy Trinity, I thank you for the gifts of faith, hope and love and ask you to make these the power by which I live and pray each day. Forgive my unbelief, my lack of hope and my many failures to be filled with your love.

THE EVENTS OF EACH DAY (CCC 2659-2660)

The final wellspring or source of prayer is simply entitled 'today'. This is not simply an exhortation to pray at different times during the day. Rather it is teaching something about the way God acts. The whole history of salvation has seen God acting through events, revealing himself and his purposes. The Catechism applies this to our individual lives. We do not rely simply on the fact that God has acted in the past, or on our hope that he will act in the future. It is in the present that we encounter him, not yesterday, nor tomorrow but today. (CCC 2659). The moments and events of our lives today are an occasion and source for prayer as God speaks to us in them.

'O that today you would listen to his voice! Harden not your hearts'
(Psalm 95:7-8, CCC 2659)

YOUCAT 494

Lord God, I believe that you are present to me through every hour of the day. Help me to see every moment and event in this way and to turn them into occasions for prayer.

DAY 349

PRAYER TO THE FATHER AND TO THE SON (CCC 2663-2669)

'The sacred humanity of Jesus is therefore the way by which the Holy Spirit teaches us to pray to God the Father.' (CCC 2664, Constitution on the Sacred Liturgy, 7)

In paragraph 2663 the Catechism states that the Magisterium of the Church has the duty of discerning the language of prayer – the words used, melodies, gestures and iconography – to make sure that they remain faithful, as ways of praying, to the tradition of apostolic faith. The Catechism also makes the point that pastors and catechists should explain this to the faithful. The next few paragraphs emphasise the fundamental principle that prayer – words, songs etc – must always be Trinitarian and rooted in the prayer and the humanity of Jesus. Prayer is ultimately to the Father, through Jesus and in the power of the Spirit.

YOUCAT 495-496

Lord Jesus Christ, Son of God, have mercy on us sinners.

The Catechism is constantly drawing us into and teaching us about the mystery of the Trinity. We can grow so much in our understanding of the Trinity through the Catechism, even though we will never exhaust the mystery. The Catechism speaks of the 'prevenient grace' of the divine person, the Holy Spirit. This is a shorthand way of saying that even before we can make any movement towards God, towards the Father, even towards Christ himself, there has to be something preparing and moving us. This is the work of the Holy Spirit. In fact, the Holy Spirit acts in us, moving us even to ask for the Holy Spirit to be poured out upon us and upon the world.

'I believe in the Holy Spirit, the Lord the giver of life, who proceeds from the Father and the Son, and who with the Father and the Son is adored and glorified.' (Creed)

YOUCAT 496

'Heavenly King, Consoler Spirit, Spirit of Truth, present everywhere and filling all things, treasure of all good and source of all life, come dwell in us, cleanse and save us, you who are All-Good'. (Byzantine Liturgy, Pentecost Vespers), (CCC 2671).

Day 351

Prayer in communion with Mary (CCC 2673-2679)

'The Holy Spirit first united God's Son with Mary, from whom he received his humanity. Now the Spirit unites us, through Christ, with Mary as our mother.' (CCC 2673, Lumen Gentium 53)

The Holy Spirit unites us to Jesus Christ in his glorified humanity. We share in Christ's filial prayer to the Father and the Spirit unites us in the Church with Mary, the Mother of Jesus. The Church from the beginning has learned, not only to pray with Mary, but also to pray to Mary. There are two characteristics or movements of prayer to Mary. The first is to 'magnify God' for the great things he did for her and, through her, for us all. The second is to entrust the praise and supplication of all God's children to the Mother of Jesus. The Catechism illustrates this twofold movement by unpacking the words of the Hail Mary.

YOUCAT 479

Hail Mary, full of grace, the Lord is with thee. Blessed art thou among women and blessed is the fruit of thy womb, Jesus. Holy Mary, Mother of God, pray for us sinners now, and at the hour of our death. Amen.

Today the focus is on the saints, who are part of the Church's living tradition. They are guides, first by the example of their lives, and then by their continuing intercession for us, which is now their role in heaven. We turn often to the saints, especially our patron saints, because it reminds us that they are interceding and praying for us and because their prayer is united with the will of God. Particular spiritualities, developed by the saints (St Ignatius, St Thérèse of Lisieux), are also guides. The Catechism wonderfully describes them all as 'refractions of the one pure light of the Holy Spirit' (CCC 2684)

'The saints developed varied spiritualities 'so that their followers may have a share in their spirit'.' (CCC 2684)

YOUCAT 497

Today is an opportunity to pray to your favourite or patron saint. Thank the saint for his or her fidelity to God and for the example of his or her life. Ask that he or she would intercede for you and for your needs.

Day 353

Servants of Prayer (CCC 2685-2690)

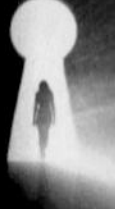

'Memorisation of basic prayers offers an essential support to the life of prayer, but it is important to help learners savour their meaning.' (CCC 2688)

It is in the family that God's children first learn to pray. Next to be considered are ordained ministers. They have a particular ministry of teaching the sources of prayer considered last week. Those called to the religious life have dedicated themselves to a life of prayer and intercession. Their witness is an example and a help to us to remember to make prayer an important part of our lives. The Catechism also mentions the essential work of catechesis and refers also to 'prayer groups' and 'schools of prayer' as signs and one of the driving forces of renewal of prayer today. Last to be mentioned are those gifted as spiritual directors.

Father, I pray that I may recognise my own role as a guide for others in prayer – not least by my example. Help me to be faithful to the role you have given me. Help me to be a wise guide.

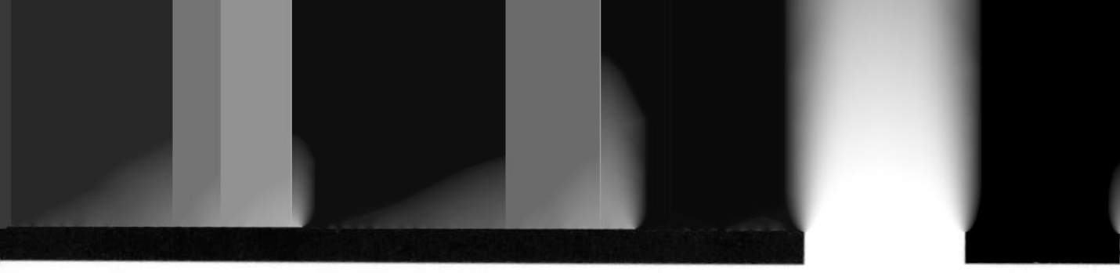

Finding a favourable place for prayer can be challenging but is crucial in helping us to turn our minds and hearts to God without the everyday distractions. The Church is the privileged place for the parish liturgy and for adoration of the Blessed Sacraments. Monasteries also afford opportunities for participation in the Liturgy of the Hours (the Divine Office) and for times of Retreat or more prolonged times of personal prayer. Pilgrimages to holy places and shrines can be occasions to renew our prayer and remind us of the journey of our lives to heaven. Perhaps we might consider a 'prayer corner' or 'a little oratory' in the home.

'The choice of a favourable place is not a matter of indifference for true prayer.' (CCC 2691)

YOUCAT 498

Father, I thank you for altars and tabernacles, and crucifixes, that turn my mind to your Son, and for those holy places – Churches, Shrines and Religious Houses – that call me to prayer.

DAY 355

THE LIFE OF PRAYER (CCC 2697-2699)

'Prayer is the life of the new heart. It ought to animate us at every moment.' (CCC 2697)

In the book of Ezekiel (Ez.36:25) in the Old Testament, God promises: 'I shall give you a new heart and put a new spirit in you'. Prayer is the activity by which this new heart, received in Baptism, is nourished and grows. One of the characteristics of the new heart is that of remembrance of God. The spiritual heart is alive insofar as remembering God happens often in the course of the day. To assist in this, the Church always proposed certain rhythms of prayer. There are several elements that contribute to this rhythm – daily, weekly and the cycle of seasons and feasts in the Church's year. We might reflect on these to ask the extent to which these rhythms are present in our lives.

Lord God, time itself is made holy through the rhythms of prayer that are laced through it. I will learn to experience your presence at all times if I practise turning to you during my day.

We are called to pray and give glory to God with all our heart, soul and strength. Our prayer needs to be expressed through our physical bodies, not least our voices. In vocal prayer our bodies become involved in the interior movement of our hearts towards God. One danger is that there can be a separation between our voice and our interior disposition. Even in the Old Testament, God warned that 'this people honours me with their lips, but there hearts are far from me' (Isaiah 29:13). It is vital that 'the heart should be present to him to whom we are speaking in prayer' (CCC 2700). Jesus himself prayed vocally and taught his disciples a vocal prayer, the *Our Father.*

'We must pray with our whole being to give all power possible to our supplication.' (CCC 2702)

YOUCAT 501

Holy Spirit, interior master of the life of prayer, grant that my heart will always seek to be attuned to the words of my prayer.

'Christians owe it to themselves to develop the desire to meditate regularly, lest they come to resemble the first three kinds of soil in the parable of the sower.' (CCC 2707, Mark 4:4-7, 15-19)

YOUCAT 502; 504

In the prayer of meditation we endeavour to engage our minds with the mystery of God, with the great truth of our redemption in Christ, and with the 'why and the how of the Christian life' (CCC 2705). The Catechism acknowledges that this is not always easy to sustain and therefore encourages the use of various aids – the Scriptures, holy icons, liturgical texts, spiritual writings, and what it calls the great book of creation and of history. In using such aids we allow God and his revelation to confront our lives in order to bring our lives and especially our thinking into conformity with God and with his will. They help us also to discern God's will for us in our daily life and decisions.

Father, you call us to meditate especially on the mysteries of Christ. Help me to rediscover the practice of the rosary and Lectio Divina (meditating on the words of the Gospel) so as to grow in love for Jesus and union with him.

Contemplative Prayer (CCC 2709-2719)

Day 358

It is hard to express summarily the content of the teaching of the Catechism on contemplative prayer. It would be especially helpful today to read the eleven paragraphs in the Catechism itself. There is a simplicity about contemplative prayer. It does not need words or even a great deal of thinking. Rather, it is a matter of making oneself present to God and turning one's heart towards him. It is 'a gaze of faith, fixed on Jesus... on the mysteries of the life of Christ' (CCC 2715). This gaze allows us also, through the Holy Spirit's power, to enter into Christ's prayer to the Father. It requires a definite effort to set aside a certain period of time and to persevere in spite of difficulties and trials.

'We must be willing to 'keep watch with [him] one hour'.' (Matthew 26:40), (CCC 2719)

YOUCAT 503

Lord, sometimes the most difficult thing to do is to sit in silence in your presence for a prolonged time. Yet, with endurance, empowered by the Spirit, my inner being becomes strengthened.

'Many Christians unconsciously regard prayer as an occupation that is incompatible with all the other things they have to do: so they 'don't have the time'.' *(CCC 2726)*

YOUCAT 505

Now we move on to explore The Battle of Prayer. The Church takes very seriously the fact that we all find that prayer does not come easily in spite of our best intentions. Prayer, then, is truly a battle – against ourselves and against the wiles of the evil one. The Catechism unpacks the reasons for this battle, including false notions of what prayer is, and the fact that we can have a 'worldly mentality' that prizes so many other things as good and desirable and chokes out the desire for God. We also face discouragement because our experience of prayer is not always satisfying. We battle for humility, trust and perseverance.

To engage in prayer is to undertake a battle. But the fruit is beyond our expectations. Dear Lord, give me the courage and the will to choose to pray and the strength to endure.

Facing Difficulties in Prayer (CCC 2729-2731)

Day 360

The common difficulty in prayer is distraction. But in reality, distractions simply reveal what we are attached to. We can resolve to turn our hearts in preference for God and ask that our hearts be purified. Dryness is another difficulty – the lack of taste for spiritual thoughts or feelings. This may be the result of a basic lack of conversion, or a call to share in the agony of Jesus, and even in his death awaiting resurrection in the tomb. This requires 'sheer faith' and clinging to Jesus. When the heart needs conversion, the word of God leads us to repentance. This battle requires vigilance – persevering in faith until the Lord comes.

'Therein lies the battle, the choice of which master to serve' (CCC 2729, Matthew 6:21, 24)

YOUCAT 508

The bridegroom comes in the middle of the night; the light that must not be extinguished is that of faith: 'Come,' my heart says, 'seek his face!' (CCC 2730)

DAY 361

FACING TEMPTATIONS IN PRAYER (CCC 2732-2733)

'Incredulity is the neglect of revealed truth or the wilful refusal to assent to it.' (CCC 2089)

YOUCAT 505; 508

The two basic temptations in prayer are lack of faith and *acedia*, which is described as a sort of depression because of our failure and carelessness about spiritual practices. In the first, many other things – labours and cares – vie for priority. Our want of faith shows that we still need to develop the disposition of the humble heart, which acknowledges that we can do nothing without God. It is the opposite of a kind of presumption, which turns to God as a last resort. Humility recognises the truth of who God really is and our utter dependence upon him. We are sinners; weaknesses and failures are a part of this. The humble will persevere in trust and steadfastness.

Rescue me, O God, from the temptations of presumption and despair. May the gift of faith grow ever stronger in me, so that I may confidently persevere in prayer.

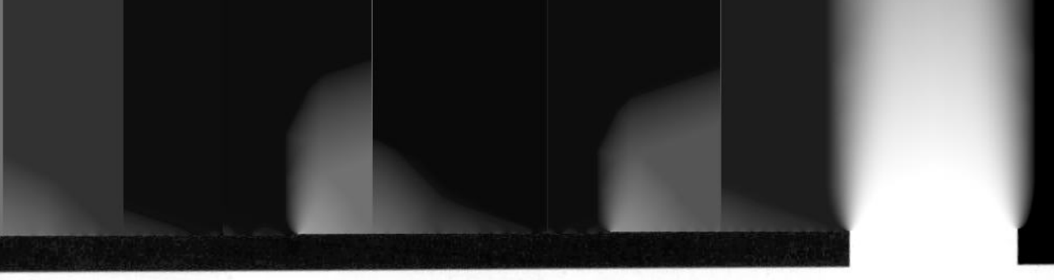

One of our greatest problems with regard to prayer is the feeling that our prayer is not being heard or answered. The Catechism invites us to ask why we think this and to understand more in what way prayer is efficacious. There is firstly the issue of the image of God that we have. Is it that we use God as an instrument to obtain what we want? Petition should be rooted in the conviction that God has already done great things in redeeming us through Christ and that he utterly and always desires what is good for us. We do not always know what is good for us. We need to pray in order to realise what he wants to give us (St Augustine).

'If we enter into the desire of his Spirit, we shall be heard.' (CCC 2737)

YOUCAT 507

Father, I ask pardon that sometimes I want you to answer my prayer as a proof that you love me. I want to trust that you already love me and to have confidence that you will grant what is best.

DAY
363

IS PRAYER EFFECTIVE? (CCC 2738-2741)

'Our filial trust is enkindled by his supreme act: the Passion and Resurrection of his Son.' (CCC 2738)

YOUCAT 507

The first effect of prayer is the transformation of the praying heart. We tend to focus on what we might be praying for, while God's desire is focused on us – transforming us into the image of his Son. Jesus, supreme among men, knows fully the Father's love and receives fully the gift of the Spirit. The more that our prayer is united with the prayer of Jesus, the more we receive all that God wants to give, in particular, the gift of the Spirit, who, the Catechism says, 'contains all gifts' (CCC 2741). We are praying with both trust and boldness when we pray believing the words of Jesus: 'Seek first the kingdom of God, and all the rest will be given to you'. (Matthew 6:33)

Father, you have already poured out the gift of your love through the Spirit dwelling within me. Teach me to trust you for all my needs.

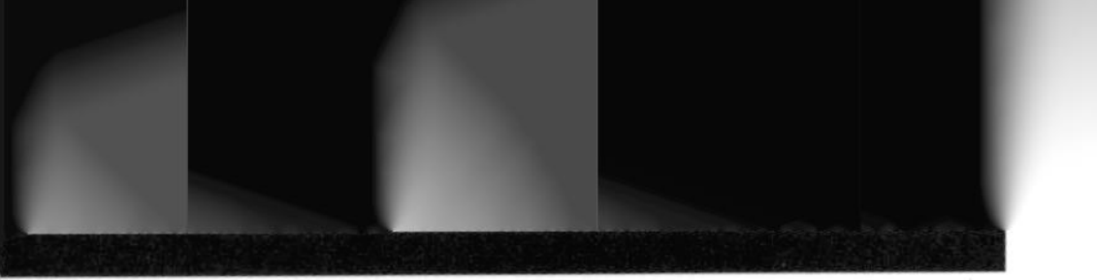

Prayer is the only thing that we have been commanded to do 'ceaselessly'. Prayer is the work of love. Only love will motivate us to endure the battle of prayer and overcome dullness and laziness; and keep us constant. This same love, which God has poured into our hearts, will open our hearts to 'three facts of faith about prayer' (CCC 2742): that prayer is possible in any situation or moment in our lives – even when troubled or occupied in our daily activities; that prayer is vitally necessary – for without prayer we will not be led by the Spirit and sin will be at hand; finally, that prayer and the Christian life are inseparable – for both draw us into union with the Father, the Son and the Holy Spirit.

'He 'prays without ceasing' who unites prayer to works and good works to prayer. Only in this way can we consider as realisable the principle of praying without ceasing.' (Origen, CCC 2745)

YOUCAT 510

'My God, if my tongue cannot say in every moment that I love you, I want my heart to repeat it to you as often as I draw breath.' (St John Vianney, CCC 2658)

DAY 365

THE HOUR OF JESUS (CCC 2746-2751)

'In this prayer Jesus reveals and gives to us the 'knowledge,' inseparably one, of the Father and of the Son, which is the very mystery of the life of prayer.' (CCC 2751)

YOUCAT 511

John 17 records for us 'the prayer of the hour of Jesus' or his priestly prayer, expressed on the evening in which the passion of Jesus began. It is the prayer that is one with the sacrifice he was to accomplish in the Last Supper and in his death on the Cross. Along with the '*Our Father*', the prayer of the hour of Jesus is the summary and gathering together of all prayer into one. It expresses God's whole plan of creation and salvation, and the perfect response of one totally conformed to the Father's will. This prayer continues in the Church's liturgy. It speaks of God's desire to bring all of us into union with God and to a share in the love of the Blessed Trinity.

Father, give me the grace today to read John 17, to study and reflect on it and so enter into your Son's prayer to you.

St Paul taught that the Spirit helps us in our weakness (Romans 8:26). He went on to say that 'we do not know what we ought to pray for' and that the Spirit intercedes for us with groans that words cannot express. We need help to pray. The disciple who made the request, 'Lord, teach us to pray' spoke for us all. In response Jesus taught the prayer we know as the *Our Father.* This prayer, more than any other, is the fundamental Christian prayer. It teaches us everything we need to know about prayer. St Matthew's version has seven petitions and St Luke's has five. It is St Matthew's version that we use in the liturgy and are most familiar with.

'The Lord's prayer is the most perfect of prayers.' (St Thomas Aquinas)

YOUCAT 511

Our Father, teach me to pray the Lord's Prayer with new conviction and renewed vigour. 'For yours are the power and the glory for ever.'

Day 367

A summary of the whole Gospel (CCC 2761-2762)

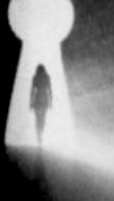

'Run through all the holy prayers [in Scripture], and I do not think that you will find anything in them that is not contained and included in the Lord's prayer.' (St Thomas Aquinas)

YOUCAT 514

The early Christian author Tertullian said that the *Our Father* 'is a summary of the whole Gospel.' The Lord's Prayer is much more than a prayer. It a kind of Creed, a proclamation of what we believe, celebrate and live. God knows that we have many needs, intercessions and petitions which are unique and peculiar to the situations and circumstances of our lives. However, the *Our Father* puts everything in its right order and perspective. God the Father knows our needs and desires before we have even asked him. We pray the *Our Father* first and then we take our own needs and desires to God.

Father, you promised that if we ask we shall receive. If we knock the door will be opened and if we seek we shall find.

St Ambrose said, 'What is more pleasing than a psalm?' He went on to say that a psalm 'is a blessing on the lips of the people.' Just as the psalms are the principal source of Christian prayer, so too is the *Our Father* at the very heart of our prayer life. The *Our Father* is a summary of all the psalms. It is the most pleasing of prayers and a blessing on our lips. Many of us have prayed the *Our Father* since childhood. There is a way in which when we are familiar with something we run the risk of taking it for granted. To be able to pray the Lord's Prayer is a wonderful blessing and joy. But it is also a great honour and privilege.

'The New Testament is latent in the Old Testament and the Old Testament is patent in the New Testament.' (St Augustine)

YOUCAT 4

Lord, teach me not to take for granted and to be grateful for the gift of being able to pray the Our Father.

DAY 369

IN THE LAW AND THE PROPHETS (CCC 2763)

'In it [the Our Father] we ask, not only for all things we can rightly desire, but also in the sequence that they should be desired.' (St Thomas Aquinas)

YOUCAT 514

Jesus summed up the teaching of the Torah (the Jewish Law) and the long history of Israel's prophets into just two great commandments. They are, as we know: to love God with all our heart, mind, soul and strength and to love our neighbour as ourselves (Matthew 22:36-40). The *Our Father,* in a similar way, is also a summary of the entire Law and Prophets. It captures succinctly and beautifully the essence of these two great commandments: our vocation to worship God and our call to forgive our neighbour. The *Our Father* is at the very centre, the heart of our proclamation of the Good News.

Lord Jesus, I give you thanks and praise for the gift of the Our Father. For within its blessed and holy words I proclaim the Good News of salvation.

The Sermon on the Mount (Matthew 5-7) is the *Magna Carta*, the blueprint, if you like, for living the Christian life. The *Our Father* is at the heart of this teaching and the centre of the proclamation of the gospel, the Good News. The Sermon on the Mount teaches us to live in the Spirit; the *Our Father* teaches us to pray in the Spirit. In the Sermon on the Mount we learn to live a new life. In the *Our Father* we are taught by the Lord himself how to pray for it. In the Sermon on the Mount and the *Our Father* we meet the Spirit, who brings order and healing to the inner movements of our hearts and our desires.

'The rightness of our life in him will depend on the rightness of our prayer.' (CCC 2764)

YOUCAT 514

Lord, help me to live in the Spirit by living the Beatitudes and pray in the Spirit by praying the Our Father.

Day 371

The Lord's Prayer taught by Jesus (CCC 2765)

'The prayer that comes to us from Jesus is truly unique' it is 'of the Lord'.' (CCC 2764)

Christian tradition is full of many masters of the spiritual life. Men and women who dedicated their lives to prayer and have left us profound and rich legacies of how to pray and how to live: St Augustine of Hippo, St Benedict, St Ignatius of Loyola, St Catherine of Genoa and St Teresa of Avila, to mention only a few. However, the true master of prayer is Jesus himself. The *Our Father* is the prayer of the Master; each word of the *Our Father* comes directly from God the Father (John 17:7). In the rich tradition of Christian prayer the *Our Father* has pride of place and is our first prayer, the foundation stone of all our prayer.

Our Father, who art in heaven, hallowed be thy name. Thy kingdom come, thy will be done on earth as it is in heaven. Give us this day our daily bread and forgive us our trespasses, as we forgive those who trespass against us. And lead us not into temptation, but deliver us from evil. Amen

We pray in the power of the Spirit (CCC 2766)

Day 372

Jesus taught that it is possible to pray in an empty, meaningless and even chaotic way. He called it 'babbling like pagans' (Matthew 6:7). He had in mind perhaps Elijah mocking the Baal prophets and those who prayed to the pagan god Baal (1 Kings 18:26-29). Our prayer to God is rooted in the Word of God (Sacred Scripture). We are taught by the Holy Spirit to pray to *Our Father*. God the Father sent the Spirit of his Son into our hearts so that we would cry out to God, 'Abba', 'Father.' (Galatians 4:6). Jesus gave us the words to pray to the Father and sent the Spirit so that these words become 'spirit and life.' (John 6:63).

'For you did not receive a spirit that makes you a slave again to fear, but you received the Spirit of sonship. And by him we cry, 'Abba' 'Father'.' (Romans 8:15)

Heavenly Father, you search our hearts and you know our minds. May your Spirit intercede for us according to your will.

DAY 373

THE PRAYER OF THE CHURCH (CCC 2767-2768)

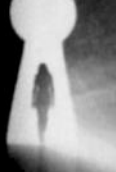

'The Lord's Prayer is essentially rooted in liturgical prayer.' (CCC 2768)

YOUCAT 514

The *Our Father* is a gift from Jesus to the Church. It has been prayed since the beginning. According to the *Didache* (an early Christian writing) the early Christian communities would pray the *Our Father* three times a day. This was in place of the 'Eighteen Benedictions' which formed part of a faithful Jew's prayer. Today the *Our Father* is an essential and integral part of our liturgical prayer. St John Chrysostom said: 'The Lord teaches us to make prayer in common for all our brethren. For he did not say 'My Father' who art in heaven, but '*Our Father*' offering petitions for the common Body.'

Our Father, from age to age you gather a people to yourself. We pray and worship not merely as individuals but as members of the Body of Christ.

The Prayer of the Church - in Baptism and Confirmation (CCC 2769)

Day 374

The Early Church Fathers wrote commentaries on the *Our Father* with the needs of the men and women who were being received into the Church in mind (catechumens and neophytes). For them the handing on (*traditio*) of the Lord's Prayer to them was a sign of the new birth and new life they had received. Indeed, when the Church prays the *Our Father*, the Lord's Prayer, it has in mind the 'new born' who pray to God and know his mercy. As St Peter taught us: 'Once you were not a people, but now you are the people of God; once you had not received mercy, but now you have received mercy.' (1 Peter 2:10).

'...for the seal of the Holy Spirit's anointing is indelibly placed on their hearts, ears, lips, indeed their whole filial being.' (CCC 2769)

Father, we praise you for the grace of Baptism and Confirmation, in which the Lord's Prayer is handed on to us as a sign of the new divine life.

DAY 375

THE PRAYER OF THE CHURCH IN THE EUCHARISTIC LITURGY (CCC 2770-2772)

'The Eucharist and the Lord's Prayer look eagerly for the Lord's return, 'until he comes'.' (CCC 2772)

The full meaning of the *Our Father* is supremely revealed in the celebration of the Eucharist. At Mass the saying of the *Our Father* is a summing up of all our prayers, petitions and intercessions. It is also a knocking on the door of the 'Banquet of the Kingdom' anticipating our receiving of Holy Communion. In the Eucharist we pray for the return of Christ; the *Our Father* is the prayer of 'the end time.' It expresses the groaning, hoping and longing for the return of Christ. Since Christ's Ascension Jesus' return in glory has been imminent. We are living in the end times and in patience and expectation we pray, 'Come, Lord Jesus, Come.'

Lord, every time I celebrate the Eucharist and pray the Our Father I proclaim your death, celebrate your resurrection and look forward to your coming in glory.

How bold are you when drawing near to God? Do you approach God with freedom and confidence? In the Old Testament the people were full of fear and trepidation. God spoke to Moses from the burning bush: "Do not come near; put off your shoes from your feet, for the place on which you are standing is holy ground.' (Exodus 3:5). Through his cross Jesus reconciled us with the Father. He crossed the threshold of the divine holiness on our behalf. He made purification for sins and brought us into the Father's presence. As it says in the Letter to the Hebrews: 'Here am I, and the children God has given me.' (Hebrews 2:13).

'Our awareness of our status as slaves would make us sink into the ground and our earthly condition would dissolve into dust, if the authority of our Father himself and the Spirit of his Son had not impelled us to this cry... 'Abba. Father'!' (St Peter Chrysologus)

YOUCAT 515

'Abba', 'Father', I come before you today in straightforward simplicity, filial trust, joyous assurance, humble boldness and the certainty of being loved.

'The new man, reborn and restored to his God by grace, says first of all, 'Father' because he has now begun to be a son.' (St Cyprian)

YOUCAT 515; 516

We all have varied and different experiences of our earthly fathers. Some have very positive experiences; others less so. Our hearts need purifying whatever our experience so that we can enter the mystery of who God the Father truly is. Our hearts need to be cleansed from certain paternal images and false images drawn from the world and which stem from our personal and cultural history. To know God as 'Father' is a remarkable grace and blessing. Human reason alone cannot conceive of this and as the Catechism teaches us, 'nor angelic powers even dimly see.' (CCC 2780). We need the grace of revelation to know God as Father.

Father, deepen in me an ever new sense of wonder that I can know and love you. We give thanks to you for revealing your name, for the gift in believing in it and for the Holy Spirit, who dwells in us.

We don't pray 'My Father' but '*Our Father*.' When we say it we join ourselves in love and solidarity to the worldwide communion of believers. We have become 'his people' and he is 'our God.' When we pray the Lord's Prayer with love and sincerity the love of God sets us free from self-centred individualism. In spite of the divisions between us, when we pray the *Our Father* we are united to all Christian believers. The *Our Father* is a prayer of love for all humankind. Every time we pray the *Our Father* we express not only our love for God but we proclaim God's love for everyone.

'When we pray to 'our' Father, we personally address the Father of our Lord Jesus Christ.' (CCC 2789)

YOUCAT 517

Father, your love has no bounds and limits. May I be a witness to the love the Father has lavished on us by letting us be called children of God.

'Heaven' could also be those who bear the image of the heavenly world, and in whom God dwells and tarries.' (St John Chrysostom)

YOUCAT 518

Blessed John Henry Newman said, 'Love of heaven is the only way to heaven.' We don't tend to dwell too much on heaven, fearing perhaps being too 'other-worldly' or not rooted enough to the things of the earth. But this way of thinking can deprive us of the hope that God wants to be burning in our hearts. The Christian life is a pilgrimage back to the Father's house. 'Heaven', does not mean a place ('space') but a way of being. (CCC 2794). Through baptism we are already seated with Christ in the heavenly realm; our lives are hidden with Christ in God. We groan and long to put on our heavenly dwelling. In the Eucharist especially we receive a foretaste of the heavenly life.

Our Father, you are in heaven and we have been raised with Christ. Teach me today to set my heart on things above, where Christ is seated at your right hand.

The *Our Father* has seven petitions. The first three focus on God not ourselves. These three petitions capture the Lord's burning desire, anguish even, for his Father. Jesus' entire mission was to make known the Father's name, to establish his kingdom, and to do his will. The final four petitions address our most profound and deepest spiritual needs. We ask God boldly to: give us, forgive us, lead us and deliver us. Our greatest needs are firstly to be fed by the Eucharist and forgiven for our sins. Then we need to engage every day in the battle to pray. We do this by being led away from temptation and delivered from evil.

'After we have placed ourselves in the presence of God our Father to adore and to love and to bless him, the Spirit of adoption stirs up in our hearts seven petitions, seven blessings.' (CCC 2803)

YOUCAT 518

Lord, every time we pray the Our Father we are strengthened in faith, filled with hope and set aflame with love for God.

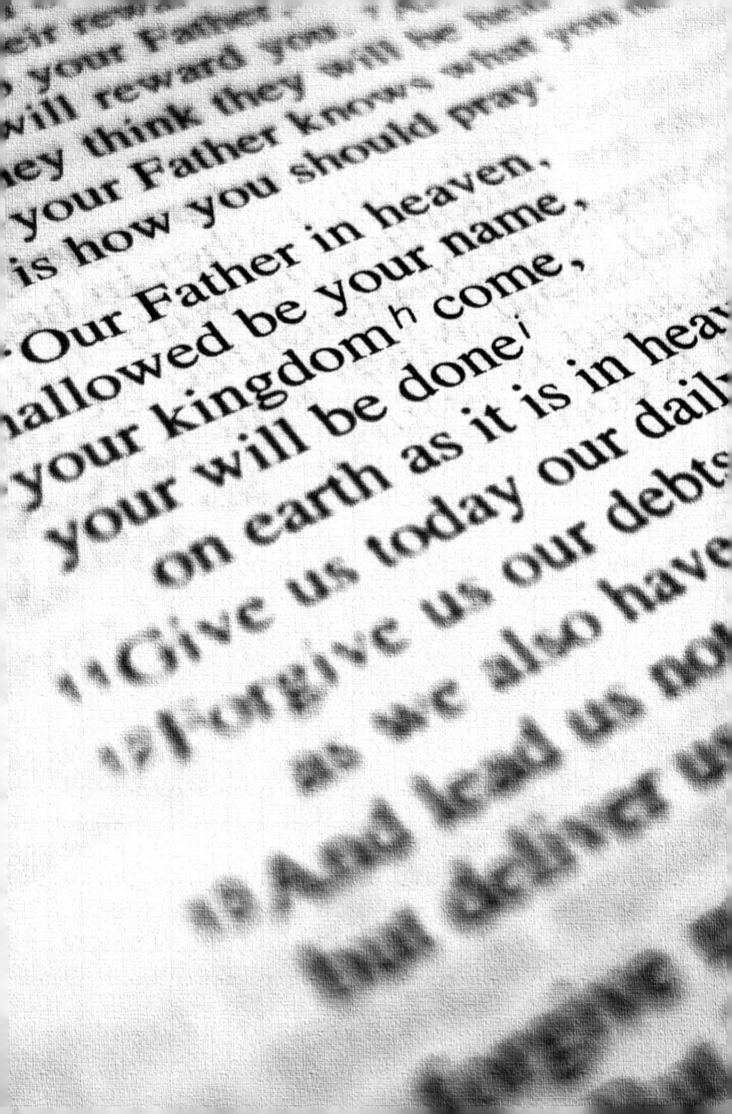

your Father
will reward you.
ey think they will be heard
your Father knows what you
is how you should pray:

"Our Father in heaven,
hallowed be your name,
your kingdom[h] come,
your will be done[i]
on earth as it is in heav
11 Give us today our daily
12 Forgive us our debts
as we also have
13 And lead us not
but deliver us

DAY 381

HALLOWED BE THY NAME (CCC 2807-2809)

'The holiness of God is the inaccessible centre of his eternal mystery.' (CCC 2809)

When we think of prayer we often think of our own needs and desires. In teaching us how to pray Jesus shows us that praise and thanksgiving are the highest form of prayer. To give God glory, honour, praise and thanksgiving, is the first response of a prayerful, grateful heart. God's name is hallowed because God is holy. God's holiness cannot be grasped merely by words or language but stands apart, it is unique, unassailable, beautiful, unapproachable, incomprehensible, unattainable. We fall silent before God's name and holiness. The right and proper response is to bow down and worship.

YOUCAT 519

Lord God, you created us in your image and likeness and crowned us with glory and honour. In your Son you revealed your Majestic Glory and restored us to the image of the Creator.

THE NAME OF JESUS (CCC 2810-2815)

DAY 382

Jesus' name is the name that is above all other names (Philippians 2:9-11). He finally and fully revealed the face and the name of God. Through baptism we were 'washed.... sanctified.... justified in the name of our Lord Jesus Christ' (1 Corinthians 6:11). We are called to live holy lives in Jesus' name (1 Thessalonians 4:7). We are ambassadors for Christ sent in his name. However, as Paul VI taught, holiness and evangelization involve proclaiming Jesus' name: 'There is no true evangelization if the name, the teaching, the life, the promises, the kingdom and the mystery of Jesus of Nazareth, the Son of God are not proclaimed.' (*Evangelii Nuntiandi 22*).

'In his priestly prayer, Jesus asks: 'Holy Father, protect in your name those whom you have given me'.' (CCC 2815)

YOUCAT 519

'The hallowed name of Jesus in not only light but food. It is oil without which food for the soul is dry, and salt without which it is insipid. It is honey in the mouth, melody in the ear and joy to the heart'. (St Bernard of Clairvaux)

Day 383

Thy Kingdom Come (CCC 2816-2818)

'Only a pure soul can boldly say: 'Thy kingdom come.' One who has heard Paul say, 'Let not sin therefore reign in your mortal bodies,' and has purified himself in action, thought and word will say to God: 'Thy kingdom come'!' (St Cyril of Jerusalem)

YOUCAT 520

How often do you pray for the return of Christ? Truth be told, most of us are too busy about our business in this world to pray for the coming of the next. However, when we pray 'thy kingdom come' in the *Our Father* we are primarily praying for the final coming of the reign of God. In other words, we are praying for the return of Christ. Does praying for the return of Christ distract us from the mission of the church right here, right now? No, far from it, rather the desire to proclaim the gospel grows more strongly in us. Since the Lord Jesus ascended into heaven the Church has eagerly awaited the return of the King.

Lord Jesus, teach me to long for, groan and cry out the prayer of the Spirit and the Church, your Bride: 'Come, Lord Jesus, Come.'

What is God's kingdom all about? St Paul taught that the kingdom of God was all about 'righteousness, peace and joy in the Holy Spirit.' (Romans 14:17). The universal call to holiness each of us has received through our baptism is at the heart of God's kingdom. In short, we are called to be saints. In other words we are called to live the Beatitudes, to put into practise the Sermon on the Mount and practice heroic virtue in our daily lives. No pressure then! The life in the Spirit is impossible without the Spirit. We can only live holy lives with the help and grace of the Spirit of God. The kingdom is within us because the Spirit is within us.

'Man's vocation to eternal life does not suppress, but actually re-inforces, his duty to put into action in this world the energies and means received from the Creator to serve justice and peace.' (CCC 2820)

YOUCAT 520

'There is no point in us travelling abroad to find heaven, or crossing the sea in search of virtue. As the Lord has already told us, God's kingdom is within you.' (St Anthony of Egypt)

'His commandment is 'that you love one another; even as I have loved you, that you also love one another.' This commandment summarizes all the others, and expresses his entire will.' (CCC 2822)

YOUCAT 521

Knowing God's will may be more straightforward than we think or imagine. What is God's will? Firstly, God desires that everyone be saved. He wants all men and women to come to a knowledge of the truth (1 Timothy 2:3-4). Secondly, God also wants us to love one another as he has loved us (John 13:34). God's will is that we strive and give our lives in loving those we live with, our nearest and dearest, but also all those we meet and encounter during our day, and those in need to whom we are called to reach out. The challenge of the vocation to love is to love as the Father cares for us, as Jesus laid down his life for us and as the Spirit comforts and consoles us.

Lord Jesus, you gave us the new command of love. With the help of your grace may I love as you have loved so that others may know I am your disciple.

Only Jesus fulfilled God's will perfectly. In coming among us Jesus fulfilled the prophetic insight of the Psalmist (Psalm 40:7): 'Lo, I have come to do your will, O God.' Only Jesus who knew no sin could say: 'I always do what is pleasing to him.' (John 8:29). In his agony in the Garden of Gethsemane Jesus consented fully and completely to do God's will: 'Not my will, but yours be done' (Luke 22:42). The Letter to the Hebrews expresses perfectly what Jesus' obedience to the Father's will secured for us: 'And by that will we have been sanctified through the offering of the body of Jesus Christ once and for all.' (Hebrews 10:10)

'In committing ourselves to Christ, we can become one spirit with him, and thereby accomplish his will, in such ways that it will be perfect on earth as it is in heaven.' (Origen)

YOUCAT 521

Heavenly Father, teach me to listen to your voice and to do your will. I know I am radically incapable of this by myself but united with Jesus and in the power of the Spirit I can surrender my will to yours.

DAY 387

GIVE US (CCC 2828-2829)

'Give us' expresses the covenant. We are his and he is ours, for our sake'.' *(CCC 2828)*

In the Sermon on the Mount, Jesus asks, 'Which of you, if his son asks for bread, will give him a stone? Or if he asks for a fish will give him a snake' (Matthew 7:9). In the question the Lord introduces us to the logic of the kingdom. Just as it would be unthinkable, intolerable and illogical for any parent to give their child something dangerous or poisonous to eat, so too God only gives good gifts to his children. God is our loving heavenly Father; we are his children. Jesus transformed the way we approach God. He taught us to go to God freely, willingly and with great confidence with our requests, needs and wants, for he cares for us.

YOUCAT 522

Father in heaven renew in me a new and exciting sense of trust and confidence in your benevolent kindness and goodness towards the whole of creation.

The history of the human race has been in a real way the struggle for daily bread. We all need food and sustenance and this is our most immediate need. We know however that we do not live on bread alone (Matthew 4:4). God gives us the bread that nourishes us physically and spiritually. We give God thanks for the gift of food when we say the *Grace before Meals*. The gift of food is a sign of God's bounty and generosity. God also feeds us spiritually. He gives us the Bread of Life, the Eucharist, the Bread of Heaven, the very source, and summit of the Christian life.

'To those who seek the kingdom of God and righteousness, he has promised to give all else besides. Since everything indeed belongs to God, he who possesses God wants for nothing, if he himself is not found wanting before God.' (St Cyrpian)

YOUCAT 522

Lord, I pray and ask only for the necessaries of life (Proverbs 30:8) and for this I give you thanks and praise, revealing as it does so clearly your goodness and kindness.

PHYSICAL HUNGER (CCC 2831-2832)

'Not to enable the poor to share in our goods is to steal from them and deprive them of life. The goods we possess are not ours, but theirs.' (St John Chrysostom)

YOUCAT 522

We pray for daily bread knowing that many of our brothers and sisters around the world are deprived of this basic human right and necessity. Over one billion people go to bed hungry every night. The Oxford English Dictionary defines hunger as: 'The uneasy or painful sensation caused by want of food. The exhausted condition caused by want of food. The want or scarcity of food in a country.' This injustice cries out day and night to be righted. We raise our voice, in an act of love and solidarity, on behalf of those who are weakened from hunger, thirst and malnourishment.

Lord, teach me always to be mindful and aware of the plight of those who hunger for food and water. I am united with them in faith. I support them with my prayers and give generously from my plenty.

One Bread, One Body (CCC 2833-2834)

Day 390

A missionary on his first visit to Pakistan was taken to a village far out in the desert. Christmas was fast approaching and he came bearing gifts. He handed out a few oranges to the older children and was taken aback by the dignified way they peeled the oranges and then distributed slice by slice to the other children. The look of gratitude, thanks and joy on their faces had a profound effect on him. He witnessed the kindness and generosity of the human spirit. We are called to show our solidarity with the poor of the world. Poverty in the spirit of the Beatitudes means sharing our abundance freely and willingly to alleviate the suffering of others.

'When we attend to the needs of those in want, we give them what is theirs, not ours. More than performing works of mercy, we are paying a debt of justice.' (St Gregory the Great)

YOUCAT 522

Lord, create in me above all a grateful and thankful heart for the good gifts you have given. Teach me to take nothing for granted and to be both a grateful receiver and a cheerful giver.

'There is a famine on earth, 'not a famine of bread, nor a thirst for water, but of hearing the words of the Lord'.' (Amos 8:11) (CCC 2835)

YOUCAT 523

Blessed Mother Teresa famously said: 'Loneliness and the feeling of being unwanted is the most terrible form of poverty.' There is within the human heart an emptiness or loneliness which can only be filled by God. There is, if you like in us all, a famine, a deep and profound hunger and thirst for God. These desires can only be satisfied and quenched by the Word of God in the Scriptures and by the Body of Christ in the Eucharist. We are beggars but once filled are to be bearers of the Good News of the gospel to others. People all around are hurting, aching and longing to hear the gospel, the life-changing message of the gospel.

'You called, you cried, you shattered my deafness, you sparkled, you blazed, you drove away my blindness, you shed your fragrance, and I drew my breath, and I pant for you.' (St Augustine)

It can be easier said than done but Jesus taught that we are to take each day at a time. 'Each day has enough trouble of its own.' (Matthew 6:34). Many centuries later Blessed John Henry Newman echoed this in a prayer: 'I do not ask to see the distant scene - one step enough for me.' Our faith is lived out in the present and daily grind we call life. St Augustine of Hippo said: 'Time is a three -fold present: the present as we experience it; the past as a present memory, and the future as a present expectation.' Each day is an opportunity to grow in trust that God will give us everything we need: our daily bread, the nourishment, support and strength to face whatever life throws at us.

'Today, do not harden your heart.' (Hebrews 3:7)

Most merciful Redeemer, Friend and Brother, may we know you more clearly, love you more dearly, and follow you more nearly, day by day. Amen. (St Richard of Chichester)

'The Eucharist is our daily bread. The power belonging to this divine food... means that we may become what we receive. This is also our daily bread; the readings you hear each day in church and the hymns you hear and sing. All these are necessities for our pilgrimage.' (St Augustine)

YOUCAT 523

The word 'daily', which occurs only once in the New Testament, comes from the Greek word *epiousios* and refers to the bare necessities of life. However, taken literally *epiousios* means that which is 'super-essential.' And what is 'super-essential' in our lives is the Eucharist, the Bread of Life, the Body of Christ, the 'medicine of immortality', food for our souls. When we receive the Eucharist we are mightily blessed because we are receiving a foretaste of the heavenly life to come. We derive our daily spiritual nourishment from two tables: the table of the Bread of the Eucharist and the table of the Word of God.

Lord, thank you for giving me the daily bread that feeds both my body and soul. May I work every day for food that lasts and does not spoil and receive the Eucharist in ever-increasing awe and adoration.

An Astonishing Petition (CCC 2838)

Day 394

Right at the very heart of the *Our Father* we find the petition for forgiveness. We ask for God's forgiveness and we confirm our willingness to forgive others. This petition is the only one with a condition attached to it. Its terms are clear: because we have been forgiven we in turn must be prepared to forgive others. Now the problem with forgiveness is that, as C S Lewis observed, 'Everyone says forgiveness is a lovely idea, until they have something to forgive.' Only the Holy Spirit can show us the depth of God's forgiveness and only the Spirit can give us the grace to forgive others. We can only forgive because we have been forgiven.

'Let no one mourn that he has fallen again and again; for forgiveness has risen from the grave.' (St John Chrysostom)

YOUCAT 524

Lord Jesus, teach me to bear with others and forgive whatever grievances I may have. Teach me most of all to forgive as you have forgiven me.

LEAD US
DEL
TATION, BUT
OM EVIL: FOR
KINGDOM, AND
AND THE
EVER.
AME

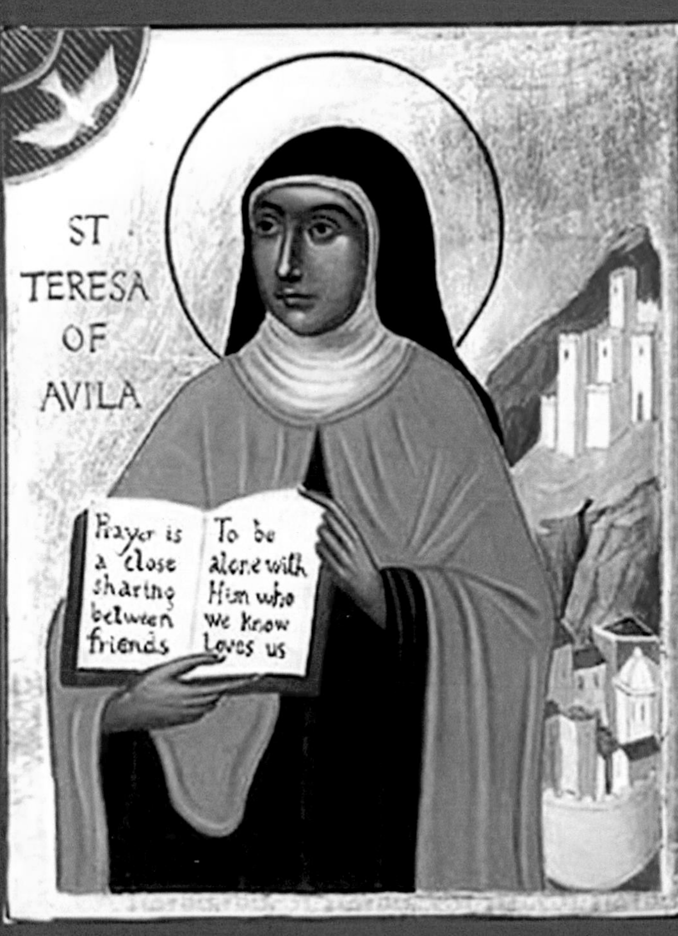
ST
TERESA
OF
AVILA
Prayer is
a close
sharing
between
friends
To be
alone with
Him who
we know
Loves us

'Our petition begins with a 'confession' of our wretchedness and his mercy.' (CCC 2839)

YOUCAT 524

The only way to understand God's forgiveness is to grasp our debt of sin. The Parable of the Unmerciful Servant (Matthew 18:21-35) sheds light on the height, breadth, length and depth of this debt. The king wants to settle his accounts and discovers that this servant owes 10,000 denarii. 10,000 denarii was an utterly impossible, immense and infinitesimal amount to repay. In today's money, it is the equivalent of the national debt of a major world economy falling on one individual. Faced with ruin and destitution he threw himself on the mercy of the king and the king took pity, had mercy and cancelled the debt.

I confess to almighty God and to you, my brothers and sisters, that I have greatly sinned, in my thoughts and in my words, in what I have done and in what I have failed to do, through my fault, through my fault, through my most grievous fault.

Forgiving Others (CCC 2840-2841)

Day 396

Forgiveness is daunting. Anyone who suggests that forgiveness is easy is mistaken. Indeed we can go so far as to say that forgiveness, this crucial requirement of the covenant, is actually impossible, but with God, thank God, all things are possible (Matthew 19:26). In order to forgive we have to know we have been forgiven. In order to be merciful we need to know God's mercy. In coming to know God's loving mercy we will discover anew the gift of forgiveness. The Spirit helps us to let go of old hurts, recurring wounds and long-standing festering resentments so that we can know the freedom and liberating power of forgiveness.

'The quality of mercy is not strain'd, it droppeth as the gentle rain from heaven. Upon the place beneath; it is twice blessed; it blesseth him that gives, and him that takes.' (William Shakespeare)

YOUCAT 524

Lord God, although I cannot see you I can see my brothers and sisters. Help me to forgive and be merciful towards them and in doing so guard my own heart from being hard, harsh and impervious to the Father's love.

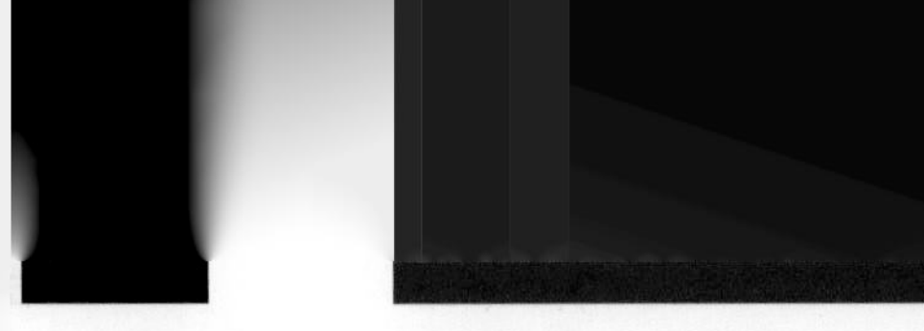

'The worst prison is a closed heart.'
(Blessed Pope John Paul II)

The adjective 'as' is an important one in Jesus' teaching. We are to be perfect *as* the heavenly Father is perfect, merciful *as* the Father is merciful and love one another *as* Jesus has loved us. Just as we ask the Father to forgive our sins, so we forgive those who have sinned against us. Our faith is a faith from the heart, reaching deep down into the very core of our being. We can't be holy (perfect) or merciful, forgive or love in a formal or legalistic way. Neither can we feign or pretend to love, forgive and be merciful. Our faith invites us into a vital participation, coming from the depths of our being, in the holiness, the mercy and the love of God.

YOUCAT 524

Lord, as you have loved me, may I love others. As you have forgiven me, may I forgive others. As you have been merciful to me, may I be merciful to others. As you laid down your life for me, may I lay down my life for others.

Forgiveness from the Heart (CCC 2843)

Day 398

The Parable of the Unmerciful Servant is a masterpiece (Matthew 18:21-35). The Catechism describes it as '[crowning] the Lord's teaching on ecclesial communion.' (CCC 2843). In other words it teaches in a most beautiful and perfect way our call to forgive and to be reconciled with each other. We should study and pray on this treasure of a scripture with renewed energy and vigour. The parable teaches us so much about grace, mercy and forgiveness. True forgiveness requires courage, strength and grace. Forgiveness of this kind is generous beyond measure, it liberates, heals memories and holds out the embrace of love and friendship.

'It is not in our power not to feel, or to forget an offence; but the heart that offers itself to the Holy Spirit turns injury into compassion and purifies the memory in transforming the hurt into intercession.' (CCC 2843)

YOUCAT 524

Lord, in the power of your grace, give me the strength to forgive any who have sinned against me, deeply, unconditionally and from the heart.

'Where there is no love, pour love in, and you will draw out love.' (St John of the Cross)

YOUCAT 524

On Wednesday May 13 1981 Mehmet Ali Agca attempted to assassinate Blessed Pope John Paul II. After undergoing life-saving surgery the Pope survived the attempt on his life. Recovering from his hospital bed he said: 'Pray for my brother (Agca)…whom I have sincerely forgiven.' He even visited him in prison. Pope John Paul showed that love, mercy and forgiveness is stronger than hatred and revenge. G K Chesterton once said: 'The Bible tells us to love our neighbours, and also to love our enemies; probably because they are generally the same people.' Our prayer makes us sensitive so that we pray for and forgive those who oppose, resist, or even hate us.

Lord, we conquer through mercy and forgiveness and we set ourselves free by forgiving our enemies, refusing to be shackled by the chains of hatred and resentment.

God's Immeasurable Mercy (CCC 2845)

Day 400

We have limits in many areas of our lives. We have speed limits, bank withdrawal limits and we all know what it is like to be pushed to the limit. St Peter wanted there to be a limit to forgiveness. Jesus transformed our understanding: 'I tell you, not seven times, but seventy-seven times' (Matthew 18:21-22). Jesus revealed that God's divine mercy and forgiveness is limitless, immeasurable and infinite. The Blessed Trinity is the source of this eternal and infinite love, mercy and forgiveness. In prayer we encounter this mystery of God's love. This knowledge becomes the fount from which we draw in order to love and forgive others.

'Do you wish to receive mercy? Show mercy to your neighbour.' (St John Chrysostom)

YOUCAT 524

Lord, by the power of the Holy Spirit may I grasp how wide and long and high and deep is the love of Christ. May I know this love that surpasses knowledge and be filled to the measure of the fullness of God.

DAY 401

LEAD US NOT INTO TEMPTATION (CCC 2846-28)

'We are engaged in the battle 'between flesh and spirit'; this petition implores the Spirit of discernment and strength.' (CCC 2846)

YOUCAT 525

Temptation can be hard to resist. We can be easily overwhelmed by desires and appetites. We have weaknesses, blind spots or shadows. We are engaged in a constant battle between flesh and spirit, between good and evil. A real tension exists between doing what is right and doing what is wrong. This is the essence of temptation. It is not sinful to be tempted; only to yield. We ask God for the wisdom, strength and discernment to make the 'decision of the heart' which turns away from that which leads to sin and death. We can be tempted to think that God is far from us when we are tempted, but God is ever close during such trials and sufferings.

Lord Jesus, you yourself suffered when you were tempted and you are able to help us when we are being tempted. Give us the wisdom to avoid temptation, the strength to overcome and the courage to say 'No.'

Prayer can be a battlefield. In prayer we come to know God, acquire self-knowledge and gain the strength to resist temptation. Jesus experienced his most intense temptations in prayer. We see this when he was tempted in the desert and in the final onslaught in the Garden of Gethsemane. The Letter to the Hebrews expresses powerfully and movingly the intensity of Jesus' prayer battles (Hebrews 5:7-9). Through baptism we are united to this battle. We are constantly invited to keep watch and be vigilant. We are called to persevere and be resilient in the face of repeated temptation. In the midst of our battles the Spirit is close, guiding, comforting and giving us strength.

'The greatest of all evils is not to be tempted because there are then grounds for believing that the devil looks upon us as his property.' (St John Vianney)

YOUCAT 525

Lord, keep me close to you by your grace and teach me to be always self-controlled and alert to the wiles, schemes and temptations of the evil one.

DAY 403

But Deliver Us from evil (CCC 2850)

'Deliver us, Lord, we pray, from every evil, graciously grant peace in our days, that, by the help of your mercy, we may be always free from sin and safe from all distress, as we await the blessed hope and the coming of our Saviour, Jesus Christ.' (Roman Missal 2010)

YOUCAT 526

The devil (*dia-bolos*) is not a figment of the imagination nor an abstraction but a person. Satan is a pure spirit, a powerful angel who opposes God. He 'throws himself across' God's plan, thwarts, spoils, but ultimately cannot prevent the building up of God's kingdom. Jesus described him as a murderer from the beginning and the deceiver of the whole world (John 8:44). In his high priestly prayer Jesus prayed: 'I am not asking you to take them out of the world but I ask you to protect them from the evil one. (John 17:15). We pray for God to deliver us from evil: meaning, protect us from it, help us discern it and lead us away from it.

Lord Jesus, through your cross and resurrection you conquered evil, and when you return in glory the definitive victory will be established and creation finally set free from all corruption and death.

In St John's Gospel Jesus spoke of the hour. They tried to arrest him but his hour had not come (John 7:30). He was deeply troubled when the hour had come: 'What shall I say: Father, save me from this hour? No, for this purpose I have come to this hour' (John 12:27). He knew when the hour had come: 'Jesus knew that his hour had come for him to depart this world to go to the Father' (John 13:1). The hour is the cross, and on the cross Jesus won victory over the 'prince of this world' (John 14:30). As we prepare to enter the Paschal Mystery we do so expectant that we will be renewed in our understanding of the cross as the ultimate sign of God's love and victory over sin, death and the devil.

'The Son of God 'loved me and gave himself up for me' (Gal. 2:20). By suffering for us he not only provided us with an example for our imitation, he blazed a trail, and if we follow it, life and death are made holy and take on a new meaning.' (Gaudium et Spes 22)

YOUCAT 526

Lord Jesus, you bore the cross so that you could wear the crown of victory. On the cross you defeated the devil and evil. Teach me to glory in the cross, rejoice in the cross and proclaim the cross.

DAY 405

DELIVERANCE FROM ALL DISTRESS (CCC 2854)

'And the peace of God, which transcends all understanding, will guard your hearts and your minds in Christ Jesus.' (Philippians 4:7)

Watching the news can be depressing. Virtually every day our media carries, stories of distress, tribulations and disasters of one kind or another. It is not difficult to see that there is a destructive and evil force or influence at work in the world. The Catechism identifies the devil as the instigator of this evil. The *Our Father* teaches us to pray with perseverance and in expectation of Christ's return in glory when evil will finally be vanquished. We are a People of the Second Coming, we pray for and long for the return of Jesus, 'who is and who was and who is to come, the Almighty' (Revelation 1:8).

YOUCAT 526

Lord Jesus, you are the Prince of Peace who conquered the prince of this world. Where there is hatred, discord and conflict may we bring peace, reconciliation and harmony.

The word doxology means literally 'glory saying' and is a short hymn in praise and glory of God. At the heart of our salvation has been a tumultuous struggle between good and evil, between God the Father and the ruler of this world. The 'prince of this world' has attributed to himself from the very beginning the three titles of kingship, power and glory. From the very beginning he has wanted to be worshipped as God is worshipped (Matthew 4:9). But by his victorious death and resurrection Jesus has restored these titles back to his Father. When we pray the doxology, we are joining the Lord in giving glory, praise and thanksgiving to his Father and *Our Father*.

'Deliver us, Lord, we pray from every evil, graciously grant peace in our days, that, by the help of your mercy, we may be always free from sin and safe from all distress, as we await the blessed hope and the coming of our Saviour, Jesus Christ.' (Roman Missal 2010)

YOUCAT 527

For the kingdom, the power and the glory are yours, now and forever.

'Jesus Christ himself is the 'Amen'. He is the definitive 'Amen' of the Father's love for us. He takes up and completes our 'Amen' to the Father. ' (CCC 1065)

YOUCAT 527

The root of the Hebrew word 'Amen' is 'I believe' or 'So be it.' Our Amen confirms our affirmation of and acceptance of Jesus' teaching. In the *Our Father* we are taught by Jesus how we should pray. Our Amen in effect says, 'Thank you Lord Jesus for the beauty and truth of your teaching and for showing us how we are to pray to our heavenly Father.' St Paul observed that sometimes we don't know what to pray for and we need the help of the Spirit who searches our hearts (Romans 8:26). This is, of course, true. However, if ever we feel that we don't know how to pray, let us say the *Our Father*, slowly, with reverence and love, for this is how we should pray. Amen.

Through him, and with him, and in him, O God, almighty Father, in the unity of the Holy Spirit, all glory and honour is yours, for ever and ever. Amen.

BLESSED DOMINIC BARBERI, PRAY FOR US
IESU XPI PASSIO
IESU XPI PASSIO

alive Publishing
Publisher to the Holy See

Editor in Chief
\+ Bernard Longley,
Archbishop of Birmingham

Consulting Editors

\+ Philip Egan,
Bishop of Portsmouth
Mgr Timothy Menezes VG
Mgr Paul Watson
Fr Eddie Clare

Censor Deputatus
Fr Paul Dean

With thanks to the Year of Faith Commitee for the Archdiocese of Birmingham
Fr Stephen Fawcett (Chairman)
Canon David Evans
Fr Pat Sayles
Fr Julian Booth
Sr Gillian Murphy
Sr Margaret Walsh
Deacon David Palmer
Teresa Kehoe
Catherine Weaver
Sue Conway
Mike Conway

Notes

tes

Notes